KU-421-576

ALISTAIR COOKE

LETTER FROM AMERICA

The 1980s—2004

For over half a century Alistair Cooke entertained millions of listeners across the globe with his weekly BBC radio programme 'Letter from America'. An outstanding observer of the American scene, he became one of the world's best-loved broadcasters and had the distinction of presenting the longest runing one-man show in radio history.

Presented chronologically in two volumes, this second volume includes Cooke's moving evocation of the events of September 11 2001 and its aftermath, which remain essential reading. The volume ends with his last broadcast in February 2004 discussing the US presidential campaign.

Imbued with Alistair Cooke's good humour, elegance and understanding, *Letter from America* is a captivating insight into the heart of a nation, and a fitting tribute to the man who was for so many the most reassuring voice of our times.

co/4/4
HAR

Please return / renew by date shown.
You can renew at:
norlink.norfolk.gov.uk
or by telephone: 0844 800 8006
Please have your library card & PIN ready.

3/07 WYMONDHAM
02. APR 07

18. APR 07.

26. MAY 07.

03. JUL 07.
07. AUG 07.

11. DEC 07

3/10/09.

NORFOLK LIBRARY
AND INFORMATION SERVICE

NORFOLK ITEM

30129 048 483 599

ALISTAIR COOKE
LETTER FROM AMERICA

1980s - 2004

BBC
LARGE
PRINT

First published
2004
by
Allen Lane
This Large Print edition published 2005
by
BBC Audiobooks Ltd
by arrangement with
The Penguin Group

973 . 92

ISBN 0 7540 9448 0

Copyright © the Estate of Alistair Cooke, 2004

The moral right of the author has been asserted

'The Cow in Apple Time', 'A Soldier' and 'Leaves
Compared with Flowers' by Robert Frost, from
The Poetry of Robert Frost, edited by Edward
Connery Lathem and published by Jonathan Cape,
are used by permission of the Estate of Robert
Frost and The Random House Group Limited

All rights reserved.

British Library Cataloguing in Publication Data available

NORFOLK LIBRARY AND INFORMATION SERVICE	
SUPPLIER	BBC AUDIOBOOKS
INVOICE No.	
ORDER DATE	
COPY No.	

LOYALTY GIFT

Printed and bound in Great Britain by
Antony Rowe Ltd., Chippenham, Wiltshire

Contents

List of Illustrations   ix
Introduction by Simon Jenkins   xi
Editor's Note by Colin Webb   xxi

The 1980s

Bringing Up Baby *2 January 1981*   3
Attempted Assassination of President Reagan
   3 April 1981   9
The Fourth of July *2 July 1982*   15

Old Man Reagan *12 October 1984*   21
Inaugurals—On and Off *25 January 1985*   27
Memories of 11 November *15 November 1985*   34
Miss Much—No Regret *3 January 1986*   40
Expert Witness *27 June 1986*   46
The Drugs Blight *19 September 1986*   53
Time to Retire *16 January 1987*   60
Martin Luther King—the Black Washington
   23 January 1987   66
Fred Astaire *26 June 1987*   72
Origins of American Slang *14 August 1987*   78

Mayor Koch at Work *12 August 1988*   84
Hurricanes *23 September 1988*   90
Chaplin—the Last Word *21 April 1989*   96
San Francisco Earthquake *20 October 1989*   102

The 1990s

Presidential Ghosts *23 February 1990*   111
The End of the Eighties—Great or Greedy?
  27 April 1990   116
Fighting in What? *30 November 1990*   122
Riots in Los Angeles *1 May 1992*   130
White House Style *6 November 1992*   137
The Irish in New York City *19 March 1993*   141
'Give me your tired, your poor. . .'
  25 June 1993   147
Thirtieth Anniversary of Kennedy Assassination
  26 November 1993   152
Boston *11 March 1994*   158
Trick or Treat *4 November 1994*   165
Fiftieth Anniversary of VE Day *5 May 1995*   171
O.J.—the Verdict *6 October 1995*   177
The Old Rocking Chair *3 May 1996*   183
Silver Watergate *20 June 1997*   189
The End of Civilization *25 July 1997*   195
The Kennedy Missile Tapes *24 October 1997*   202

The Evolution of the Grand Jury *31 July 1998*   208

The President Will Address the Nation
  21 August 1998   214

New Words for Objects New and Old
  16 October 1998   220

Loneliness, Male Companionship and the Hunt
  30 July 1999   227

Park Avenue's Colourful Christmas
  24 December 1999   234

2000–2004

The Death of the Old Media *14 January 2000*   243

Running Mates and Carpetbaggers
  11 August 2000   248

The Day of Judgement *3 November 2000*   254

The Origin of the Continental Blow-out
  24 November 2000   260

America's Day of Terror *14 September 2001*   265

America on Standby *21 September 2001*   270

The Stars and Stripes *9 November 2001*   276

Messiah at Christmas *21 December 2001*   282

Ringing the Changes *4 January 2002*   288

Arise, Sir Rudolph *22 February 2002*   293

The Day the Money Stopped *8 March 2002*   299

Memory of a True Great *15 March 2002*   305

The Last of the Old-Time Gangsters
   14 June 2002   311

Farewell to San Francisco *18 October 2002*   316

Remembering a Dear Friend
   13 December 2002   323

Meeting the Stars *4 July 2003*   329

The Pledge of Allegiance *17 October 2003*   335

Towering Glass and Steel *31 October 2003*   339

Charlie Addams *23 January 2004*   345

The Democrats' Growing Confidence
   20 February 2004   349

List of Illustrations

1.   In the studio, 1970s. (Copyright © Penny Tweedie)
2a. AC and President Eisenhower during the filming of 'General Eisenhower on the Military Churchill'. (Courtesy of the Alistair Cooke Collection in the Howard Gottlieb Archival Research Center at Boston University)
2b. AC with Attorney General Robert Kennedy. (Courtesy of the Alistair Cooke Collection in the Howard Gottlieb Archival Research Center at Boston University)
3a. Adlai Stevenson's 54th birthday. (Courtesy of the Alistair Cooke Collection in the Howard Gottlieb Archival Research Center at Boston University)
3b. AC interviewing LBJ about Vietnam. (By kind permission of Alistair Cooke's family)
4a–c, 5a–c.   AC in his study at 1150 Fifth Avenue. (Copyright © Penny Tweedie)
6a. AC putting in the long gallery at 1150 Fifth Avenue. (Copyright © John Byrne Cooke)
6b. AC practising his swing in Central Park. (By kind permission of Alistair Cooke's family)
6c. AC chipping out of a bunker at Island's End Golf & Country Club. (By kind permission of Alistair Cooke's family)
6d. AC after a round with Bing Crosby and Robert Cameron. (Courtesy of the Alistair Cooke Collection in the Howard Gottlieb

Archival Research Center at Boston University)

7a. On the roof of 1150 Fifth Avenue, overlooking the reservoir. (Copyright © Penny Tweedie)

7b. In the living room of 1150th Fifth Avenue. (Copyright © Penny Tweedie)

8. Portrait by long-time friend Roddy McDowall. (Copyright © Roddy McDowall courtesy of the Roddy McDowall Trust)

Introduction

Alistair Cooke was the classic Anglo-American. He embodied the cultural and political bond that linked Britain and the United States during the long half century from the Second World War into the twenty-first century. In the great game of current affairs, he was an observer, not a player. But like the best observers, he helped define the game.

My parents were ardent Americanophiles. As a result they would sit each week listening to *Letter from America*, like wartime refugees glued to a message from a land afar. Cooke kept them in touch with Strong America in the 1950s, Rich America in the 1960s, Questioning America in the 1970s and Uncertain America in the 1980s and 1990s. He never preached. He was accused of ignoring the dark side of American life, but his bias throughout was that of an East Coast liberal conservative. It was the bias of most of his British listeners.

Alistair Cooke's writing was extraordinary. He wrote in conversation and he spoke in prose. In fifty-eight years of *Letter from America* he perfected the journalism of personal witness, adapting it brilliantly to the medium of radio. His mellifluous mid-Atlantic voice treated Britain and America as if they were two armchairs talking to each other, with 'the Pond' as coffee table. Above all, he knew his craft. He never wrote a dull sentence. He never lost touch with narrative, with the commentator as storyteller, learned from his love of theatre and movies. He understood that listeners wanted more than the old standbys of anecdote and opinion. They craved context and history. As his years lengthened into decades, Cooke's journalism acquired a depth inaccessible to younger practitioners.

Here was a man who could recall Hoover and Roosevelt. He could compare Churchill and Truman as orators, for he had heard them both. He could remember the arrival of air conditioning, the building of freeways, the exploding of the atom bomb and Bobby Jones making the green in one. His letters from America brought the New World into the drawing rooms of the Old, not as a series of sensational events but as a rounded culture. His journalism published and broadcast in the United States returned the compliment. It brought British culture to American attention. In periods when the two countries seemed at risk of tearing apart from each other, he linked hands and held them tight.

Cooke's work and outlook were rooted in his past. He was born with the name of Alfred in 1908 in Salford, Lancashire. His father was a metalworker, Methodist lay preacher and teetotaller. His early theatrical and writing talent was noticed by his teachers, who encouraged him to a Cambridge scholarship. The upwardly mobile Cooke changed his Christian name to Alistair and applied himself furiously to acting, producing and writing. He founded The Mummers and edited *Granta*. By the age of twenty-two he was suggesting himself to the *Manchester Guardian* and the BBC as a contributor on theatre, poetry and literature.

In 1932 he struck gold. He won a Harkness Fellowship to Yale and Harvard. The curtain opened on what seemed an even more glittering stage. For the drama of theatre he exchanged the drama of America.

Cooke's early ambition was to become a leading theatre director. This ambition was cursed by his success in transatlantic journalism and the people he met thereby. He was taken up by another British refugee, Charlie Chaplin, and wrote scripts for him. Cooke married an American model, Ruth Emerson (a relative of Ralph Waldo), and moved back and forth between London and America in search of work, becoming the film critic for the BBC in 1934. He wrote a *Letter from London* for NBC, allegedly clocking up 40,000 words for American outlets at the time of the Abdication in 1936. Back in America, he suggested a similar venture in reverse, for the BBC. With the outbreak of war he risked his reputation on both sides of the Atlantic by taking out American citizenship, granted in 1941.

Cooke's career in America was initially that of a normal foreign correspondent. In the 1940s he worked variously for *The Times*, the *Daily Sketch* and the *Daily Herald*. In 1940 he also began regular broadcasts for the BBC, titled *American Letter* (they became *Letter from America* in 1950). Early records show the producers remarking on 'a tendency to be allusive and glib'. Yet throughout the war Cooke built up an audience approaching six million. In 1945 he was asked to cover the opening of the United Nations for the *Manchester Guardian*. Three years later he became that paper's chief American correspondent at the then huge salary of $14,000 a year, a happy homecoming for a son of Salford. He retained this post for a quarter-century.

Working for the *Guardian* in the 1950s and 1960s allowed Cooke to cover the emergence of the new global superpower. He was never a normal news hound. Most correspondents in America were, and still are, 'Beltway fanatics'. They paced the corridors and smoke-filled rooms of Congress and the White House, and saw little else. Washington at the time was still a town with a single industry, that of politics. This was not the sort of town likely to appeal to a man with Cooke's wider interests.

He duly covered America from New York, a fact crucial to the content and style of *Letter from America*. This was controversial. The *Manchester Guardian*'s Washington correspondents at the time were Max Freedman and Richard Scott. The fact that the paper's 'Chief Correspondent' was resident in New York was the source of much bickering. It gave Cooke a reputation among journalists as problematic, indeed 'a nuisance'. He was rarely at the scene of events. His witnessing of the murdered Bobby Kennedy—'like the stone face of a child lying on a cathedral tomb'—was exceptional. He called it 'a casual chance in a thousand'.

Washington reporting, like British 'lobby journalism', was that of politics and the gossip of the political street. Such coverage is necessary, but never sufficient in depicting a country. Cooke's view of America was different. His America was rich in politics, but politics seen as ordinary Americans saw it, including from television. It was from television that he wrote his celebrated Letters after the death of JFK. To Cooke, the most important event of the week rarely happened in Washington. He travelled to every state, missing only Alaska. America was 'happening' in Little Rock or Dallas or Los Angeles or Chicago. It was Ali versus Frazier, or the death of Dorothy Parker. It was a movie or a ball game or the changing leaves of a New England fall.

*   *   *

His presence in New York was also crucial for Cooke's work beyond journalism. Most Americans knew him as a writer and television presenter. He hosted a weekly arts programme, *Omnibus*, for CBS. In 1972 he produced *Alistair Cooke's America*, a television series screened in thirty countries. Recordings are in every public library in America, and the resulting book sold two million copies. He had stopped working for the *Guardian* to produce the series. This in turn led to *Masterpiece Theatre* for the PBS network. In this role millions of Americans came to associate Cooke with the canon of English literature, mostly through the medium of BBC costume dramas. This tweedy, amiable intellectual seemed the perfect custodian of the temple of English drama, from Shakespeare to *Upstairs, Downstairs*. He was to receive four Emmys for his work.

Cooke's lifestyle was that of an East Coast aesthete. His hobbies were American and fanatical: jazz, movies and golf. His first marriage failed, leaving a son, and in 1946 he married an artist, Jane White Hawkes. She came with two children by a former husband and together they had a daughter. The couple moved between a comfortable (rent-controlled) apartment on Fifth Avenue overlooking Central Park and Jane's weekend house on Long Island. The Cookes would 'season' in San Francisco and visit Britain twice a year to see their British family—such visits usually coinciding with Wimbledon and the major golf tournaments.

Letter from America formed a most remarkable sequence of sustained commentary. Its original remit from the BBC was to record 'the passions, manners and flavour of another nation's way of life'. The mission was hardly innovative—witness Cooke's own heroes Mark Twain and H. L. Mencken—but Cooke put it on radio. The result was not a 'column'. Nor does it merit the pompous style of essay. Though the Letters make much use of the first person singular, they have none of the cloying self-regard of modern 'I-journalism'. Cooke is the observer of events, not a participant. I would apply to the Letters the honourable journalistic term of stories. They tell a tale, sometimes two or three. They are one man's take on the world 'as I saw it'.

Cooke accepted the retort that this made him seem ambivalent, a fence-sitter, 'a moral coward for refusing to take a stand'. He was criticized as pussy-footing on Vietnam, and his biographer, Nick Clarke, records the *Guardian*'s view that 'he had a blind spot about the civil rights movement'. As the years rolled by he moved progressively to the right. His early adoration of Adlai Stevenson was later settled on Ronald Reagan. At the end of his life he accepted the Pentagon line on Iraq. But to every critic he cheerfully replied that 'once every four years . . . I vote'. Beyond that was only 'the discovery that in life the range of irreconcilable points of view, characters, flaws, idiosyncrasies and virtues is astounding'.

The style of the Letters was influential and much imitated in both print and broadcasting. It has come near to parody in its BBC offspring, *From Our Own Correspondent*, anecdotal, herbivorous and mildly self-indulgent. Cooke's version was in a class of its own. Though written and rehearsed for speaking, the Letters remain 'writings', owing a debt to Cooke's tutor, Arthur Quiller-Couch, a champion of simplicity and clarity. They have the laconic touch of Cooke's hero, the Baltimore columnist H. L. Mencken, and display Mencken's hatred of cant and love of plain-speaking. But the mastery of cadence and colour which made *Letter from America* so fluent on the ear was, in my view, born of Cooke's love of theatre. There is no better training for any writer than to listen to the cry of the actor and feel the lash of the newsroom. Cooke benefited from both.

The shared Anglo-American culture is rooted not in politics but in history. *Letter from America* was never a 'home thought from abroad'. It showed no Browning nostalgia for 'the chaffinch on the orchard bough' from a land of the 'gaudy melon-flower'. Nor was Cooke a post-imperial Kipling. His Fifth Avenue apartment bore little comparison with 'an old Moulmein Pagoda looking lazy at the sea'. The surprise of Cooke's America was its familiarity. It was written for and heard by those who knew America from the cinema, music and newsreels.

Britons still look to America before they look anywhere else. They visit America, they absorb American culture, they enjoy American exports, they marry American spouses. More Britons could name the Mayor of New York City or the Governor of California than the leader of any English provincial city. The metropolises of New York and London are Siamese twins, two districts of one city, two venues of one culture. They have more in common with each other than with their respective hinterlands. Hardly an American magazine or newspaper is without a British byline. Hardly a British radio programme is without an American voice. Business, academia, music, art and architecture operate by mid-Atlantic values from mid-Atlantic institutions.

At the end of the Cold War it was asserted that Britain would now 'choose' Europe. Within a decade, in the so-called war on terror and in Iraq, it was emphatically choosing America. The burst of anti-Americanism which accompanied the war was an aberration, not a norm. Indeed, much of the protest over the Iraq war was itself Anglo-American in origin. At the time of Cooke's death the Atlantic bond seemed as tight as ever and the gulf with the rest of the world as wide.

Former Secretary of State Henry Kissinger, with his long experience of office, called the bonds between America and Britain 'matter-of-factly intimate', to a degree 'probably never practised before between sovereign states'. He was echoing de Gaulle's view that Britain 'neither thinks nor acts like a continental nation'. The most recent custodian of the special relationship, Tony Blair, would tell his staff that not to be by America's side through any crisis or travail was 'simply unthinkable'.

Cooke's lifework was to be Boswell to that relationship. *Letter from America* was his diary and his testament. There may be no one America, single and true. But Cooke's America is the truest we have.

Simon Jenkins
July 2004

Editor's Note

The last collection of Alistair Cooke's *Letter from America* was published in 1979 (*The Americans*) and, along with two earlier collections (*Letters from America*, 1951, *Talk About America*, 1968), has been long out of print. Alistair had always intended to complete a fourth collection of letters taken from the 1980s and 1990s—a collection that he liked to refer to as 'The Last Post'—but as time moved on his energies became exclusively dedicated to the writing of his weekly broadcast letter. He maintained this focus of attention right up until the last letter, number 2869, broadcast on 20 February 2004, just six weeks before he died. When he appointed me as his literary executor he also assigned me the task of preparing this volume selected from the entire period of his broadcast letters, 1946–2004. As his book editor and last British publisher of his two collections of essays (*Fun and Games*, 1994, and *Memories of the Great and the Good*, 1999), Alistair knew that I understood his requirements and fortunately he left clear guidelines for this collection.

In his first published volume Alistair wrote in the Preface: 'A good many of the letters I have had from listeners to the series were from people who can hardly put pen to paper. Their taste seemed to coincide with my own: they got pleasure from talks which I felt had managed to convey some human experience in a language most people can understand. These successes average about one in five, but they are not necessarily the ones that look best in print. But by the time the series had run to two hundred there appeared to be a good handful that would survive the translation into black and white. Accordingly, the pieces that follow were selected by this test. They were chosen on no other principle.' With this in mind, for the years 1946–1980, there was no need to go further than to select those letters that I consider to be the best taken from the earlier books. In this process I was much helped by the writer and editor George Perry, who proved, as always, a sound adviser.

The selections made from 1980 to 2004 required more detailed review. Several folders of manuscript letters marked on the outside in Alistair's handwriting as 'The Chosen' were found and then typed up 'squeaky clean', as he had requested, by Patti Yasek, his redoubtable assistant. I have been supported in making the final selection not only by Patti but also by Alistair's daughter Susan Cooke Kittredge. They have both provided huge encouragement and I was relieved that this final selection agreed with so many of Susan's own choices. In addition Stuart Proffitt, Publishing Director at Penguin, has contributed many recommendations and has provided valuable advice in relation to the overall selection. With such wealth of material it has been difficult to achieve a perfect balance for each decade and I have decided to give more emphasis to the second part of Alistair's career where none of the letters has, until now, been published in volume form.

As on his earlier collections I have tried my best

to apply Alistair's principle, in choosing those letters that work best in print. I have also provided a wide range of contents, and indeed tried to include some surprises that might correspond on the page to the experience of tuning in on a Friday evening or Sunday morning to hear the often unexpected topic that Alistair was addressing that day. As with the earlier collections the letters 'except for a little trimming and polishing, appear here as they were broadcast'.

There is no better preface that can apply to this collection than Alistair's original opening to the first collection published in 1951 which included the following passage:

Some months after the war was over the BBC asked me to go to London and discuss the sort of broadcasting I might do in what was then called the peace. I had been talking about America to Britain since 1934 and from America to Britain since three years after that. My one-man band met the same fate as everybody else's in the autumn of 1939. And through the war years I doubled in brass and learned to play the solemn trombone of a political commentator. Politics will undoubtedly bedevil us all till the day we die, but when General MacArthur stood on the deck of the *Missouri* and said in his resounding baritone, 'These proceedings are closed,' I took him at his word and, like most other people, yearned to get back to the important things in life. Even the prospect of early annihilation should not keep us from making the most of our days on this unhappy planet. In the best of times, our days are numbered, anyway. And it would be a crime against Nature for any generation to take the world crisis so solemnly that it put off enjoying those things for which we were presumably designed in the first place, and which the gravest statesmen and the hoarsest politicians hope to make available to all men in the end: I mean the opportunity to do good work, to fall in love, to enjoy friends, to sit under trees, to read, to hit a ball and bounce the baby.

The suspicion that these things are what most men and women everywhere want led me to suggest, in London in 1946, that Britons might be more honestly enticed into an interest in America and Americans by hearing about their way of life and their tastes in these fundamental things than by suffering instruction in the procedures of the American Senate and the subtleties of the corn-hog ratio. Mr Lindsay Wellington, then director of the Home Service, responded so promptly to this that he suggested I forget politics altogether and accept an assignment to talk about anything and everything in America that interested me. To do this for a large and very mixed audience, ranging from shrewd bishops to honest carpenters, was a challenge to explain in the simplest and most vivid terms the passions, the manners, the flavour of another nation's way of life. It was a formidable assignment, for though a man might make sense of his travels in his own way for his own friends, broadcasting demands of him, if he respects the medium at all, that, as the old Greek had it, he 'think like a wise man and talk in the language of the people'. I don't know whether this has ever been done, except at various times by minstrels, the greatest religious teachers and comedians of genius.

But out of this bold ambition grew a series of weekly talks to Britain which I called Letter from America. They were commissioned in March 1946 for a tentative run of thirteen weeks; and by the grace of the BBC, the receptiveness of the British listener, and the stubborn endurance of the pound sterling, they still at this writing go on. After a year or two the number of listeners asking for copies of scripts began to strain the mimeographing resources of the BBC's New York office. Some people took so kindly to them that they urged me to put them out as a book. This has the same effect on a broadcaster as a nomination for the Presidency of the United States on a first-class cement manufacturer. The thing is patently absurd except to his cronies, but the idea first flatters, then haunts him, and he ends by feeling he must accept a sacred duty to save the Republic.

Most of these pieces were written at the end of a week's work without my knowing, as I faced the typewriter, what I was going to talk about. But they were all written in freedom and in pleasure.

Alistair Cooke's *Letter from America* was an astonishing and unique achievement that reached a listening audience of some twenty-two million worldwide. It would have been his hope that these letters will be read, as he wrote them, 'in freedom and in pleasure' throughout the world.

Colin Webb
July 2004

The 1980s

Bringing Up Baby

2 January 1981

You wake up under a strange ceiling and pad over to a strange window and look out on a sun just chasing the night away and suddenly lighting up a landscape that blinds your eyes. The valley's bone white and the forests on the mountains like stockades of thistledown. Every branch of every tree is bearing a sword of snow. The road that curves past this old farmhouse and up into the mountains is gleaming with ice. A car comes scudding by, and if you were brought up in what they call a temperate climate you may wonder for a moment how any car could hold a foot of the road. But in this part of the world, work and life have to go on in a planet of snow, and you couldn't drive anywhere if you didn't have snow tyres and four-wheel drive. You go off to the bathroom and take a peek at the two-way thermometer in the window. On the left column is the indoor temperature, on the right the outdoor. The left says 70 degrees precisely, and that's what the thermostat says, set for every room in the house. The outdoor temperature is ridiculous. Below freezing, the column turns blue. Below zero, it turns red. Well, something must be wrong. Turn on the radio and hear the man giving the ski conditions and then the weather forecast. He says, 'Twenty-eight inches base, six inches of fresh powder, the lifts are holding.' That's something you've never heard before. Lifts holding! My son-in-law tells me that

3

means 'no downhill skiing'. A very rare prohibition, I gather. Why? The man goes on: 'Happy New Year, people. The temperature stands now at 34 degrees below zero and that's considerably warmer than it was during the night. But cross-country skiers should be warned that the wind chill factor is such that it feels like 80 degrees below zero.' This is so preposterous that it's impossible to take in, until you go out later in the brilliant midday light. We go out in turns, my son-in-law having warmed up the car. Ready, Adam, go. Zeb, go. Next their mother with a ten-week-old baby, a fat, faceless bundle of clothes. Then grandma. Then the old man. We're off, to call on a neighbour.

You'll gather we're in northern Vermont, and one of the striking things about life here during the Christmas holidays is that people shop and visit and hardly mention the weather. Any more than people in the Caribbean mention the temperature of the sea they swim in. This time, though, we did shake hands with this neighbouring family, and an old man said, 'a little nippy out there'. A young relation, visiting from Alaska, says, 'it's almost a relief to me. Where I come from it's been 60 below zero every day for the last three weeks.' The old man, if *I* call him an old man, he's an *old man*. He reminisces. He's a Vermonter, and he recalls the most biting cold he ever experienced. 'Once,' he says, 'I was in Scotland in July. It was my first and only time there. And we were in a little hotel by the sea. Well, it was a holiday, so what do I do but go in swimming. Holy smoke!' he says, 'you ever tried that? I went and bought a thermometer. I couldn't believe it. The water was 55 degrees—55 degrees! I was out of that water quicker than a dog with fleas.

4

It left a lifelong impression.'

This is my contribution to the theory of relativity. All such words as hot, cold, sweet, sour, dry, wet have no absolute meaning at all. They depend on what you heard from your parents in the place you were brought up in. You do wonder how they, the English, of all people, ever colonized and settled northern New England (a famous photographer once said that if America had been discovered at California and the colonizers had then moved east, New England, with its glacial soil and Arctic winters never would have been settled). But living up here for some days, you don't wonder that there's little talk about Mr Reagan's Cabinet appointments, or the hostages, or who's going to be or maybe has just been appointed Secretary of the Interior. Survival is all.

Missiles and laser beams are another matter. The first morning I came down to the kitchen, I found on the icebox (the refrigerator) door two notes, one practically a thesis written by my grandsons. The 8-year-old has printed his thesis out with painstaking precision. It says: 'The Cosmos is ever expanding, even as a tree grows, as a rocket is zooming through deep space, as a satellite is launched. There are more wonders on space, like we will send men to Saturn. We'll send people to stars or other universes. The vast Cosmos has more stars than there are single grains of sand on Earth. Isn't that unbelievable?' He's obviously hooked on Carl Sagan. The other note is from the 5-year-old and has been there since Christmas morning. It says: 'Mother, I am thankful for my X-wing fighter, my brown suit, my Millenium Falcon, and Eliza.' (Eliza is the new baby.) Both the boys are hipped on *Star Wars* and in all the reams of political stuff that comes on the evening television news. There's only one sort of item that makes them perk up: anything about the M-X missile or the proposed deployment of a new intercontinental what not. I set this down as a fact, without comment, except to say that I was once close to a scientist, a very good scientist and a sweet serious-minded man and devoted father. He forbade his sons ever to play with toy pistols or soldiers. One boy was frightened for life. The other went into the Marines.

I suppose every generation of young parents proceeds on a theory of bringing up children. I have in my time watched the waxing and waning of several fashions, but may I whisper to grandparents that it's important never to use that word in relation to the serious business of how to bring up a child. Every first-time mother is grateful for the fact that after centuries of trial and error, her generation has arrived finally at universal truth. I go back to the dark ages when babies were slapped for wetting their pants; then to the time when mothers stayed in the hospital with their newborn for about ten days. Then the pendulum swung and mothers were told to sit up and dangle their legs the first day and get out the third day at the latest. I am ashamed but secretly relieved to say that, in my time, the father stayed home and brooded, whereas it is now compulsory for the expectant father to attend fatherhood classes for several weeks beforehand and assist in person at the birth. My children's baby doctor was an enormously tall, gangling bony man with an amiable loose-limbed manner who regarded nothing that happened to

6

babies as odd. He seemed to us, anyway, to sweep away, with his affable presence, dense fogs of Victorian superstition and old wives' tales. His physical presence did, however, terrify my daughter for a time. But we were as dogmatic as all young parents and thought he was one in a hundred. His name was Ben Spock, and I understand he went on to make quite a name for himself.

I don't know how far we've come from old Ben, but my daughter is up on every new movement in diet, environmentalism, baby care and the rest. And I must say I was astonished, when the baby cried, to see at hand an object which I thought had been banished since about 1920. It was what we in England called a dummy, and what Americans called a pacifier. The wheel, one of the wheels anyway, has come full circle. Thirty years ago, it was thought to be the most witless, primitive and ruinous device ever given to a baby. It was said to pull the upper teeth out, and it may well have been the reason why some of my college friends, otherwise fairly handsome, came to resemble Bugs Bunny. Well, Eliza has a dummy, but it is an orthodontic pacifier, approved by dentists. It is not just a blob of rubber. It looks more like the snout of a dolphin, curving up to stay under the upper gum without requiring too much outward pull to keep it in. (I hope they're right about this one.)

You'll gather, from these intensely domestic concerns that Washington, which is only six hundred miles south of here, seems as remote as Peking. I feel like Captain Scott at the Pole, except that if Captain Scott had had central heating, as well as a Swedish stove, and snow tyres, and an electric typewriter, a word computer, not to mention lashings of shrimp, pâté, chicken, geese, cakes and a huge plum pudding (because of grandpa's English origins, this un-American item is considerately included in the Christmas fare), Captain Scott would have retired to the House of Lords and died in bed.

Since we do not choose to drive into the village in what is now 31 degrees below zero to pick up the *New York Times*, we must fall back on the local paper, which is delivered to the door, come 30 below or 90 above. It is a journal not to be sneezed at. Apart from the usual international and Washington stories, and the numbing pictures of the hostages, there is a local item that makes a four-column headline. A federal court has struck down a law, which banned highway billboards in the neighbouring state of Maine. This disturbs Vermont, whose extraordinary beauty has gone unsullied since 1968 when it passed a law banning every form of outdoor advertising throughout the state. The court's ground is that outdoor advertising is a form of freedom of speech, guaranteed by the Constitution. We can only hope that if it goes to the Supreme Court, the nine old men will decide that the screaming defilement of the highways and byways and valleys and mountains is not a form of free speech the Founding Fathers were eager to preserve.

The art students of the local high school have put on an exhibition of a life-size group of Jimmy Who, Donald Duck, Richard Nixon, Abe Lincoln and Mick Jagger playing a silent hand of stud poker. And the local church of the Nativity has still on display a crib to remind us of what Christmas is about. If this is rather a humdrum thing, we see on

8

the television that in Bethlehem, there were soldiers (in full battledress) on duty at the site of Jesus' birth, to keep an eye on the crowds flocking around Manger Square—which is now a parking lot. Well, as the taxi drivers say, 'You can't stop progress, can you?'

Attempted Assassination of President Reagan

3 April 1981

Our plane was coming in from San Francisco, nosing in through endless layers of cotton wool, with the rain streaming against the windows and no land in sight, till we suddenly spun out of a ground mist and hit the runway. As the brakes roared on and the plane slowed to make the long taxi to the terminal, the captain came on the public address system. He said there was something he wanted to tell us, 'not by way of sensationalism' (he said), about something that had happened in mid-afternoon. I assumed there'd been some trouble with the plane, and he had sensibly waited to tell us about it till we were safe and sound. He was mumbling very low into his microphone. I think he didn't want to sound 'sensational', but unfortunately he could hardly be heard. It was something about the President and a secretary. Then he said a little more clearly that two and a half hours ago an assassination attempt had been made on the President, and he was now in surgery in a Washington hospital. It was something he

9

thought we ought to know.

At Kennedy (which used to be Idlewild Airport before the assassination of that President), people waited for their baggage, and I don't think the most imaginative or hyped-up reporter could have seen anything different in the behaviour of the people, from that of any other day. Maybe there was less jocular small talk. Most people looked tired and patient. Perhaps by now we are resigned to atrocity, as infantrymen get used to seeing dead bodies.

We happened to get possibly the only Chinese cab driver at the airport who spoke little English and had no radio. So it was nearly an hour before we were home, and turning on the television and seeing there—almost like a cruel replay of Dallas, 1963—startled Secret Service men, people falling to the ground, and a sudden scrum of men huddled over a young man.

Fortunately, for the country, the anxious hours were blessedly few. The first authoritative spokesman, the man who conducted an evening press conference at the hospital, was one Dr Dennis O'Leary, the dean of clinical affairs at George Washington University Hospital. By great good luck, he was one doctor in a thousand, in that he had an immediate air of candour and authority; he sensed in a flash what sort of language would enlighten people without alarming them. He had humour, when it was appropriate to have it; he was responsive to intelligent questions and courteously non-committal to idiotic questions. And he was able, as doctors very rarely are, to translate the abominable jargon of his trade into sensible and even subtle English that any of us could understand. Of course, the fates were with him.

10

The President had been jaunty about his wound, he had the luck of what Dr O'Leary called 'fine physiological health . . . a very young 70-year-old', and the bullet had stayed inches away from a fatal point of entry. Still, looking back on it, I think we all owe an enormous debt to Dr O'Leary. He is young enough to have come to take for granted what actually scandalized an older generation: the expectation that the press would want to know all the medical details and had a right to have them. This tradition is very new, though we were already inured to the historical shift in journalistic practice when President Eisenhower had his heart attack. Day after day in Denver his doctor came before the media, and described everything in great detail, down to the consistency of the President's bowel movements. Ever since then, a public man hides from the press the symptoms of any affliction, however mild, at his peril. Obviously, it has become harder and harder for a doctor to instruct the layman in the facts without leaving little loopholes through which the dumber sort of journalist will fish out lurid inferences.

So what Dr O'Leary did, on the evening of the wounding of the President, was to restore the morale of the country in a decent and authoritative way. He was helped, of course, by being able to report the heartening fact that the President had shown an almost puckish bravery of spirit. Dr O'Leary deserves the Medal of Freedom— especially because the scene in the White House, where you would properly expect authority to take hold, was a muddled, and for a time, a faintly alarming one. I'm afraid the culprit here was General Haig, the Secretary of State. It is quite

11

true that he was, very shortly after the shooting, the senior member of the Cabinet who happened to be on hand. He at once decided that since the Vice President was flying back from Texas, he—Mr Haig—was now in charge of the government. Of course, he wasn't; President Reagan was, until either the President declared himself disabled to continue in office, or the Vice President and a majority of the Cabinet told (in writing) the pro tem President of the Senate and the Speaker of the House that the President was unable to discharge his duties. Then, and then only, the Vice President becomes Acting President. This is all set forth quite precisely in the 25th Amendment to the Constitution. And suppose that the President dies, and after him—or with him—the Vice President, the succession then goes to the Speaker of the House. *He* is third in line. But Mr Haig, when all about him might have been losing their heads, rushed on to television with darting eyes and a sweaty forehead. He was nervous and he was dogmatic. He was, he said, 'in control'. He could have been in control in a purely practical sense at the moment, but his fatal remark came when he was asked why. He mentioned the Constitution and repeated the gaffe that the Secretary of State succeeds after the President and the Vice President, thus showing, as one commentator put it, 'an incredible lack of understanding of constitutional succession'.

There is, however, another line of succession, which has to do with the command structure of the military, the Pentagon. When Mr Haig got away from his unfortunate performance on television, he went back to what is known in the White House as

12

the Situation Room, the place where crucial military decisions are made, invariably in the presence of the President, who, we should remember, is the Commander-in-Chief of all the armed forces. There, the Secretary of Defense, Mr Weinberger, felt it his duty to tell Mr Haig that he was not in charge of that structure either. The command passes from the President to the Vice President and then to the Secretary of Defense—nobody but Mr Weinberger. Altogether, an acutely unhappy time for Secretary Haig. But he, and the people, were put right at once by the chief Washington correspondents of two networks.

One of the more stupid but I suppose inevitable questions put to Dr O'Leary, of all political neutrals, was whether or not there was evidence of a conspiracy. He wouldn't think of commenting on that. And from what we know, and we know a great deal about the life and character of the pathetic John Hinckley, he was no more of a conspirator than the equally pathetic 18-year-old bartender who fired twice on Constitution Hill at the very young Queen Victoria and missed. Edward Oxford (this was his name) did not have a repeater. Unlike John Hinckley, he did not have the means to spray half a dozen shots in two seconds at several targets. Hinckley, at this time anyway, appears to be a sick, and lovesick, young man acting out a fantasy with a girl he had never met, and meaning, more than anything, to make himself important by a violent act.

Inevitably, old arguments have been brought up and old morals have been drawn. The campaign for stricter control of handguns (Washington, DC, by the way, has one of the strictest laws, as strict as

13

anything that might be written into a federal law) takes on new strength, through indignation, after every murder or attempted murder of a prominent person. It raged after John Kennedy's death, then waned; raged again after the assassination of Martin Luther King, Jr., the paralysing of Governor George Wallace, the death of Bobby Kennedy, the shooting of John Lennon. But these crusades always fade away, not, as many angry people charge, because the rifle lobby is very powerful in Washington, which it is, but because millions of Americans are scared enough of violence on the streets and against their homes to feel that a law to ban handguns would render the citizen helpless against the criminal, who will always get a gun somehow. At any rate, there is not likely to be much success in the next crusade, since President Reagan himself is strongly against gun control. His solution, as Governor of California, was, and still is, a compulsory sentence of from five to fifteen years in jail for anyone committing a crime while in possession of a gun.

I leave the grave and undoubtedly sincere moralizing about the sickness of this country, of our time, to others. If violence is indeed a special sickness of our age, it is universal, and nobody so far has come up with a cure. But I will end by reminding you that such characters as John Hinckley seem to be around at all times, especially in a country which offers to a fugitive the escape-hatch of a continent. The proper comparison between violence in America is not with any one country but with the whole of Europe. On any given day, the Protective Research Section of the United States Secret Service has on file the names

14

of not less than fifty thousand persons who have written threatening or obscene letters to the incumbent President. Fifteen hundred new letters are added every month. Repeaters are tracked down, simply from their letters, and the Secret Service claims an average of 98 per cent of such people are apprehended, many of them tried and put away. John Hinckley, it appears now, was one of the 2 per cent who slipped through the net.

The Fourth of July

2 July 1982

Next door to my apartment house, or, if it helps, block of flats, is a small three-storey house in a French style, what used to be called a carriage house. Thirty years ago or more, it was owned and lived in by a wealthy New York eccentric. His most endearing habit was that of dressing up, as men did in those days, dressing up in white tie and tails for the first night of the Metropolitan Opera season, going down there and standing on his head on the sidewalk outside the opera house. This feat was always received with applause by the passers-by. Well, he died years ago, and the Metropolitan openings have never been quite the same since. His house was sold and turned into a school. It was the first private school in Manhattan that truly integrated whites and blacks. Through the 1950s and 1960s there'd been several so-called progressive schools (disciples of the theories of John Dewey) which boasted a few token blacks

15

who were there if their parents could afford the fees. This massaged the social conscience of the whites and presented the black children with the unenviable task of pretending to belong to the upper-middle-class white WASP culture, without emotional strain. But the people next door, the young couple who twenty years ago set up this mixed school, started with something like 30 per cent black children and now the races are about equally divided; I mean integrated. The blacks come from—I was going to say all sorts of backgrounds, but the social range of blacks anywhere in this country is pretty narrow. (I don't want to seem to be making a snide comment; we should still not forget that at the last count I'm aware of, about ten years ago, more black children went to college in this country than white children in the British Isles.) However, whereas the first lot of black children next door were nearly all from poor Harlem families, by now there's more than a sprinkling of the new black middle class, whose parents work in offices, banks, the professions, all the places where, thirty years ago, the work force was uniformly white. How do the majority of these poorish black children get to the school? They are there on financial support, scholarships and the like, raised by the school itself.

Well, I was coming along the block to my entrance the other morning and could barely thread my way through a pile-up of duffel bags and kitbags and battered little suitcases and string bags and—bags. Sitting on them were the tots, holding hands or sulkily refusing to hold hands, with their mothers. But most of them were hopping around as merry as crickets. They were waiting for a bus, a

16

bus half the size of a city block, which eventually glided up. It looked like an air-conditioned mausoleum with its dark brown tinted windows. It had printed on the side 'Adirondack Bus Tours Inc.' I knew then what the children were doing with their duffel bags. They were off like a vast army of young New Yorkers between the ages of, say, 7 and 12, to summer camp. And this lot was off to the Adirondacks: a lush, mountainous region of upstate New York, much of it protected by state law, where 4,000–5,000-foot mountains are carpeted —bristled would be better—with forests of spruce, pine and hemlock and tower over a couple of hundred lakes, naturally, a summer mecca for tourists and campers and school camps (a winter mecca, by the way, for such things as Olympic skiing).

The sight of all these small fry bundling themselves and their bags into the bus was a gladsome one and a sharp reminder that school was out everywhere, and that this is the weekend of the Fourth: Independence Day—the Fourth of July, falling this year on a Sunday and therefore, according to recent custom and union insistence, making Monday a holiday too. The Fourth is understandably the oldest of American national holidays, since it celebrates the adoption by the original thirteen colonies of the Declaration, signed two days earlier, that proclaimed their independence of England. Of the especially American national holidays, there are only three that are truly national: the Fourth, George Washington's birthday and Thanksgiving. Columbus Day, hailing the discovery of the New World itself, is not celebrated in Alaska. Certainly

17

the word has got there by now, but at five or six thousand miles from old Christopher's landfall, it must seem unreal. Lincoln's birthday, a stranger might assume, is a cause for national celebration, but to this day it is politely ignored in the South. George Washington's birthday, you would swear, is celebrated in all the fifty states. And so it now is, but only since 1955, when the Governor of Idaho had to be nudged, by yours truly, with the sinister reminder that his state was the only one in the Union that failed to recognize Washington's birthday as a legal holiday. I'm proud to say that I have in my possession, suitable for framing, a letter from the then Governor with a hasty postscript, in his own hand, which says: 'A bill is now before me for signature. It will have my approval, and February 22nd, 1955, will be a legal holiday in Idaho.—Robert E. Smylie, Governor.'

But there have been no such oversights about the celebration of the Fourth of July. The Fourth of July is for everybody. Within a year of the signing of the Declaration, the main cities of the thirteen emancipated states got busy with parades, the firing of guns, ringing of bells, the explosion of fireworks. Boston started the custom of getting things going with a prayer. Charleston, South Carolina, was I believe, the first city enlightened enough to require the drinking of thirteen toasts by way of saluting the independence of the thirteen colonies. Philadelphia twisted the knife in the wound of the British lion by forcing a German band to provide the music. (They were Hessians, and the Hessians, unlike the French and, at the last minute, the Spanish, had bet on the wrong winner. The Hessians had been hired by England to fight the colonial rebels, and the Philadelphia band was made up of musical prisoners of war.)

After the new nation got its second and its permanent form of government, with the adoption of the Constitution of the United States, the custom of high jinks on the Fourth spread to smaller towns. And by the time, during the next sixty-odd years, that pioneers had pushed through the Appalachians, across the prairie and the Rockies and the High Sierras, the annual festival had reached California. Once the festivities spread to country towns, the celebrations became less formal and less grand, but no less fervent. The bawling politician, who made a heyday of the Fourth, came in and only gradually faded away. But there were everywhere picnics, potato-sack races, and contests in eating the most watermelons or catching the greasiest pig. Most of this has gone now and been supplanted by rock concerts, jazz festivals, in the Western states by rodeos, and in California by giant barbecues, log-rolling contests, Hollywood Bowl Super-recitals, and supermarket specials of two jumbo burgers for the price of one.

An early piece I dug up, from a historical dictionary, says: 'Throughout the two centuries, however, fireworks, great and small, have held a foremost place.' So they have, but not without much hand-wringing from the city and state fathers. Fireworks, including even crackers and sparklers, are illegal in New York, New Jersey, Connecticut and many more states.

But this is a fact of life that most people consider, as they considered the prohibition law, more of a nuisance than a prohibition. There's something grave and dotty, and typically American, it seems to me, about a government commission (the Federal Consumer Product Safety Commission) and the statement it put out this weekend. Fireworks are illegal, right? Right. So, the commissioner says: 'Fireworks sometimes do things they are not supposed to. People should be extremely careful.' Last year more than eleven thousand Americans were treated in hospitals for injuries from fireworks that did things they are not supposed to. The Commission, acting responsibly in the knowledge that fireworks are illegal, has now put out seven rules or precautions to help people set off fireworks safely, such as: make sure the fuses are attached; don't use leaky fireworks; have adults on hand to supervise fire-cracking children; ignite fireworks outdoors. And, my favourite: 'Call the local police or fire department if you are unsure about the law.' The law, that is, that you are going to break.

Of course, I guess the big deal on the Fourth of July weekend for most Americans is neither a watermelon contest nor a rodeo nor a rock concert. It is flocking to the stadiums to watch baseball, or, and I should guess many more millions are doing it, sitting in the living room with two or three buddies, getting out the six-pack of beer, pulling down the shades against the intrusion of the noonday sun and *watching* baseball on the box. A big minority will be watching the Wimbledon finals on the box, and a smaller minority will be watching golf. A smaller minority still, say no more than fifteen million, will be banging a tennis ball or scuffing a golf ball, and wishing they'd stayed with tossing horseshoes.

An odd minority, showbiz stars and agents and

20

such, at the end of a winter run, will be off to open up their houses at the end of Long Island. This is the weekend they used to trek like homing pigeons to the Adirondacks where the little blacks and whites are going. That reminds me of a story involving the great musical comedy, rather operetta, composer: Sigmund Romberg. He had a summer house up there in the Adirondacks. He was a bridge addict, and had a favourite partner. One time, they played through the night, and as the final hand was dealt, Romberg and his pal gambled all or nothing on the last hand. They were about to make a killing. The partner picked up his hand. He had one heart, leaned back, and as airily as possible, started to hum the tune of Romberg's great hit: 'One Alone'. No visible recognition from Romberg. They lost. The furious pal took Romberg in a corner afterwards and said, 'Rommy, what's the matter with you? I gave you the sign!' What sign? 'I started to hum, "One Alone", my heart was yours, for Pete's sake.' Romberg, a vain man, said, 'Ach! Who knows from lyrics?'

Old Man Reagan

12 October 1984

We have just over three weeks to go to the Presidential election, which is always the first Tuesday in November. And while all the reporters travelling with both camps, and all the commentators and all the pollsters, have unravelled and re-ravelled every possible 'issue'

21

that might decide the outcome, suddenly, out of the blue, there comes looming up an issue that was dead and buried four years ago. A man from Mars who knew nothing about American politics might have guessed at it as an important issue, but that would only have shown his charming ignorance of the whole subject. It is the issue of President Reagan's age.

Surely it's always been there. Well, no, it hasn't. Of course, when Mr Reagan was nominated by the Republicans four years ago, it was a lively theme. Here was a man who, if he was elected, would within a month or so of his inauguration be the oldest President ever to have lived in the White House. In other words, no other President, at the very end of his term, had been older than this one would be at the beginning of it. The issue no sooner came up than it gradually, and then quickly, began to disappear. Let me remind you how this happened. Many of you will recall what turned out to be the crucial television debate between President Carter and Mr Reagan. Mr Carter was then 56. Mr Reagan was 69. Many months before that debate, in the late winter when the primary elections were getting under way, the Democrats were going around with mock glum faces masking secret giggles and saying, 'Just think, by the end of this man's first term, he'll be 73.' Mr Reagan's campaign team, whom nobody knew much about at the time (except the California politicians who knew it was a very smart team indeed), quickly thought up an artful tactic. They encouraged Mr Reagan, as he barnstormed around the country, to bring up the issue himself, in the form of chuckly jokes. He'd say something like: 'Neither George

Washington nor Thomas Jefferson would have stood for the abuse of government we've been seeing in the past twenty years. I know, because both of them told me so.' Things like that. It was a winning ploy in both senses of the term. The clincher was the Reagan team's decision, just before the New Hampshire primary, to organize and advertise public celebrations of Mr Reagan's sixty-ninth birthday, when he was seen on television acknowledging well-wishers and cutting a cake with a comically shaking hand. That ploy dissolved the issue in the most effective way that a grave topic *can* be dissolved—in laughter.

Of course, the Democrats went on mumbling warnings about the enormous strains of the Presidency and what it was likely to do to the health of a man over the turn of his seventies. Anyway, we'd all get a good long look at both men in the coming Presidential debates. What I've called the crucial debate was the one in which Mr Reagan responded to warnings from Mr Carter of what life under Reagan might be. Usually Mr Carter would hint at a statistic which Mr Reagan would then disarm, suggesting Mr Carter had got it all wrong. The telling, the triumphant phrase, accompanied by a regretful, almost a forgiving shrug was: 'There you go again.' But what was far more powerful, far more reassuring as a sign of Reagan's health, and blitheness, was the sight and sound, the demeanour of Reagan matched against the demeanour of Carter. What we saw was Reagan as a natural optimist against Carter, a cautionary school principal. Reagan, the confident purveyor of half-truths (and sometimes of howling boners) against a Carter insisting that life is real

23

and earnest and painfully complicated. Reagan the broadcaster, who had learned through years of practice and as many as fourteen speeches a day on the road as a salesman for General Electric, had learned to be his best self talking to neighbours in a room, against a more thoughtful but verbose lay preacher addressing a congregation. And—here was the rub—a seeming young Reagan against a seeming old Carter.

None of us enquires about a man's age before deciding how bright or healthy or vigorous he is. We react to his appearance of life, and only then ask how old he might be. And, those of us who know 60-year-olds doddering in mind or body or both never get the feeling, watching President Reagan, that he is any special age at all. At least, we didn't get the feeling until last Sunday. That's when 'the issue' raised its wrinkled head again.

The debate. The television debate between the two principal nominees—the so-called Presidential debate—is by now not only a fixture every four years, it has become as compulsory a duty as if it had been laid down in the Constitution. It is, of course, a new thing. I don't know why I say that! Those of us who were already mature or sentient, shall I say, in 1960 must realize with a shock that there is a generation, already in its mid-twenties, that was imbibing mother's milk when the first television debate took place, between Vice President Richard Nixon and Senator John F. Kennedy. What most of us recall from that debate is the *appearance* of Nixon against the appearance of Kennedy. There were other debates after that first one, but the contrasting appearance of the two men, and what their appearance implied, was as the lawyers say, controlling. Before we saw them together, Kennedy was suffering from the age issue, in reverse. He was only 43. If he won, he would be, after Theodore Roosevelt, the second youngest President, on the day of his inauguration. Mr Nixon was 47, a fact that now shocks oldsters to recall, because on television he looked a generation older than Kennedy. Mr Nixon, that first and, as it turned out, fateful, evening had been campaigning between the Pacific and the East Coast. He'd had a very short night. The make-up man had failed to mask what was then known as a five o'clock shadow, but which looked at the time more like a three-day shadow. In short, Nixon looked like Bela Lugosi. Kennedy looked like a choirboy. Even President Truman had wondered whether the Republic could be safely entrusted to such a youngster. Lyndon Johnson, who had lost the nomination, felt similar misgivings about the safety of America in the hands of what he called 'eh beardless youth'. Well, in the result, Kennedy's boy-scout appearance worked for him: he was completely unintimidated by the expertise of the Vice President. His grasp of facts and policies was at least as firm. So the impression he left was that of a boy prodigy.

Last Sunday, before the Reagan–Mondale debate, I didn't read anything by way of commentary, or speculation, that even hinted the age issue would rise and dither from its grave. If we had a preconception about the failings of both men, it was one summed up in a cartoon. Two boxed pictures: one showed Reagan asleep at a Cabinet meeting; the other showed Mondale addressing his potential Cabinet, and the Cabinet was asleep. The public image of Mondale, which has bedevilled him since the start, has been that of an earnest speaker, chop-chopping away at his opponent, one stroke at a time, with no emotional rise and fall to a long speech. Everybody knows by now what is most successful about President Reagan: the ease, the intimacy, the emotion rising almost against his own wish, the directness and simplicity. Reagan turned from a 'B'-film actor into an 'A'-film actor of the quality of Gary Cooper.

Well, on Sunday we saw a new Mondale: a courteous and firm debater, gutsy and graceful at the same time. We saw a Reagan, as an incumbent President must always be in these debates, on the defensive. He had no script beautifully printed on a wrap-around, invisible teleprompter. He was on his feet and on his own. And he was nervous, and hesitant. And when he pulled out of the bag his old, famous line 'There you go again', Mondale was ready for it, like an outfielder ready for the catch that would clinch the World Series. Mr Reagan did not know (until later) that the Mondale team, working on a mock debate, had given Mondale six different ways of reacting to just that line. In the event, he leaped in with, 'D'you know when you said that? D'you know when you said that? When President Carter said you were going to cut Medicare. And you said, "oh no, there you go again". And what did you do right after the election? You went out and tried to cut twenty billion dollars out of Medicare!' (In fact, 'right after the election' was two years later. It didn't matter on Sunday night.)

So, the result has been a whole literature, from columnists, and gerontologists, and various medical men, on the quality of physical stamina and mental alertness to be expected from a man, a President, between the ages of 73 and 77. The White House pretended, for a day or two, to regard the whole thing as frivolous. But on Wednesday it released the latest medical report on the President, backing up its assertion of a robust physique and a sharp mind with enough statistical details to satisfy the fussiest clinician: from alkaline phosphotase through segmented neutrophils to mean corpuscular haemoglobin. This means he's in great shape! But what Sunday's debate recalled to me was not the physique, it was Benjamin Franklin's 'By my rambling digressions I perceive myself to be growing old'.

The consensus of the pollsters that Mondale was the overwhelming winner last Sunday has certainly brought a spark of life to Mondale's campaign. It will tantalize a larger audience for the next, and last, debate between the two men. It probably won't in the short run of three weeks cut significantly into Reagan's handsome lead. It may, however, stir new misgivings in a lot of people about the *image* of President Reagan they'll be seeing in the long run, two, three years from now.

Inaugurals—On and Off

25 January 1985

'Beautiful but dangerous.' It's a phrase that's been used, I imagine, about every siren from Cleopatra to Ava Gardner. I doubt it has been used before, as it was last Monday morning, about Washington, DC. Thomas Jefferson was one of the old colonials who were disgusted with the choice of Washington as a capital city. He called it 'That Indian place in the wilderness'. More often it was called a swamp, or 'a notable hotbed of vapors and disease'. These nasty words objected to the fact that Washington is nowhere more than a few hundred feet above sea level, and being on a river on the edge of the South, it has, in summer, such a humid stew of a climate that for many years—it may still be so—the British Foreign Office gave the ambassador to Washington and his staff a special tropical allowance, the idea being that they could retreat in summer to a hill station, which they did, to the Blue Ridge Mountains of Virginia. Since the arrival of the jet aeroplane, however, they've tended to escape to the hill stations of the Cotswolds.

In winter, as all the books and the records will tell you, Washington has a mild, damp, shivery climate, much like London, somewhere in the high thirties, low forties Fahrenheit, rarely getting very much below freezing. But last Monday it went to 34 degrees below freezing, or 2 below zero Fahrenheit. A high wind on Sunday evening and a whirl of snow flurries reduced the feel of the air, what we now call the wind-chill factor, to about 15 below zero. It's no weather for man or beast, and especially not for five thousand participants—half of them youngsters—in uniformed jackets and miniskirts. On the Sunday morning, one or two hardy detachments of these high school cheerleaders and bands had been out on the streets rehearsing for the great inauguration parade. They didn't stay there long. Some of them discovered that if you

28

don't have ear muffs, or a ski mask, and something to cover the nose, it would take only about five or six minutes for the first burning sensation that precedes frostbite. The valves on wind instruments froze up. The skin of several drums cracked. Rifles jammed. An ensign had the unique experience of watching the standard he was bearing snap and break in mid-air.

So, on Sunday evening, the President sadly called in the Senator from Maryland who was in charge of the Presidential Inaugural Committee, and they sat down with a doctor or two, and the whole thing, the four-hour outdoor triumphal parade, was called off. The doctors were not thinking primarily about the President—he would be cosy in a heated reviewing stand behind a six-inch layer of bulletproof glass. They were thinking of the five thousand soldiery, the teenagers on floats, the marching delegations from most of the states, the need for fleets of ambulances and heaven knows how many people carried indoors for emergency treatment. The only delegation that could be confidently certified as fit for public exposure was an Alaskan dog-sled team. And, of course, they were gung-ho and ready to go. But it would have been odd and pretty funny, to have only the Alaskans mushing down the vast emptiness of Pennsylvania Avenue. So the word went out, only a little before midnight, that the huge festival, which took three months to plan, was off, and that a makeshift demonstration of high school and other bands would be put on in a sports arena outside Washington. A hundred and forty thousand spectators were instructed to turn in their tickets for a refund. Every one of them would have

29

been required, on Monday morning, to pass through the sort of metal detectors they have at airports. The loss of money from the intending spectators was figured at about two million dollars. Anyone who has ever put together even a band concert in a town square can only guess at the hundreds of organizers who got no sleep on Sunday night. The most frantic of these insomniacs were the presidents, or more probably, the executive vice presidents in charge of sales at the television networks. In all, more than a hundred sponsors had to be re-slotted or reimbursed. The only consolation for thousands of people from the hinterland who had flown into Washington over the weekend, and were now comfortably marooned in their hotels, was that they were not back home. For most of the continent, including, freakishly, the South all the way down to the Gulf of Mexico, was assaulted by an atrocious storm, in the South worse than anything this century. The happiest refugees I talked to were from Chicago, where it was 27 below zero Fahrenheit—the whole city cloaked in ice— even the fire engines and their gear petrified to look like huge abstract sculptures from the Ice Age.

I must say, speaking as a tucked-up viewer in a warm room overlooking the ice of the Central Park reservoir—that the effect of taking the inauguration ceremony indoors, inside the Rotunda of the Capitol, was to give this usual circus an unintended dignity. Only about eight hundred people could be got in there. And the sequence of events—a prayer, a hymn, the swearing in first of the Vice President, then of the President, his speech, the Lord's Prayer, a

30

benediction. I think it's one of the very few Inaugurals, perhaps the only one of modern times, to which old Thomas Jefferson would have given his blessing. Jefferson, the third President of the United States, but a young man very much in on the founding of the Republic—he did the final draft of the Declaration of Independence—had very firm ideas about the limits of ceremony and public display that were proper for a republic. George Washington, the first President, arrived for this first Inaugural in full dress military uniform. He had a coach flanked by outriders. It was a small, smart military ceremony, but by our lights not much more elaborate than a performance by an amateur dramatic society. Nevertheless, it was too much for Jefferson. And, when soon afterwards, Washington held levees, made a formal speech to the Congress, and enjoyed watching the procession of Congress in a body to reply to it, Jefferson was so upset by what he took to be 'symptoms of a change of principle' that he wrote to the President saying that (these things) 'are not at all in character with the simplicity of republican governments, and looking as if wistfully to [the practices] of European courts'.

When the time came for Jefferson's own inauguration, he renounced all such pomp. He got on his horse, rode up to the Capitol, tethered his nag, went inside, made his speech—almost inaudibly—went out, mounted his horse and rode off back to his boarding house, where finding the places at the head of the dinner table taken, he sat down below the salt.

I suppose the last glimpse we've had of anything like such 'republican simplicity' was the memorable scene, at the inauguration of Jimmy Carter, when he got out of his gleaming limousine and walked down Pennsylvania Avenue hand in hand with his wife. A gesture such as that would not possibly be allowed today, when two or three millions of those inauguration dollars went on electronic and weapons security the like of which there has never been before but which there will certainly be again.

When it was all over, the television commentators—deprived of the parade, and the Cadillacs and the chinchillas and the crowds and the clothes and uniforms and bands and general glitz—these poor professionals, found that the cameras stationed all over town could show nothing but the enormous wide avenues in the sunlight empty of all humans, as if the bomb had dropped. They checked in from time to time with their own roving commentators on the streets. They were there, muffled to the eyebrows, lonely steaming sentinels. 'Anything happening out there?' one anchorman cried hopefully. The man came back: 'Nothing out here but us electronic chickens.' It was sad and comical. All these millions gone to erect miles of stands nobody would sit in, the grandeur of a block-long reviewing stand, with nobody there to review except, just for a quick darting moment, I noticed, one small, bewildered sparrow.

So the commentators had to fall back on talking about the mostly invisible hero of it all. Ronald Reagan. The enormity of his landslide. How come this 'B'-movie actor had swept the country twice? Old liberals who had spent four years scorning or pitying Reagan now thought again. The most interesting of the rafts of big men brought in to meditate was the old Governor of California whom Reagan had trounced seventeen years ago, Edmund 'Pat' Brown. 'We Democrats in California', he said, 'made the mistake the whole Democratic party made a dozen years later: we mightily underrated him as a politician, as a leader.'

And now that the party's over, the most beetle-browed writers and commentators are looking at inflation, down to an eighteen-year low, unemployment holding steady, employment up at about 350,000 a month, the promise, at least, of talks with the Russians. But mostly, the old pros and the old politicos look at him and listen to him and have come to envy his effortless gift for being, like no other living politician, as natural, and easy, and affable in public as he is in private, before a crowd or before two or three. So that when they hear him say, looking all of us straight in the eyes, that his own vision of America is of a country 'hopeful, big-hearted, idealistic, daring, decent and fair' well, we forget much of the dubious shenanigans of some of his Cabinet, and the CIA. We see Ronald Reagan standing in for Jefferson, and Lincoln, and Gary Cooper as the marshal, and Robert Redford as a fearless reporter, and we say, as an ageing Washington friend of mine said, 'I hunger to believe—or hope—it's so.'

Memories of 11 November

15 November 1985

As I sit down to record this talk—a little earlier than usual, since I am in San Francisco, six thousand miles away from its destination at Broadcasting House—I cannot help noticing the bizarre coincidence that it is the one thousand nine hundred and eighteenth talk in this series, and that it is being recorded on Monday the 11th. So, if this were a newspaper dispatch, it would bear the dateline 'Letter from America 1918, the 11th of November.'

I suppose that is a date which now has to be taught in schools, since most of the people who lived through it, in France, in Russia, in every part of Australia, India, New Zealand, not to mention Germany and Austria and Turkey—are dead and gone. But for those of us still around, it is as solemn and as indelible as any date in our lifetime. On the eleventh hour of the eleventh day of the eleventh month, in 1918, what *we* called the Great War, and then the World War, and then ruefully, the First World War, and now what is known to younger generations as simply 'The 14–18 War' was all over. I was up at the first flicker of dawn, because our newspaper had promised the day before that it would print on the 11th the terms of the Armistice. I took out several pages of what we then called cartridge paper, and, in a laborious but pretty fast script for a 9-year-old, I copied out the entire document. I gummed the pages together in a

34

long scroll, rolled it as stage plays and early movies had taught us to believe was the proper shape of a diplomatic document, tied it with a little red, white and blue ribbon, and marched off around our seaside town, my left hand in my mother's hand, my right clutching this state document. (It should have been to the neighbours an early warning signal of the emergence of a ham.) It was, I recall, a crisp and sunny November day. But the only other memory, which is as sharp and mouth-watering as last night's dinner, is a shop window. After our walkabout—on the way home—we passed by what was then called the confectioner's. I imagine today they are called pastry boutiques, just as in Paris, the chicest boutique I know calls itself simply Le Shop. Anyway, a confectioner's window was, of all shops in wartime, the most barren, the most pitifully denuded of all shops' windows. Sometimes, there were two or three loaves of brown bread. And sometimes, there was none. But, on that still, blissful, bright November morning, there stood, glistening in the centre of the empty window, a cut-glass cake stand. And on the stand stood a bun, a round bun. And on the top of the bun was a circle of snow? Ice? No, of white icing, something I had never seen before. It was an iced bun, what Americans call a cupcake. It was, for the long moment we stared at it, a thrilling symbol of the fact that we had come through.

Last Monday, I paused in this reminiscence, as the clock of San Francisco's nearby Grace Cathedral struck eleven. I paused and looked out down on the graceful little rectangular park that surmounts Nob Hill. The hour struck, but nobody else was pausing. Two tots were being pushed on

35

the swings. Two mothers were chatting away. An old Chinese man in a black suit was doing his morning exercises under a tree in the grave, slow-motion dance style of his race. The cars whisked by. People bent forward, staggered up the practically vertical incline of Taylor Street, or leaned back and pattered down. Nobody went in or out of the cathedral. I felt uncomfortably like a visitor from another planet, another century. I don't know for how many years, at that hour, on that day, and in how many countries, everything stopped for precisely two minutes. Streetcars, buses, motor cars, people—the men doffing their hats, everybody standing stock-still. There was the most unearthly silence in all great cities. And two minutes later, everything started up and soon the cities were roaring again. It must be twenty years, at least, since this stunning and admirable custom ended. Perhaps it isn't admirable, after all, or after a time. To forget old enmities, old wars, is necessary for the sanity of the living. At any rate, the two-minute silence is long gone, and I should guess, forgotten by most of the world's peoples. And, you can't go on for ever calling 11 November Armistice Day. In this country, it has been re-christened Veterans' Day, to commemorate the veterans of all the American wars, from the first, the triumphant one that ended two hundred years ago, to the last, Vietnam, the bitterest lost one. And on Sunday in Washington, on a balmy morning, several thousand men and women and children, a silent troop of unforgetting mothers and widows and sisters and fathers, took their turn to touch what is surely the boldest and most sombre of all war memorials, the vast, black stone wall on

36

which are chiselled 58,022 names, the men who died in combat in Vietnam.

In the past day or two, I have read a lot of newspapers. Because of its place in the time zones, San Francisco can offer you at breakfast not only the *Los Angeles Times* as well as the local newspapers, but also that morning's *New York Times* and London *Times*. I have read, or scanned, hundreds of pages but only here in the *San Francisco Chronicle* have I seen a piece devoted entirely to recalling the first Armistice Day, the eleventh of November, and what it meant to a generation or two that is now white-haired or gone for good. This was a piece by Herb Caen, a local columnist, who is San Francisco's resident Mr Pepys. He remarked on how the importance of the day has waned and added regretfully that 'too many of our [national] holidays are disappearing or becoming homogenized. As school kids, we were so proud to remember the 12th of February as Lincoln's birthday, and February 22nd as Washington's, but now they have been telescoped into a long weekend, so much better for business, so much more convenient.'

This is literally true. Whatever day of the week 22 February fell on, the entire nation used to close its businesses and schools. Store windows displayed pictures or busts of George Washington and gave him a swag or drape of the Stars and Stripes. (I ought to tell you, though, that while on Lincoln's birthday many states performed the same obeisance for old Abe, 12 February was never a national holiday; and no President ever dared proclaim it as such, so long as the South retained its own resentful image of Lincoln as a tyrant at

37

worst, at best a Northern conqueror. To this day, one hundred and twenty years after the end of the Civil War—most Southern cities and towns, and they are embraced by a third of the nation's geography, don't exactly make a fetish of ignoring Lincoln's birthday: they pay it the passing tribute of a nod, and go about their business.) So it seems that while many decent solemn dates dim and vanish, the bitter taste of others keeps its tang.

I noticed in the long spring commemoration of the end of the Second World War in Europe, the hideous fate of the Jews in the Holocaust was, properly, retold and mourned over till, however, there came a point when I, for one, began to feel uneasy that this necessary but prolonged act of remembrance might have the opposite effect to what was intended: to stir, in sullen or bigoted people, their old anti-Semitic impulses. This is not the sort of fear that respectable commentators put into print or over the air, but I mention it because several friends, mostly Jewish friends, confidentially felt the same way. The fear came very vivid to me when, after one of the many documentaries we saw (about six million people being treated like pigs on a spit), one New York television station showed a family of Armenian-Americans celebrating, or bemoaning, their own particular annual festival. It was the seventieth anniversary of the infamous massacre of the Armenians by their Turkish conqueror. It had been going on since the 1890s, but in 1915, the Turks, in a final spasm of hatred, slaughtered all the able-bodied Armenians in sight and drove the rest out into the Syrian desert on the wholesale charge that all Armenians existed to help the Russian armies.

Hundreds of thousands of Armenians died in the desert of starvation and/or sunstroke, and in the end the official estimate of the Armenian dead was over a million. This outrage was, of course, thoroughly reported at the time in Britain, all the more colourfully since Turkey was a fighting enemy. But after the war the indignation cooled and the war hatreds eventually languished and died—in Britain, I mean, but not in America, where there were, and are, large colonies of immigrants from every part of Southern and Central and Eastern Europe. They feel acutely the sufferings of their relatives, partly no doubt from the guilt of not being there to share them. When I came to this country in the early 1930s, small children everywhere were scolded for not cleaning their plates: 'Think', the parents used to say, 'of the starving Armenians.' And in several great cities, and in one valley of California almost entirely populated by Armenian immigrants, the old grievance against the Turks was nursed and kept green. But not, I should have thought, into 1985. However, on the television programme I mentioned, a great-grandfather and a grandfather were, on a night last spring, instructing their small grand- and great-grandchildren, slowly, patiently, as you might teach them a nursery rhyme, in hatred of the Turks.

I don't know why this scene horrified me, whereas the recall of the Nazi Holocaust seemed timely and right. Do an extra thirty years make all the difference? When will the Germans feel free from the stigma of the swastika? They are, to me, unanswerable questions.

One thing was painfully clear last weekend. The

war in Vietnam ended ten years ago, but the wound to American morale is only partly healed. It was the first great military defeat in the country's history. The Veterans' Administration calculates that between 300,000 and 400,000 of the men who served are still afflicted with what they call 'post-trauma stress disorder', what in the First World War was more bluntly called 'shell shock'. One veteran who touched the black stone last weekend called it 'a memorial to desolation'. So, Veterans' Day this year did at least remind us of the tenacity of old hatreds, and leave us with the uncomfortable question: when will the Turks, and the Germans, and the Vietnamese, be welcomed back as equal members of the human family?

Miss Much—No Regret

3 January 1986

I hope I'm not stretching to find good news in a wicked world when I say that the happiest sentence I've read in the New Year comes from an anonymous—until now—office worker in his mid-thirties who has a wife and a 12-year-old son. His name is Gadany. He lives in Moscow. 'Quite frankly,' he told a British newspaperman, 'we were amazed when we turned on the 9 o'clock news and saw this friendly face staring out at us, speaking what sounded like a genuine message of peace.' It's not too much to say that the man was in shock, in the pleasantest way. He went on: 'My family noticed [too] that despite what we have always been told, he looked friendly and quite normal.' This may not be an earth-shaking confession to most of us, but consider who was saying it, and about whom. The 'friendly face' which appeared to be that of a 'normal' human being was none other than that of Ronald Reagan. Mr Gadany is an ordinary Russian, intelligent, educated—we are told—but yet he was amazed by this strange, this wholly unexpected face and manner. We know it well, but consider the weight of that phrase 'despite what we have always been told'. Mr Gadany, and surely millions of other ordinary non-official Russians, had never before been talked to by this President of the United States and, on a New Year's Day, they discovered that he does not have horns and fangs. Other correspondents in Moscow, both British and American, confirmed the general amazement at seeing the leader of the other superpower as nothing like what—since 1980—'we have always been told'. Namely, a leering warmonger with a six-pack of missiles in his hand, a figure hardly less terrifying to the Russian people than Attila the Hun. I'm not joking. I don't know where the suggestion came from that the two leaders should go on television and talk to each other's people. But whether it came from the American side, or the Russian, the decision to let Reagan be Reagan in full view of the Russian people could not have been taken lightly in Moscow. Only the resident fly on the Kremlin wall could tell us whether it was the result of intense discussion and back-and-forth arguments by Mr Gorbachev's inner circle, or whether it was a single bold decision by Mr Gorbachev himself. And what amazes me, as distinct from Mr Gadany, is the subsequent decision to permit the whole text of Mr Reagan's talk to go unedited, most of all to allow him to be seen and heard saying that 'both the United States and the Soviet Union are doing research on the possibilities of harnessing new technologies to the cause of defense'. This means, meant, only one thing: that both superpowers have been busy working on a strategic defence initiative, on what—in the teeth of Mr Reagan's pleas to drop the term, has been, and will always be, known as Star Wars. I suppose that the phrase 'harnessing new technologies' was thought sufficiently vague by the boys in the Kremlin to mask what it means to us.

Another passage in Mr Reagan's talk must have given them (the Kremlin elite) thoughtful pause. It was this: 'Our democratic system is founded on the belief in the sanctity of human life and the rights of the individual.' That's all right; from everything they've been taught, the Russian people could take this to mean that the Soviet state is most concerned for the right of its people to have free education, free health care and a home, however humble. But then the President went on: '. . . the rights of the individual, such as freedom of speech, of assembly, of movement and of worship.' Perhaps 'freedom of speech and assembly' are untranslatable as new and daring freedoms to a people who from birth have never known them. I'm sorry to say that neither Mr Gadany nor any other man in the street appears to have been questioned on this vital difference. I certainly wish some correspondent, on our side, or anybody's side, would go around Moscow or Leningrad or Yalta or wherever and ask the people: 'What do freedom of speech, freedom of assembly, of movement, of worship mean to you?' There must be a confident, plausible answer that any Russian official could give, because in most of his or her contacts with the West, they hear it from their point of view, ad nauseam. Well, it's not ad nauseam to us. And I dare to think that it can come as a revelation, of a wholly new kind of life, to a Soviet citizen who for one reason or another is allowed to leave his native land and take up life in another.

This brings irresistibly to mind a cab driver I rode with a couple of months ago. I've often thought back to him and felt at one time I must talk about him. My problem here was that to give the flavour of the encounter, I should have to be able to mimic his thick and floundering English as well as it could be done, by say, Peter Ustinov. I can't do this, and if I could, I'm afraid that he would inevitably come out as a comic vaudeville character. I think I ought to have a shot at it, mainly because it moved me, and it moved me to think again about this very topic that most of us take for granted.

Quite simply, I hailed a cab at my door, as I do every week at the same time, to drive downtown to the BBC to do my talk. A cab drove up and I was not merely nodded in, but welcomed in by a driver who smiled and even managed to bow in his seat. This is not standard practice among New York cab drivers, however amiable they may be. I did notice the man's name on the registration that is fixed above the dashboard. It was a Russian name. I've forgotten it. No matter. In an accent like molasses trying to pour itself through a tea strainer, he wanted to know 'Where, please, pleasure to be

43

taking you.' We didn't exchange any words for a few minutes, till this sturdy middle-aged man, who was jolly and intense at the same time, half-turned over his right shoulder and said: 'Please, sir, to be telling me if you long in America.' A very long time, I said, but that like him I was born and grew up abroad. 'Ah, England,' he said, and nodded approvingly. 'And how about you?' I said. 'One year only,' he said. Then he was off, or rather he struggled to give me his story. About 50 (a bad time, I should guess, for a national of any country to emigrate to another), he had two children, grown. Not much to go on there. Then a traffic light changed, a cab in the adjacent lane squealed to a halt and just missed a carefree pedestrian. The driver, the other driver, snarled some obscenity, and my man gave a shrug, halfway between a chuckle and a sigh. 'Some', he said, 'very rude, very sharp, some very nice. But no can tell. No sure what manners may be for all.' It was, you can guess, heavy going. I'd already sensed that this man was a sensitive, nice man incapable of a cliché and anxious to express his difficult feelings in a language that stretched before him like a marsh of alternating bogs and hidden islands. I made a quick mental resolve to reduce my own part in the conversation to words of one syllable and to the simplest English idioms. The trouble here is the assumption that the English he'd learned had started with plain talk. A man who has landed here and never heard anything but having his wages 'inflation-indexed in the shortest possible time frame' is not likely to know what you're talking about if you say, 'And do your wages go up as soon as there's more inflation?'

44

Anyway, after several hopeless, strangulated pauses, we managed to hit on an understandable common language. He sensed I was on his side. And his story came out, in a wonderful, thrashing, staggering, procession of sentences. He *was* 50. It was a hard decision to make to leave Russia, his own country which loving very much. Missing very much. The people. The friends. All people, ways, food very different here. Very troubling. He was not Jewish. He was not political. But his two children, a son, a daughter, were now getting to college age. Both were very bright. But he saw no future for them except in some branch of the civil service and in Moscow. This would not have upset him, but he caught stuff on the big radio of his brother on the Voice of America. He also, to my alarm, said he had also listened, when it was not jammed, to an Englishman who did a talk from New York. It was called 'I think, Letter—Letter from America'. Believe me, I wasn't going to take the blame for yet another soured, embittered immigrant. Truthfully, I said I'd heard of him, but he was not heard in America. This amazed him. He went on. Why had he left? Because he'd heard children—studious ones—could try in America many colleges, could travel to get in, and could then choose what to do. He even heard, from that man, that it was a common thing for New York taxi drivers to take a week or two or a month off in winter and go to Florida. He had a distant cousin in New York. He and his wife took the risk. Now, his daughter was at Hunter College, didn't have to say yet what she wanted to be. His son was in premedical, going to be a doctor. But life was hard, he so missed Russia, the country, the people, the

45

'ways I brought up'. I asked him if he regretted the move. And he swivelled round in something close to alarm. 'No, no, no, no,' he said, 'miss much, but no regret.' Why? Why? 'How can I tell you? Listen, please. I talk to cab drivers. I visit the store. I meet on the street. People talk, all the time, they argue. On the TV. People fight in words. Like the government, don't like the government. Say good things, bad things. Say anything. Nobody follows. Nothing happens. My daughter no like Reagan. I like Reagan, I think great man. He say all the time why I here. What you call it?'

He was writhing in his seat reaching for some difficult impossible word. Freedom, I hinted. He positively shouted, 'Freedom!' I saw that his face was streaming with tears. I sniffed myself. 'I do know what you mean,' I said. Though, as I say, we take it for granted. This naive, shaken man did not.

Expert Witness

27 June 1986

Some years ago I had the extraordinary—for me, unique—experience of appearing as an expert witness before a judge. I immediately hear prim old gentlemen saying, 'And pray, what expertise can you claim in any field whatsoever?' A good question. A journalist, a foreign correspondent especially, is expected to pick up something across as wide a range of knowledge as possible. He is by definition a jack of all trades. And so, to complete the definition, he is assumed to be master of none.

46

But nobody is a born journalist. And before I was stricken by the urge to enlighten the general public on every conceivable subject, from medicine to golf, from professors of religion to practitioners of politics (which is about as wide a gamut as exists in our society), I was a scholar, in a special field of study. It was linguistics. Which is not quite the same as being a linguist. Linguistics is the scientific study of how languages come about and how they change. Why the Greek 'k' goes over into English as a soft 'c' and kinema turns into cinema. Why do the French put a circumflex accent in the word 'côte'? To show that between Old French and later French, an 's' got dropped, and the original word was the one that passed over into English as 'coast'. How did it happen that the Spanish looked at the basic Roman word for a sheath and turned it into 'vanilla'? Look that up and you are in for a startling discovery.

Well, my special study was pursued under an American linguistic scholar who was, in his time, the American Henry Higgins (you'll see in a minute why that name came up). My special field was the history of the English language in America, following, most obviously, the growth or development of a new vocabulary to describe the new landscape, and the effect on English of having daily contact—first with Indians, then with the Spanish and the French, and then the Dutch and arriving Germans, and in time, Poles, Russians, Hungarians, Italians and so on, all of whom contributed words to the English of America.

But the most fascinating part of the year I spent doing practically nothing else, was the history of the seventeenth-century *pronunciation* of England

—among incoming lawyers, divines, carpenters and mechanics. Offhand, you'd say it would be impossible to know about this because there were no movies, no recordings of sound anyway. Well, yes, there was. We have the written records of the earliest town meetings, two in Massachusetts, one on Long Island. The town meeting was, still is, in almost all small towns and villages, the basic body of democratic government. Anybody could come and have his or her say, on any topic that was disturbing or exciting the neighbourhood. They were conducted in the early days usually by the lawyer or the parson—by the educated types. The record, in longhand abbreviated, was usually kept by a farmer or mechanic. And the pronunciations of the chairman were, naturally, written down in a rude phonetic way. So when the English parson, or whoever, said 'lib-rairy', we know that that's how educated Englishmen of the time spoke the word. That pronunciation, like many another old English pronunciation, stayed on in America, while down the years, the centuries, it changed in England. More often than not, that was the story: the Americans retained the old English pronunciations, and the English changed them.

Well, to my expert appearance. An old friend of mine, a theatrical lawyer, was planning to revive in New York the masterpiece of his long-time client, the late Alan Jay Lerner. That masterpiece, as at least three continents are well aware, is Lerner and Loewe's adaptation of Bernard Shaw's *Pygmalion*: *My Fair Lady*. Whenever you decide to bring an English play to New York, or an American play to London, you instantly have trouble with the actors' unions. The general rule here is that an

Englishman will be allowed to play his part in the American production if it can be demonstrated—before the actors' union—that he is sufficiently distinguished to be irreplaceable by an American playing the part.

This is not a regulation restricted to actors. It is a regular requirement of the immigration service (same in England). It applies to a doctor, a carpenter, anyone of foreign citizenship seeking to do a temporary job in the United States. The immigration service gets in touch with the appropriate union, and if the union agrees that the man, the woman, has some skill not likely to be matched by an unemployed American, he, she, will be allowed in. This applies all the way from labourers to nuclear physicists, though it would probably not be hard for the Pentagon and the President's chief scientific adviser to prove, or maintain, that Herr Schmidt or Joe Parkinson is uniquely qualified to take on the job they have in mind. For instance, there would be no ban on a nuclear physicist from any (non-Communist) country who knew why cockroaches are immune to radiation (and don't think there aren't in many countries men bending over test tubes and microscopes and bits of cockroach tissue trying to solve that puzzle).

When it comes to proving here that an English actor or actress can play a role with unequalled skill, that is a tougher assignment. There are, after all, not only unemployed American actors who would like to strut their stuff but also, in or around New York, literally hundreds of English actors at large (resting, as they say) who also have the prime requirement of being American citizens. Well, in

49

this case, in this play, *My Fair Lady*, Mr Lerner and my lawyer friend wanted to bring over Ian Richardson as Higgins and a young Englishwoman who had been chosen from a series of auditions, given in London, to over thirty English applicants for the part of Eliza Doolittle. They'd also had extensive auditions here, among Americans, but couldn't find one as good as the Englishwoman they chose.

The immigration service telephoned the actors' union. The union, after some thought, was quite willing and quite right too, to let Mr Richardson play Higgins. But they balked at the Englishwoman. The procedure then is to call for a so-called arbitration meeting, at which one arbiter, chosen by the union, will hear the case from the author's/producer's side, on why the Englishwoman could play Eliza better than any of the Americans who'd been auditioned. The union challenged this assertion.

Came the great day, for the first and only time in my life, of the confrontation (one on one) between the union arbiter and the 'expert' that Mr Lerner and his lawyer had decided could best sustain their preference. A few other members of the union, as well as Mr Lerner and his lawyer, were allowed to sit in. The lawyer presented the credentials of the expert, never, to the arbiter's surprise and curiosity, mentioning such things as journalism or broadcasting, except to say that their man had been here for many, many years, had closely followed the theatre in both countries, but mainly because he had started, and pursued, down the years a special study of British and American speech.

Very good. Now proceed. I was required to

50

detail the work I'd done at Harvard, and the fieldwork on a mighty work of sound (in both senses) scholarship called *The American Linguistic Atlas*. And so on. All this led to my contention that I could think of no living American woman who was capable—in a play uniquely about the social significance of spoken English—who was capable of moving without effort from genuine Cockney to believable Mayfair. The arbiter, at the peak of the discussion, called off American actresses he obviously admired, and challenged me to question their great gifts. I turned 'em all down as tactfully as possible, while expressing my own passion for his favourites on other grounds. At last, he looked at me, as the song says, square down in the eye and pronounced a name which (he probably never knew) was mentioned mockingly on Broadway, fifty years ago, as the name of a non-actress but who, down the decades, has been elevated into a pantheon all her own. He mentioned the English and Scottish roles she had played, from Mary, Queen of Scots down—or up. How about, he said, Katharine Hepburn? 'Impossible,' I said, 'was never any better than an upper-middle-class New Englander trying strenuously to sound British.'

At the end, he thanked me profusely, said he was impressed, and he would let us know the verdict within twenty-four hours. I blushed becomingly, and the lawyer and Mr Lerner took me out to a celebration lunch. 'Tremendous,' they said, 'We're in.' They saw me off with gaudy expressions of admiration and promises of lifelong devotion. Next day, need I say, the arbiter turned us down. The part would have to be played by an American. And so it was. And she was good, more than adequate.

But the Cockney was studied, and the Mayfair could just as well have been Kensington or Bette Davis.

When it was all over, and the three of us met again, we fell to talking about the opposite problem: how to find English actors who can talk American. To Americans, it is an equal problem. Many British actors are wonderful mimics—of Cockney, North Country, West Country, whatever. Peter Sellers and Peter Ustinov could do Spanish-English, Italian-English, and German-English. But the best of them, for some reason, never exactly discovered or could do more than one sort of American. And whether they were being a judge, an ambassador, a president, a Southerner, a cab driver, it always came out—to Americans— sounding like George Raft, or some other gangster's henchman.

Last weekend, a great friend, an Englishman who has lived here for a dozen years or so, shed a beam of light on this dark problem. 'Even good English mimics', he said, 'are not prepared to think of Americans as individuals. They think of Americans as one type of variation on Englishmen. They are always the same: tough, Midwestern. They act out a theory in their heads, that Americans are nasal and rough-hewn. They don't listen.' So it was, and is, and no doubt for ever will be. Ah, me—and amen.

The Drugs Blight

19 September 1986

One of the sparkling sights at this time of year, around the equinox (it can vary by a day or two), is to see the boats go out from the marinas and inlets into the blue expanse of Peconic Bay, which divides the forks at the end of Long Island. The boats are owned by the so-called 'bay-men' and what they go out now to garner is the first harvest of a delicacy about which a friend of ours, a visiting Frenchwoman, once said: 'If they were as fine as this in France, tourists would come from all over the country.' The delicacy is the tiny Peconic Bay scallop, in its maturity no more than an inch in diameter. And on the first day of the season, the bay-men usually bring in hundreds of thousands of this tender, delectable, bivalve mollusc, which is not matched anywhere.

The Peconic harvest provides more than 30 per cent of the bay scallops, seared, just in butter, in restaurants around the country. At any time of the year, you can see 'bay scallops' printed on menus everywhere; but the fresh Peconic variety is not available before the third week in September. What you get at any other time is either frozen scallops or calicos from the Carolinas. Most often the title 'bay scallops' is a cover-up for the large sea scallops cut up into small chunks.

Well, this past weekend it was a sad sight on the shores of the Bay. The four hundred bay-men, whose livelihood depends on this late and abundant harvest, stayed home. No boats went out, for the simple blunt reason that there are no scallops. None. Or to be fussy, one boat did go out, piloted by one Christopher Smith, a marine specialist. 'We were out in Orient Harbor,' he said. 'Normally, you'd find hundreds of thousands of scallops, both young and adult, in there. We find two. It was like we were holding nuggets of gold.'

This is the third autumn of our discontent. In the late summer of 1984, we'd look out from any cliff or bluff and see something new and puzzling: instead of the blue waters lapping in, we looked down on what we came to call 'the brown tide'. It was the first invasion in human memory of what the marine biologists call a bloom of algae, so microscopic and so dense that we assumed we were the late victims of some pollutant, of spreading industrial waste, which has deprived us, for instance, of our finest eating fish: the noble striped bass. They spawn in the Hudson River in what are now polluted stretches, but even when they swim out along the ocean line and into the bays along a hundred miles of Long Island, their catch has been prohibited.

But this is not the case of the bay scallop. Nobody knows where the brown tide came from. One marine scientist has a theory, but is ready to admit it's only a hunch. He thinks it's meterological in origin, and follows on a succession of dry winters and dry springs. But we've had—we had in the mid-1970s—three or four such dry seasons. We also had a million scallops later on.

There's no mystery, however, about what the algae do. They choke out the normal phytoplankton, the microscopic plant life on which

54

the scallops feed. So, simply, they starve to death.

In the fall of 1984, the scallop harvest was pitifully small. Last year, there was none. Same this year. The expert theory, not a very cheerful one, is that in some mysterious but dependable way, the scallops would learn to overcome, or enjoy, the algae and would recover on their own, but not much before the end of the century. So, at the understandable pleading of the four hundred bay-men, who together will lose the two million dollars they earn at the dock, New York State has done something about it: an experiment conducted with skill and crossed fingers. Last Monday, in the late afternoon, a single-engined plane flew into Montauk, the last—the most eastern—settlement on Long Island. It had come from the state of Maine. It carried eight hundred thousand minute bay scallops taken from a nursery on a river in Maine at eleven in the morning. They were packed in foam coolers, and the pilot was nervous about their expectation of life, for they can live outside salt water for no more than eight hours. He landed at Montauk just after 4.30. That left two and a half hours to get them into pens in a saltwater lake on Montauk Point. It took two hours to unpack, separate and open up the scallops. In the last half-hour, the divers started plunging into the lake. By 7 o'clock, just when the sun was sinking (as it does at this latitude, as fast as the divers), and to everybody's relief, the minuscule molluscs were feeding away in their new home. It is a re-seeding project, and the hope is that if it works, and *if* the brown tide that killed all the native scallops doesn't come back next summer, there could be a sizeable crop of these mature immigrants by the fall

55

of 1988.

I appreciate that the sudden impoverishment of four hundred men and their families is not a matter of great pain to 99.9 per cent, or more, of my listeners. But it was happening to us. And as we all come to know, four hundred thousand people killed in an earthquake in China is a horrid, but bearable, statistic. A child you saw killed by a motor car is a memory that stays with you for life.

There is one form of pollution that is drastically affecting this whole nation. And if it's true, as somebody said, that 'in America we see our future, good and bad', then this blight will soon overtake the other countries of the Western world. In fact, there's lots of evidence that in Germany, in Scandinavia, in Britain, in Holland, it has already started. I mean the drug blight, which sixty years ago was a small sinister symptom of the decadent 1920s in Hollywood, and among the arty-society Bohemians of London. (Dorothy Sayers wrote one of her novels, an untypically tart one, about them: *Murder Must Advertise*.) But now, we are talking about a country, this one, in which one high school pupil in five has tried cocaine, in which one in twenty or thirty is likely to become an addict. A treatment programme in Florida, which has over six hundred teenagers under treatment, found that most of them had started a drug habit by the age of 12. As against 7 per cent of a similar group that had used cocaine in 1984, today 63 per cent have done so. Two in three of them used drugs of one sort or another before their parents suspected it. Most— 70 per cent—were introduced to drugs, not on the street or by pushers, but by friends.

Cocaine has become the drug of choice of the

middle-class teenager (not to mention, of course, prosperous yuppies, rock performers and showbiz parasites, and an alarming minority of star footballers and baseball players), and finally President Reagan has decided to propose a national battle against drugs. 'Finally' is not meant to imply a sneer. Mrs Reagan, since the first month she was in the White House, has devoted all her spare time to travelling far and wide, talking to youngsters in and out of school, in and out of treatment centres, about drugs. And, consequently, her husband is probably more aware of the blighted lives of the young than most husbands.

And of course, the White House, through the Department of Justice, has for long had a programme of trying to stop the importation of drugs into the United States from South and Central America. It's an effort which—in view of the size of the country with its enormous wriggling borders, the impossibility of patrolling the twenty-five-hundred-mile southern border of the United States with anything like enough radar-equipped helicopters, the ruthless ability of South American growers and organized crime to mount fleets of small boats and larger fleets of private aeroplanes on secret night-flights, in view of this tidal wave of drug entry into the country—has so far been about as effective as mopping up the ocean with a pocket handkerchief. One official, trying to plug the innumerable gateways to Florida by air, by sea, by every sort of roadway from four-lane motorways to dirt roads, said that the plugging-up process was like squeezing a balloon: 'You press in one place, and it bulges out in another.'

What the President has now done, in a

determinedly dramatic appearance with Mrs Reagan on national television, is to announce what he called a national 'crusade' against drug abuse. It went far beyond the long battle with foreign importers, suppliers and pushers. For the first time, it turned to the users. It was a powerful sermon against drug abuse and a warning, especially to the young. As such, people who have spent half a lifetime with addicts doubted that the young— temperamentally curious and likely to try drugs— will be stopped by sermons, however eloquent or well-intentioned. One stoical youngster spoke for what I suspect is a large percentage of actual or potential users when he said: 'Nothing can be done for my drug-using friends. They do it for fun.' And when you say, 'Don't they realize it will ruin their lives?' they say, 'Well, it hasn't happened to me yet.'

The Presidential programme, which must go before the Congress, would stiffen the laws against drug-related crimes; give more money for research and treatment centres; and—in its most controversial proposal—require about a million government workers in sensitive jobs to take drug tests. That means routine urinalysis. This suggestion at once provoked an outcry in Congress, from civil libertarians, and from one government union that has already filed a suit. They all protested that compulsory testing would violate a citizen's constitutional rights by invading his or her privacy. The House of Representatives, which is controlled by the Democrats, no sooner heard about the President's forthcoming address than it rushed, three days before the address was given, to prove quite suddenly it was more alert than anybody to the nationwide drug abuse. It passed, helter-skelter, its own anti-drug programme. It was more specific than the President's, and tougher on two counts, both of which had other Congressmen and civil libertarians protesting against an unconstitutional use of the military, and a federal return to the death penalty. The House bill proposes the death penalty for pushers of drugs to children. And it sanctions the use of the military, instead of only the local police and the FBI, to stop illegal drugs coming into the country.

I'm afraid both the House bill and the President's crusade represent less of a considered cure than a rush to righteousness. The entire House of Representatives comes up for re-election in November. And a Congressman voting against a drug-abuse bill today would be about as popular as a Congressman who voted against mother and Santa Claus. Maybe, when the election is over, both houses of Congress will sit down and look at all the facts, ponder, and write a thoughtful, effective programme. At the moment, the government's anti-drug programme and the House's response to it have been launched in the headlong, vote-catching atmosphere that characterized the passage of the 18th Amendment, which prohibited 'the manufacture, sale or transportation of intoxicating liquors'; and which plunged the country into a fourteen-year orgy of self-righteousness, hypocrisy and prosperous crime.

Time to Retire

16 January 1987

A letter from a friend in England caught me napping between two emotions. It was the sort of letter that normally calls for congratulations. But in the moment of writing back to say, 'Well done, good luck!' I felt something of a fraud, because my first emotion was one of shock, verging on alarm. I suppressed this feeling in the interests of common courtesy.

So, what was the letter about? It simply announced with evident pleasure, not to say pride, that he was retiring. What do you say to a friend who retires? There are so-called greetings cards available at every stationer's in this country, and I don't doubt in many other countries, for every conceivable and inconceivable occasion. I recently had a flock of them on my birthday; my favourite being one that came from my daughter. On the outside, it showed a drawing of a simple, cheerful-looking dope. And above the drawing, the inscription: 'At your age, you've got a lot going for you.' Turn the page, and on the inside, it said, 'Your eyes are going, your back is going, your knees are going, your hearing is . . . Happy Birthday.'

But there are no greetings cards for people about to retire. For in a nation that coined the phrases 'over-achiever' and 'under-achiever', a man who retires has announced that from now on, he's going to be a 'non-achiever'. Not quite a disgrace, but nothing to cheer about either.

I can best explain my feeling of shock at the news of this vigorous, dapper man on his way out by recalling one of the last acts passed by the expiring 99th Congress (which died in December). It was a measure which received so little publicity here that I didn't think to remark on it at the time: a federal, a national, act which forbids an employer to require anyone to retire at the age of—wait for it—70. Unless the person can be medically pronounced to be incompetent or disabled from doing his or her job, if he or she wants to go on, so be it.

I don't know what the law or custom is in France or Mexico or the Australian outback, but Englishmen, at any rate, will now appreciate my shock. My retiring friend is about to be 60. I mentioned this to many friends here—from the naive to the sophisticated—and they too either registered shock or suggested that I'd got it wrong. One determined sceptic practically demanded proof, so I got out *Who's Who* and looked up various men we knew, or knew of, who had been in the Foreign Service. Subtract their birth date from the retirement date, and sure enough, the answer was always 60, except for one or two brave entries which briefly stated 'called' or 'recalled' out of retirement to take on one more job for old England's sake. How about Churchill, somebody asked, who formed his last ministry in his seventy-seventh year, which is what Ronald Reagan will enter in another three weeks. Doesn't apply, I said, to elected officials.

It's an interesting difference between the two countries, because it reflects such a dramatically different view of the limits of a person's stamina

61

and usefulness to society. A sharp American friend of mine immediately asked what is the normal expectation of life in Britain, because that would seem to be the most realistic gauge of how long you can do your job effectively. The answer is, of course, that in Britain and America the expectation of life at birth (the only true measure of a nation's increasing or decreasing lifespan), is just about the same, give or take a percentage point. And because in both countries, as also in the Scandinavian countries—in fact all of Western Europe, I believe—people are living very much longer than they did eighty, even fifty, years ago, the actuarial tables of insurance companies have been adjusted accordingly. My friend assumed, and so did I, that the general view of a proper retirement age has similarly changed.

Of course, the age at which you officially become one of the old folks, or as we now ridiculously say, a 'senior citizen', remains, in this country as elsewhere, 65. And that's the age when you get a card from the government entitling you to medical benefits—by Act of Congress (Medicare)—and the age at which, even more agreeably, you start receiving a monthly cheque to return to you the benefits that have accrued from your payments under the Social Security Act of fifty years ago. One even more agreeable novelty which I still don't quite understand is that when the male of the family reaches 72, his wife, whether she has ever been employed in a salaried job or not, also gets a cheque. I imagine it's the same in all countries: communications between a human being and his government are so impersonal that you never know whom to write to, either by way of gratitude or protest. Such communications normally have no signature. They are printed. They do manage to print your name at the top, but everything else is a form letter that could have gone to anybody. Sometimes there's not even a date. Imagine, then, the comic shock we had when, about a week after my seventy-second birthday, a letter—nay, a telegram, Mailgram as it's called—arrived for my wife. She tore it open hoping it was no bad news about any of the children, who live three and six thousand miles apart, or any of our brood of grandchildren. It was, in fact, a telegram from the government. Remember, there'd never been any 'Dear Mr C' or 'Dear Sir' or any recognition of me, in previous correspondence, except as the bearer of Social Security number 066-14-1674. This Mailgram said, with almost weepy intimacy, 'Dear Jane, now that Alistair is 72 you will be entitled to and will receive a monthly Social Security check.' In the interest of not getting my block knocked off, I stopped myself saying: 'What have you done to deserve this?' The answer, of course, is everything: from bearing, rearing, maintaining, nursing, feeding, schooling, laundering, etc., etc., a family. This carries the official status on government documents as 'non-working housewife', which recalls the memorable question, at Christmas time, of a vivacious young woman at a small, quick party which my daughter, mother of five, was able to attend for an hour or so. 'Tell me,' asked the vivacious one, 'do you work?' 'Sort of,' my daughter replied, 'from about 4.30 a.m. to 10 p.m.' 'Really,' exclaimed this vivacious dumb-bell. 'What at?' No answer.

Still, it's a pleasant surprise to know that both of

us will, till death do us part, get a monthly cheque from the government. And mine keeps going up. I don't write to the government and ask them why. Like every other concerned citizen, I believe that the administration should drastically cut the budget, so we can do something about our appalling $150 billion deficit, but wherever else they make the cuts, we're dead against reducing *our* slice of the pie.

Well . . . expectation of life. That certainly would seem to be the logical test of when people should retire. At the turn of the century, I mean around 1900, and on—certainly until the First World War—successful businessmen usually retired between 45 and 50, since the expectation of life for men was then between 55 or 60; for women, a few years longer. When the American Social Security system was started, a regular percentage was taken out of your pay-cheque, on the understanding that it would go into a giant piggy bank in which all those withheld payments would sit and collect interest until the accumulated money would be paid back in the form of retirement benefits. This is the general understanding, and it is false. No wonder this is the popular myth, because the system, when it was first established, was called 'an intergenerational income transfer program' to which most beneficiaries replied: 'How much is in it for me when I'm old?' What it meant, and means, is that in the beginning and now, active workers have a part of their salary withheld in order to support people already retired. And when today's workers retire, they in turn will be supported by a future generation of workers. I remember at the time—the mid-1930s, at the peak of

64

Roosevelt's New Deal—the President translated 'intergenerational income transfer program' in a masterly way, using one of his typically homely figures of speech. 'The Social Security system', he said, 'is no more and no less than a national attempt to observe the Fifth Commandment: "Honour thy father and thy mother."'

It worked fine for about forty years. The trouble began about ten years ago, when it was recognized that more people than ever were living longer. Today, the expectation of life at birth, here and in most of the Western world, is 69 point something for males, 74 point something for females. So, except for the early years of the Great Depression, the system used to take in more money than it paid out. But increasingly, during the past decade, because there are millions more retired than was originally figured on, the system is paying out much more money than it's taking in. Therefore the government keeps drawing and drawing on reserves. It's got to the point where something like 40 per cent of the national budget is devoted to Social Security. No Senator or Congressman dares say it must be cut. The popular cry now is to cut military spending, which is a little more than half of Social Security. Maybe the federal extension of the compulsory retirement age (it's been extended twice in the past twenty years) is, in essence, not so much an assertion of the rude health and vigour of Americans as a rather desperate way of taking in more deductions from the old in order to help the older. It's a brave effort, anyway. I can't imagine what the burden is going to be on the working population of the young in Britain who pay to maintain, in pensions, all those sturdy people who have to retire at 60. I forbear from mentioning the medical fact that men, at least, who retire in their prime tend to keel over; or the social fact that they amaze their wives by suddenly becoming household nuisances, wanting, for instance—lunch!

Martin Luther King—the Black Washington

23 January 1987

If you had arrived as a stranger, in just about any American city or small town last Monday, you'd have been puzzled to see some banks open, some not, some offices closed. Over public buildings, flags flying at half mast here, and there, a flag flying high and free. In New York, in San Francisco, the two financial centres of the East and West coasts, there was no trading on the stock exchanges. If you had been in Phoenix, the capital city of the Arizona desert, you would have seen a march of thousands of people—fifteen thousand was the police count—leaning into freakish, freezing winds and trudging towards the state capitol, the Arizona legislature. The march there was led by the former Governor of the state, a Democrat. 'Let's all keep coming back here,' he said, 'until we have in Arizona a holiday in his memory.'

The memory they were invoking was that of the Reverend Martin Luther King, Jr., the black leader, who was assassinated in the spring of 1968, and who would have been 58 last Monday. That day, 19 January, has been designated by the Congress, in a bill signed two years ago by President Reagan, as a national holiday: a federal holiday, that is for all workers in the federal government. Most of the states, well over forty, have seconded the motion and declared it a holiday for all workers in state government. Last Monday was the second national observance of Martin Luther King's birthday. Why then the to-do in Phoenix, Arizona? Because, it is the only state that first followed the federal government and then, last November, elected a new Governor who has rescinded Martin Luther King Jr. Day as a state holiday. It has produced an uproar and, inevitably, charges of insensitivity and racism. The new Governor says he has no prejudice, no emotion at all about his act. He says that a state holiday may only, in law, be declared by the legislature, and therefore the former Governor did wrong in proclaiming it on his own initiative. 'Let the people decide,' says the new Governor. (Arizona has a population of just over 5 per cent blacks.)

When the idea of a national holiday was first proposed, several years ago, there was, remarkably, not much opposition. And it came, mainly, not from old segregationists; of course it came from pockets of declared white Christian supremacists and the small, frenzied remnants of the Ku Klux Klan. But in the main, it was from a Senator or two, a Congressman or two (in states not dependent on considerable black populations), who pointed out, quite correctly, that Dr King was about to be given a distinction which, in the whole of American history, has been accorded only one man: George Washington. True, Lincoln's birthday

67

is a legal holiday, but only in twenty states, nowhere I believe, in the South, in any of the states of the old Confederacy. To be absolutely accurate about the custom, and the procedure, there are no national holidays in the United States. The President and Congress can legally designate holidays for government: federal employees only in Washington, that is, its district, the District of Columbia. Each state has the right to follow suit or not to.

So, while thirty states still hold out against Lincoln, there are no more than half a dozen that do not officially recognize Dr Martin Luther King Jr. Day. Of course, federal government workers everywhere take the day off. But as the first objectors pointed out, there is no Jefferson Day, no Benjamin Franklin Day, no Madison Day, and no Franklin Roosevelt Day. Why, they asked, should one man be singled out, above a roster of distinguished Presidents, for this amazing honour? The answer cannot be minced into fine legal English. The answer is simple and resounding. Dr Martin Luther King, Jr., in his late twenties, thirty-one years ago, led a black boycott against a bus company down in Alabama and that led to other boycotts, and marches, and jailing for Dr King and others, and a vast rebellion that we call the Black Revolution. This happened, by the way, two years after the United States Supreme Court came through with its historic ruling that segregation was, at last, unconstitutional.

There was instant and formidable resistance to the Court throughout, at first, the whole South. The little matter of the Montgomery bus boycott turned out to be the spark that ignited the revolution. And in that little matter, as happens in every nation, one obscure person, as obscure as Wat Tyler or Ned Ludd, lit the charge. Her name was Rosa Parks. Let me reach on the shelf and look over a very browned-off page of a newspaper. It is eerie to read it now, because it was written, from Montgomery, Alabama, by a reporter who had not a flicker of foresight about where this humdrum incident would lead. It was written by me. It was written in the spring of 1956, and was in the main about a church service, or rally, which I attended as, by the way, the only white in the congregation. But it went back to the beginning of the boycott, which was still going on five months later. It goes like this:

On December third last, four Negroes went aboard a city bus and sat in its forward section. This is a flexible area marked off by cards that snap on to the central poles; they may be moved back and forth according to the racial majority that lives along the bus's normal route. The bus driver asked them to move back into the colored section. All but one, a woman, complied: one Rosa Parks. The driver acted in accordance with a city law, which may be flouted at the risk of fine and imprisonment and the loss of the city's operating franchise. The bus driver tried again, and failing, called in two policemen. When the woman still refused to move, they arrested her. The same afternoon thousands of printed handbills mysteriously dropped on the doorsteps of colored homes urging a boycott of the bus line, to start two days later.

It accordingly began on Monday the 5th.

Well, it was still going five months later when I was down there to cover the story, which by now was a national concern. It would not have grown so, I believe, if it hadn't been for the man who kept coming back there to strengthen the resistance of the blacks, all of whom went on, day after day, month after month, walking to work. In the evening of that spring day, I went to the service—a sort of service of rededication—in a shambling coloured section of town, a squat, ugly Victorian church, the Mount Zion African Methodist Episcopal church. The place was jammed to the doors. For an hour or more, there were chants and hymns, and single figures rising as the spirit moved them, to shout and 'testify' in many a Bible sentence sung in the minor chords and heaving melancholy of the blues. Then they all sang 'Old Time Religion' and there was a rustle of leaders at a side door, and out came three parsons who prepared the way for the coming of the leader. The side door opened again, and the roar might have been for Victory in Europe. He was a young man with solemn good looks. The roar eventually died into a breathless silence, and this young Dr King read out a petition that was to be, he said, 'a constitution for our cause'. At the end, I walked out with one of the clergymen. 'Tell me', I said, 'about Dr King.' With a steady look and absolute seriousness, he said: 'God took time to prepare him a man. God had to find him a Leader. And having looked, he chose Him a man, young, dynamic, wise and Christian. He is second only to Lincoln as the Great Emancipator.'

70

Well, it was a rousing, seething evening, not to be forgotten. But the rhetoric did seem a little heady at the time to one reporter who was moving through the South to see how well or badly the states, the cities, the country towns were complying with the Supreme Court's already famous judgement.

Since that evening in darktown Montgomery, Dr King's so-called 'constitution', which meant only to demand equal treatment in public transportation, came to force equal rights across the whole social span of American life. He stands alone as a black leader, and he triumphed with no more, but no less, than the weapons of Mahatma Gandhi: steadiness, unwavering courage, jail terms, abuse, patience, an absolutely iron refusal to meet violence with violence. When the resolution came before Congress to declare his birthday a federal holiday, there were very few Congressmen who dared oppose it. President Reagan himself was against it, and when asked at a press conference if he thought (it was a common, scurrilous rumour) that Dr King was a Communist, he replied: 'Well, in about thirty years or so, I guess we'll know, won't we?' When the resolution was passed, the President signed it. And last Monday, he spoke movingly about the lessons we had learned from Dr King, a man who united us in tolerance and understanding. Down in Atlanta where Dr King was buried, there was an ecumenical church service, from which Mr Reagan's Secretary of State, Mr Shultz, took Dr King's message out to South Africa. 'Our objective', he said, 'is to encourage the extension of the full benefits of citizenship, which white Americans so rightly

71

cherish, to all their countrymen.'

There have been, around the time of the King birthday, some sporadic flares of racism—whites beating up blacks in a New York City borough; one small county in Georgia swears it will let no black family live there. This county is now practically under siege. Thirty years ago, it would never have made the news. There would have been thousands of counties all over the country similarly minded.

So, the revolution has been won? No. So things are much the same? No. Black unemployment is still twice that of whites. Four black families in ten have no man in the house. But beyond any other white society I know, blacks are no longer the obvious pool of menial labour. They have spread their ablest through every sort of profession and job, up from businessmen and bank clerks to editors, sheriffs and mayors—of five of the seven biggest cities—to the Supreme Court. No cause yet to crow. But it is a vastly different, more colour-blind society from the one I took for granted when I left Montgomery that spring evening thirty-two years ago, and waited for my train in a waiting room marked, 'Whites Only'.

Fred Astaire

26 June 1987

Movie stars don't make it. Nor statesmen. Not Prime Ministers, or dictators unless they die in office. Not even a world-famous rock star, unless he's assassinated. But last Monday, none of the three national television networks hesitated about the story that would lead the evening news. On millions of little screens in this country and I don't doubt in many other countries around the world, the first shots were of an imp, a graceful wraith, a firefly in impeccable white tie and tails.

And for much longer than the lead story usually runs, for a full five minutes on NBC, we were given a loving retrospective of the dead man, ending with the firm declaration by Nureyev that 'He was not just the best ballroom dancer, or tap dancer, he was simply the greatest, most imaginative, dancer of our time.' And the newsmen were right to remind us of the immortal comment of the Hollywood mogul, who, with the no-nonsense directness of an expert, reported on Fred Astaire's first film test: 'Has enormous ears, can't act, can't sing, dances a little.'

That Hollywood mogul, long gone, spent his life ducking round corners, to avoid being identified as the oaf who looked in the sky and never saw the brightest star. However, that expert opinion was, as the lawyers say, controlling at the time and in Astaire's first movies, there was no thought of allowing him to act or sing. But not for long. And thanks to the invention of television, and the need to fill vast stretches of the afternoon and night with old movies, it has been possible for my daughter, for instance, to claim Fred Astaire as her favourite film star from the evidence of all the movies he made fifteen, ten, five, three years before she was born.

When I got the news on Monday evening here, and realized with immediate professional satisfaction that the BBC had smartly on hand a

73

musical obituary tribute to him I put together eight years ago, I couldn't help recalling the casual, comic way this and similar radio obituaries came about.

I was in London at the end of 1979, and Richard Rodgers—one of the two or three greatest of American song writers—had just died, I believe on New Year's Eve or the night before. Britons, by then, were getting accustomed, without pain, to making what used to be a two-day Christmas holiday into a ten-day much-needed rest. For all laborious research purposes, the BBC was shut up. And there was no retrospective programme on the life and music of Richard Rodgers in the BBC's archives. Of course, in a gramophone library that looks like an annex to the Pentagon, there were hundreds, perhaps thousands, of recordings of his songs. The SOS went out to a writer, a producer, and—I presume—a man who had the key to the gramophone library. The silent place was unlocked, and the three of them laboured through the day to put together an hour's tribute to Richard Rodgers. It was done. It was competent enough, but rushed to an impossible deadline. This hasty improvisation happened just when my own music producer and I, who had enjoyed working together for six years or so on American popular music, were wondering what we could offer next. We'd done a sketch history of jazz, through individuals. We'd gone through all the popular music of the 1920s, 1930s and 1940s, and were stumped for a new series, at which point I asked if we mightn't go and talk to the head of the channel, network or whatever. We went in, and the genial boss asked me what we had in mind. 'A morgue,' I said. A what? 'Where', I asked, 'is your morgue?' He was not familiar with the word, a newspaper term. 'Well,' I said, 'all newspapers have them.' 'How d'you mean?' 'If', I explained, 'Mrs Thatcher died tonight and you woke up and read a two-sentence obituary, you'd be rightly outraged. But if you saw a two-page obituary, you'd take it for granted. When d'you suppose it was written?' 'That's right,' he said thoughtfully. What I was proposing was a morgue of the Americans eminent in popular music and jazz, so they'd not get caught short again. A splendid idea, the man said; pick your stars. We made a list and were commissioned to return to America and finish all of them. Naturally, we looked at a calendar, and birthdates of Hoagy Carmichael, Earl Hines, Harold Arlen, Ethel Merman, Stephane Grappelli, Ella Fitzgerald. But then, in a spasm of panic, we thought of two giants—if the word can be used about two comparative midgets: Irving Berlin and Fred Astaire. Berlin was then 91. And Fred Astaire was just crowding 80. The boss man, to whom the idea of a morgue had been, only a few minutes before, quaint if not morbid, wondered what we were waiting for. Better get busy, at once, on Berlin and then on Astaire. I remember doing the Astaire obit, then and there, while I was still in London. Meanwhile, we'd simply pray every night that the Lord would keep Irving Berlin breathing till I could get home and get busy. I remember being picked up in a car by a charming young girl to get to the BBC and record my Astaire narration—there wasn't a moment to lose. She asked me, in the car, what the script was that I was clutching. 'It's an obituary', I said, 'of Fred Astaire.' 'Fred Astaire,'

75

she shrieked, 'dead?' and almost swerved into a bus. 'Of *course*, he's not dead,' I said, 'but he's going to be one day.' She, too, was new to the institution of a morgue. I recalled that when I was a correspondent for a British paper in the United States, and when for example, Dean Acheson was appointed Secretary of State, the first cable I had from my editor said, 'Welcome Acheson obituary soonest.' How ghoulish, she said.

I imagine that to two generations at least, it's assumed that Fred Astaire, this slim, pop-eyed newcomer to Hollywood who couldn't act, couldn't sing, danced a little, only made a fool of the mogul through the movies he made, with Ginger Rogers, in the mid- and late 1930s. But long before then, from the mid-1920s on, he was already an incomparable star—as a dancer—to theatre audiences both in New York and in London. Perhaps more in London than anywhere, certainly in the 1920s, with the early Gershwin hits, *Funny Face* and *Lady Be Good*, and lastly, in 1933, in Cole Porter's *Gay Divorce* (which was the title of the theatre show; Hollywood would not then allow so shocking a title and called the movie version, *The Gay Divorcee*). Of all the thousands of words that have been written this week, and will be written, there is a passage I went back to on Tuesday night which, I think, as well as anything I know, sums up Astaire's overall appeal—the appeal that takes in but transcends one's admiration for his dancing and for his inimitably intimate singing style. This was written in November 1933, by a theatre critic who had so little feel for dancing that he marvelled why London should go on about 'Mr Astaire's doing well enough what the Tiller Girls at

Blackpool do superbly'. The critic, the writer, was James Agate, the irascible, dogmatic, opinionated but brilliant journalist, and I believe the best critic of acting we have had this century. He is writing his review of *Gay Divorce*, after declaring yet again his contempt for musical comedy as an entertainment for idiots, deploring the play's plot and the acting and hoping 'Micawberishly, for something to turn up'. 'Presently,' he wrote, 'Mr Fred Astaire obliged, and there is really no more to be said.' Except—'a very distinguished colleague began his criticism of this show by asking what is Mr Astaire's secret. May I suggest that the solution hangs on a little word of three letters? Mr Astaire's secret is that of the late Rudolf Valentino and of Mr Maurice Chevalier—sex, but sex so bejewelled and be-pixied that the weaker vessels who fall for it can pretend that it isn't sex at all but a sublimated projection of the Little Fellow with the Knuckles in His Eyes. You'd have thought by the look of the first night foyer that it was Mothering Thursday, since every woman in the place was urgent to take to her bosom this waif with the sad eyes and the twinkling feet.'

As for the unique quality of Astaire's dancing—something impossible to put into words—I think the near-impossible has been achieved by an American critic of films and jazz, the late Otis Ferguson. He wrote: in reviewing *Top Hat*: 'He has given the best visual expression that has been generally seen of what is called The Jazz, as a man who can create figures, intricate, unpredictable, constantly varied and yet simple, seemingly effortless. Whenever the band gathers its brasses and rhythm section and begins to beat it out, he is unequalled anywhere, with his soft-shoe sandman number, and when before the line of men with top hats, he swings up the steps . . . Fred Astaire, whatever he may do in whatever picture he is in, has the beat, the swing, the debonair and damn-your-eyes violence of rhythm, all the gay contradiction and irresponsibility, of the best thing this country can contribute to musical history, which is—the best American jazz.'

Origins of American Slang

14 August 1987

In the spring of 1984, there was a new television commercial, for one of those three or four fast-food chains that compete savagely and endlessly like religious factions in a holy war, for the favour of teenagers who seem to survive mainly on hamburgers, French fries and gaseous soft drinks. This short, I think, only thirty-second ad, was an audacious exercise in a new type of television commercial in this country which doesn't cry up its own product so much as cry down the product of its competitors. Very often, this type of ad names the chief competitor and sneers at its claims, a technique that, a dozen years ago, would have appeared likely to offer grounds for a libel suit.

In this particular ad, you saw two women looking down at a very meagre hamburger, and at their side a little old lady with a craggy face. You sensed at once from her scowl that she was the representative of the chain that was making the ad.

She was, apart from her angry carbuncle of a face, tiny: in life, only four feet ten. So all we saw of her, above the counter, was her bobbing angry face. She had obviously had enough of the pitiful object her friends had been served. And she suddenly barked at them: 'But where's the beef, where's the beef?'

It touched the hearts of those millions of us who, when eating out, very rarely come on the genuine article, a plump patty of chopped sirloin or filet, but more often a sliver of a patty that could be mistaken for a coaster to rest your drink on, and composed usually of pounded cereal and other foreign bodies impregnated with a shred of meat. The line 'where's the beef?' must have been echoed in a thousand lunch counters and roadside restaurants. It suddenly, however, became a national idiom when Mr Walter Mondale, in a televised debate with Mr Gary Hart, another contender for the Democratic nomination, listened a while to Mr Hart's visionary, and rather vague, blueprint for running the country (Mr Hart's rhetoric was always a little short on substance). Mr Mondale heard him out, but then turned to him and said, 'Yes, but where's the beef?' It brought the house down, and the director of the hamburger commercial said later, 'If Walter Mondale could have said the line like Clara, he'd have been our president.'

Clara was Clara Peller, a child immigrant from Russia, and for most of her life, a manicurist, who in her sixties, got into television commercials as a non-speaking, practically invisible, extra. In 1984, when she was 83, her head appeared above that lunch counter, and she barked out her famous line. She died in Chicago the other day at the age of 86,

79

and achieved the dignity of a two-column obituary in the *New York Times*. A clip of her ad, and another of Mondale's adoption of it, was shown on all the national networks.

Clara Peller's famous three words are a reminder that the television ad is only the latest source of American popular idiom. I can now think back to a dozen or more catchphrases in the past ten years or so that came out of television commercials and, since millions of people heard them, passed into the language, for the time being. American slang, especially, has traditionally sprung from what is most characteristic in the experience of people doing different jobs in different climates. From the timber workers in the Northwest, we got 'on the skids'—planks of saplings on which the logs could be rolled down the river. The cowboy gave many expressions to the language, and one of them—I should guess the last of them—remained into my own time. I remember when I first came to Yale, if you asked somebody to do a favour which might be troublesome, he'd say: 'No trouble, it's a cinch.' This came from the cattlemen in Texas who, a century ago, rounded up their yearling calves for the long trail to the feed lots in the lush pastures of the Midwest, where they would be fattened up for you and me. When the whole company, the outfit, was ready for the journey north, the cowboys strapped up the belt around the girth of their horses, the saddle girth, and were on their way. In Spanish—and remember, the Southwest had once been New Spain—in Spanish a saddle girth is a 'cincha'. So, 'it's a cinch' came to mean, ready to go, and then by extension, as we now say, 'No problem.'

However, the word is long gone and I doubt that any American under 40 has ever heard of it. It appears that once an idiom no longer calls up a picture of the condition that bred it, it dies. And the cowboy and the cattle kingdom and all their customs and talk are dead and gone. Hence, young people are the first to drop their parents' slang and catchphrases because they don't recall the life that spawned them. I'm not sure whether this is so true in older countries. There must still be old gentlemen in England who talk about somebody being 'hoist with his own petard', but I'm pretty sure that few of them get a mental picture of what is meant by the phrase, and fewer still who know the very rude origin of the word 'petard' from the French. I've heard even young people, in England, say they were 'on tenterhooks', but I'll bet only young Lancashire men or Yorkshire men with fathers or grandfathers who were in the mills know what a tenterhook is and why it produces tension.

In my early time here, the Prohibition gangsters of the early 1930s splattered the language with phrases that, through the early sound movies, passed over to England and were used, often with unconscious comical effect, even by respectable officers of the BBC. Staff members who were sacked were said to have been 'taken for a ride' or 'bumped off'. Somebody getting quickly out of an awkward situation decided to 'take it on the lam'. But certainly, what you might call the classical language of the gangsters has passed away with the gangsters of the Chicago vintage. You'll notice I don't say with the gangsters. They are still with us, but today they are not crude and flashy. They dress austerely, like the conservative businessmen they are. Their sons have probably gone to Princeton or Columbia. They don't merely eat at fashionable places, they quite likely own them. Their offices are not in suburban warehouses. They are in Wall Street. They run such diverse and essential enterprises as—in some cities—the building industry, the docks and waterfront stevedores' unions from Maine to New Orleans. They have a hand in such seemingly innocent fronts as ski resorts and pizza parlours (which have proved to be wonderful cover-ups for drug sales). Only the sleazier heirs of the old Capone days specialize in the gambling and prostitution rackets of Las Vegas and Atlantic City. For the others, whatever slang they generate is indistinguishable from the daily jargon of takeovers and insider trading.

Prison slang has always been a very fertile source of the American vernacular, and all of us use, quite innocently, many of the jailbird's expressions, the original meaning of which the most brazen of us would blush to learn. We won't go into that. New York City itself added new words to the language in the beginning because the Dutch had owned the place before the English. And such words as the 'stoop' (of a house) and 'cruller' as a kind of cake have stayed with us, and every child who learns to say 'faist' and pronounces turmoil as 'toimerl' knows that Brooklyn is an English corruption of Breucklein. But the main source of new entries into New York English was the fact that in the past hundred years this city has been the port of entry for immigrants from many countries of Europe. And because about half of all the Jews who arrived here settled here, many Yiddish words passed into everybody's slang. I hadn't been here a month

82

before I knew what a schlemiel was, and when playing cards, learned to watch out for kibitzers. The cloak-and-suit business alone produced catchphrases that are still with us.

Coming up to today, I was going to say that since the administration was taken over by Marines and Navy men, but that would be an outrageous exaggeration. However, in the recent testimony before the Iran-Contra committees, we kept hearing naval expressions from three ex-Marines: Secretary Shultz, former Chief of Staff Don Regan, not to mention the third man—what's his name?— Colonel North. At one point, Mr Shultz differed with Admiral Poindexter over the meaning of the phrase 'stood down'. The Admiral had said that there came a time when the Iran arms deal was 'stood down', by which he implied it had been put, for the time being, on the shelf. Mr Shultz said that when he was told it was stood down, he assumed it had been abandoned. Why, he was asked, the difference in understanding? Because, he said, 'I'm a Marine, not a Navy man'. Out of those hearings there has come an old phrase which will for ever be attached to what the President now calls the Iran-Contra 'mess'. 'The buck' comes from poker. It was a marker, often a silver dollar, to show who had the next deal, and it could be passed by someone who didn't want the responsibility of dealing to the man on his left. Hence, 'passing the buck'. President Truman made the word immortal when he made it clear that the President alone is responsible for his administration. 'The buck', he said, 'stops here.' In this administration, and in its 'mess', we had come to believe that the buck stopped with Admiral Poindexter. 'Not so,' said Mr Reagan on

Wednesday, 'it stops with the President.' It will send a huge sigh of relief throughout the country. After nine months of doubt, we know now that the President *is* the man in charge, and that he is responsible for what happened, as the old Marines kept saying, 'on his watch'.

Mayor Koch at Work

12 August 1988

The other morning, caught on Fifth Avenue in a hopeless traffic jam, the driver and I panting away in the furnace of his taxi which must have been well over 100 degrees, the driver said, 'If you'll excuse me, mister, but I'm going home.' I didn't blame him, paid him off, and padded down the Avenue with all the alacrity of an infantryman tiptoeing through a minefield.

Later in the day, I had occasion to be going by Gracie Mansion, the Mayor of New York's graceful colonial house that sits in a little park on the edge of the East River. The ordeal of the morning, the traffic jam, and the sight of the Mayor's white house bristling like a mirage among the trees made me think back to a time, I think the last time, I was a guest in the house with the then Mayor, and one or two of his young aides. We were going on about the increasing traffic density everywhere in the city, and I was complaining—as I've been doing ever since—about the meaningless signs, posted every two blocks, on Park and Fifth Avenues, which said, in bold print: 'No Commercial Traffic.' No truck driver I can remember has ever been stopped. I suggested there was an enormous amount of revenue available from a campaign to enforce the signs and hand out hefty fines. The trucks and vans, I said, go ten, twenty, forty blocks, two miles down Fifth Avenue and nobody does anything. The Mayor shook his head: 'It's not possible', he said, 'to do anything anymore. You'd have unholy congestion on every avenue that allows commercial traffic.'

That must have been twenty years ago, and presumably Mayor Koch feels the same way. As we tilted our drinks that evening long ago, and gave up yet another local issue as a bad job, I suggested, 'Why don't you do what they did in Rome? Prohibit all commercial deliveries between dawn and sunset.' Say, said the youngest of the aides, how about that? The Mayor looked pityingly at this young, this very young politician and said, 'Oh, great! First, you'd be paying golden time, triple pay, to all the truck drivers. The price of everything would shoot up. Then you'd have protest marches about the city's inflation rate being way above the national average. Pretty soon, I can imagine somebody in Albany getting out a bill—Teamsters Marriage Compensation Act—for all the drivers whose marriages went bust through the guy sleeping by day and being out all night. The Parent-Teacher Association would move in on that one. And citizens' groups protesting all those delivery vans and trucks barrelling through the streets in the dead of night. And extra help needed at the toll stations and the tunnels across the rivers, at double pay. Shall I go on?' 'Well,' said the young aide, 'they did it in Rome.' 'When?' asked the Mayor. 'I think,' I said, 'it was around 30, 40 BC.' Another bright idea bit the dust.

The other night, I watched the present Mayor, the beleaguered but indestructible Ed Koch, in a packed schoolroom up in Harlem doing what he does once a week, which is primly described as the Mayor's question-and-answer show, on the city's television station. You might have thought you were present at an interrogation session on the West Bank between Israeli soldiers and a pack of young Palestinians. Everybody was fanning themselves in the atrocious heat. The Mayor was continually mopping his face and neck with a handkerchief the size of a tablecloth. And the questioning, so-called, a screaming siren of protests, about the drug pushers taking over this bit of park, no street lights in that lady's block on Staten Island, an old man threatened with eviction and what was the Mayor ever going to do about extra night police at such an intersection, and why was a big condominium—a high-rise for the well-off—going up by a tenement that had no water pressure. The questions were very rarely put as questions. They were defiant, disgusted speeches, bawled at this sweating figure on a rostrum, and the Mayor never paused or backed away: 'Listen, lady, if you'll listen, when this meeting is over, get a hold of Commissioner So-and-so, he's right here, and give him the details. You, no the man in the red shirt, okay, okay, lady, that's enough, shut up. Next: the young woman over there, what's your complaint?' She was the one screaming about the street lights on Staten Island, and she also joined in on the water-pressure problem, which the Mayor said was 'absolutely unavoidable with the

86

enormous draw on the power grid in this heat—you'll be lucky if you don't wake up one night with all the lights out'. The young woman, a Hispanic with blazing black eyes, howled: 'My father tell me don't go live New York, it's hell on earth.' She was screaming on and the Mayor cut in: 'Okay, listen to your father next time. You—the old lady in the corner. Yes, Madam?'

There are many mayors of cities, governors of states, who regularly submit to the questions of citizens from all over but in the air-conditioned sanctuary of a television studio with an emcee monitoring the incoming calls, and the questioners, the attackers, at the long, safe, distance of a telephone wire. I don't know of another politician who goes through this face-to-face, nature-red-in-tooth-and-claw performance more than once in a while, as an unpleasant necessity of political office. But to Mayor Koch, it's a necessary weekly joust which, he fervently believes, is the essence of his being: being a politician. When the meetings are over, within a few days his office is flooded with letters from people who saw the show on television, and the various officials who stood warily beside him that night are confronted by the complainers who were told to take their troubles to the responsible department. This is, of course, a mere item in the Mayor's daily grind, which starts at dawn and is lucky to end at midnight. Just now, today for instance, he's trying to recruit seven hundred new policemen in the narcotics division of the city force to stem the outrage over open drug dealing in the streets of many neighbourhoods. He's just apologized for the excessive force he believes the police used in putting down a

87

demonstration against a curfew in a small but dangerous park. He's just begged people to stop giving money to street panhandlers and contribute instead to city charities. He's ordering the hospitals to report on their methods for disposing of hospital waste, which has been washing up in noxious quantities along some of the Jersey and Long Island beaches—and now, by the way, has appeared lapping the shores of Lake Erie, seven hundred miles inland in Cleveland, Ohio. That has spurred the United States Senate to get out a bill prohibiting, from 1990 on, the disposal of hospital wastes in all seas and lakes.

Meanwhile, the Mayor faces a constant battle with the people in every borough who want new prisons but don't want them in their neighbourhood—just like the aroused citizens of several New England states who believe, in principle, in nuclear power but have mobilized to resist having an essential nuclear waste dump in their neck of the woods.

Two or three evenings a week, the Mayor has, in theory, time off, which means attending a dinner to distribute to eminent immigrants the city's medal of freedom; the ducking into an Italian-American dinner; then a Puerto Rican dinner; an Irish protest meeting about his outrageous remark that the British in Northern Ireland did not constitute an army of occupation. That observation alone probably lost him a hundred thousand Irish votes; in the next year's election, he backed off. And, the unreal, the incredible thing is: he wants to run again, after eleven years of presiding over this seething cosmopolis, and after two years of fighting charges of corruption in his administration. During that time, several of his closest aides and city officials have gone to jail, resigned under fire or committed suicide. He has, by his own admission, too often put his trust in the wrong people.

Why would he want a shot at another four years? Because, I think, after all the wear and tear of trying to take care of seven million people, he remains an irrepressible romantic, who has had the tonic experience of sometimes seeing romance turn into reality. He did pluck New York from the brink of bankruptcy and is not going to let you forget it. But unlike President Reagan, another romantic, he does not cling to an old and simpler picture of America and yearn to restore it. He gets as excited over the prospect of housing a hundred homeless families in a rundown Harlem hotel as Mr Reagan does over the vision of Star Wars.

Mayor Koch, in his racy, egotistical and never dull autobiography wrote:

The City of New York included nearly two hundred religions, races, and national groups. It used to be said that New York City was a melting pot. It never was, and it isn't today. Our fathers and mothers, and some of us, wanted to believe we had lost our own racial and ethnic traditions and had become homogenized. That never happened. What happens is, you gain respect for the traditions of others but don't lose your own. Today, black is beautiful. Spanish is the language of the future. Women want to be astronauts, and are. Jews play golf. God made us whatever we are. Being Mayor of the City is a very special experience, and I'm lucky.

89

By the way, the Mayor—one of the leading Democrats of the nation—did not go to the Atlanta Convention. Sobbing rhetoric and a thousand balloons are not his style. As for the weekly brawl with those rocking, bawling, aggrieved citizens, the Mayor finds it a stimulus. If nobody had ever invented the now worn-out phrase, he could truthfully say: 'That's what government is all about.' If he were a demagogue, which he isn't, he might call it 'democracy in action'. As it is, if you put it to him, he'll say, with a stoical smile, his eyebrows up, and his shoulders shrugging: 'Well, it's nothing else.'

Hurricanes

23 September 1988

If you can imagine yourself in an aeroplane flying from the tip of Cornwall to the north of Scotland, or more accurately, from the toe of Italy up the seven hundred and fifty miles to Milan, and seeing the greater part of the land you flew over under water, you would have an idea of the monstrous scale of Hurricane Gilbert after it had done its frightful wrecking job on Jamaica, the Yucatan peninsula, and the Mexican towns on the Gulf coast. Most of central Texas and on through western Oklahoma had, in twenty-four hours, between 10 and 18 inches of rain. Something like 32 inches is the annual quota of London and, by the way, New York. The result, of which we saw only 30-second glimpses, was of an endless landscape of little Venices with people wading or getting from here to there on improvised rafts. The only good (for the United States) that blew in with this ill wind was a deluge of rain dumped on the farm states of Kansas and Nebraska and Iowa (we are now fifteen hundred miles north of Yucatan), whose immense crops have withered in this summer of unrelieved drought.

As for Mexico, the plight of hundreds of small towns and villages is hardly to be pictured. The heartbreaking item was the fact that the worst casualties, now mounting two hundred, were of people who'd had the sense to flee from the coast and were already a hundred and eighty miles inland in Monterrey, when their buses were overwhelmed by the roaring flood waters.

For a storm that was a thousand miles in diameter when it crossed the Gulf of Mexico and packed winds of over a hundred and fifty miles an hour, it must appear that the casualties were astonishingly, blessedly low. And so they were, compared with, for instance, a hurricane that swooped on to the coastal city of Galveston, Texas, in 1900 and took six thousand lives in that small city alone, one-seventh of the population, leaving, the official report said, 'not a single house undamaged'. Well, even if all the people had fled, I suppose the physical, structural damage would have been the same. But the death rate was due to a simple failure, incapacity of the time: the inability to see it coming. The weather forecast for 8 September 1900 in the Galveston papers read, 'Sunny and warm'. And so it was for all the great recorded hurricanes from 1938 back to 1848—a monster that destroyed much of Florida and did damage for the next thousand miles of its northward trek.

All that people knew, for the years that records had been kept, was that these hurricanes arise in August and September in the West Indies and move north or northwest. The meteorologists could track them only when they hit land. Not until 1932 did a radio station in Florida, working with a couple of the university's engineers, and financed by the WPA (the New Deal agency for the unemployed) start a rudimentary hurricane research station whose job was to maintain short-wave radio communication with Puerto Rico. Even then, they were dependent on reports from the West Indies of what people had seen happening to them. The course and intensity of the storms, once they got up into the Gulf, were a mystery. Only in the past thirty years have we had a National Hurricane Center in Florida, now on permanent duty, a staff of hurricane experts equipped with high-tech devices and, the really new and vital adjunct, a crew of Coast Guard pilots trained to fly over and then drop into the eye of hurricanes and to bring back the details of their forward speed, rotary speed, and their course. Even then, even now, after Gilbert was buccaneering into Oklahoma, the head of the National Hurricane Center remarked that we can accurately predict the direction of a hurricane only for the next twenty-four hours. Beyond that, we still do not know if it is going to turn, and where, and why. So, once the thing had torn through Jamaica and across the Yucatan peninsula, the Hurricane Center could do no better than suggest the evacuation of the coast populations round an arc of the Gulf from northern Mexico along all the Texas and Louisiana Gulf coasts, a broken stretch of over five hundred miles. By Friday of last week, about half a million people were on the move. As Gilbert stubbornly maintained its west-northwestern course, the alarm was called off for New Orleans and the Louisiana coast.

By the way, last weekend I asked a young European who broadcasts to his native land if he had, at any point in his early reports, said what a hurricane is. He was startled. Surely, he said, everybody knows that. Yet, I've noticed, even some of my friends imply that a hurricane is a very high wind, high in the sense of speedy. I was told by English meteorologists that the great storm which ravaged southeastern England last autumn was not technically a hurricane, which must be scant consolation to the curators of Kew Gardens. We have weathered six hurricanes on Long Island in the last fifty years, and while they've detached shingles, broken windows and let the rain in, it was not a hurricane but a simple though ferocious northeast wind that five years ago ripped off the whole bayside porch of the house, crashed it through the roof and deposited much of it in the living room. Luckily, we weren't there. We were sitting in a hotel room on the coast of California watching pictures of people in boats ferrying between houses and flooded shops. 'Wonder where that can be?' we said. 'Riverhead, Long Island,' the announcer obliged. 'Poor old Riverhead,' we said. When we got back to New York and drove down to the Island, we said, 'Poor old us!'

The main point about a hurricane is that it is not

a furious, fast and damaging wind moving like an army. It is shaped like a doughnut, a doughnut whirling around anti- or counterclockwise at speeds above 73 miles per hour (Gilbert got up to 180 at one point). The hole in the middle of the doughnut is the eye and the eerie thing about it is that it is dead calm. The forward movement of the whole system is very much slower, usually not more than 20 miles per hour. The damage comes from the whirling motion, and the worst damage happens to very tall trees, which can be spun and plucked up by their roots.

It's an odd coincidence that even if there'd been no Gilbert, I'm pretty sure that this week I should have talked about hurricanes—about one hurricane, the memory of which made those of us who came through it shudder a little last Wednesday. Just fifty years ago, on that day, I was sailing to New York on the great French liner, the *Normandie*. The sea was a little choppy, and the sky was overcast and stayed so the next morning when we woke up to receive the breakfast tray and the ship's newspaper. Those of you who have ever taken a cruise or sailed the transatlantic ships in the old days will know what I mean when I say that a ship's newspaper could be a source of much hilarity. Scraps of international news picked up by radio overnight—most of the copy about fashions or sport. Spelling mistakes abounded, pieces stopped in mid-paragraph. So, when we saw a headline, 'Hurricane à New-York', we knew that the French had got their information badly fouled up. We did not have hurricanes 'à New York'. But I read on, and it talked about the devastation of towns on 'le Fork du Nord' (the North Fork, which

94

is where we live) and the lifting of a cinema on the Fork du Sud (the South Fork) at Westhampton out to sea. They were right—twenty-odd people at a matinée, and the theatre, projectionist and all, landed two miles into the Atlantic and drowned. There was flooding of Providence, Rhode Island, huge destruction of the forests of New England, and so on.

Next morning, we were practically jolted out of our beds, and the public address system announced that nobody must try to go on deck. The hurricane blowing out across the Atlantic had hit us. What I most remember, for an hour or two, was that the *Normandie*, the second largest (I believe) transatlantic liner afloat, simply got up out of the water, shook itself in the air like a drenched mastiff and plunged back into the deeps. On and on. Five people out of close to three thousand went down to dinner.

The following morning, as always seems to happen, was a brilliant and beautiful day, and we sailed up the bay and into the harbour, and there my father-in-law was waiting for us. A ramrod-straight, austere old New Englander who scorned ever to show emotion for any hurt done to him, he told us briskly with a moist eye about his ninety wooded acres, 'a lifetime to plant, a few years, perhaps to clean up and plant again'. Well, it wasn't quite that bad, but it was about ten days before we could drive through the main street of our nearest village, Southold. The towering American elms had been whisked and plucked and brought up by their roots and the sidewalks with them, so that the streets were trenches with tilted pavements as their walls. The devastation everywhere was

95

indescribable. A third of the American feather-duster elms through Rhode Island and Massachusetts were destroyed, half the New Hampshire stands of white birch. More than six hundred people were drowned. The *New York Times* weather forecast, on the morning of 21 September 1938, said: 'Cloudy, chance of rain'.

My sharpest, the most indelible memoir of a hurricane, which to me dramatized the wind force more than a hundred panoramic shots of toppled trees and floating houses, was my recollection of a pencil-thin something that had pierced the bark of a tree and lodged deep in there like a struck arrow. It was a straw.

Chaplin—the Last Word

21 April 1989

About a month, six weeks ago, I was surprised to get a call from a newspaper—and in the following weeks pursued by a flurry of calls from other papers and television stations, all asking the same question. Would I like to contribute to the coming great celebration, the centenary of the birth of you know who? I knew who, but I put them off by saying: 'Oh, so you're going to do a big feature on Hitler?' Everybody was baffled. Hitler? Why Hitler? Because, I said, 20 April 1889 is a date that will live in infamy. They may have changed now, but none of them at the time had any plans to observe (shall we say), if not celebrate, the hundredth anniversary of the arrival on the continent of Europe of the human who did more than anybody in this century to shatter it.

No doubt by now, this weekend most of the media will be making up for this omission. It would be an omission. After all, most of us who live through the exploits of our youthful heroes and villains go into middle and old age remaining constantly amazed that the next generation, or the one after that, has never heard of them. I well remember the envy I felt for the bliss of my daughter's ignorance when, thirty-some years ago, when she was about 6, she had been watching a television programme and came running into my study saying, 'Daddy, what's Hitler?' What's? Wonderful! She learned.

Of course, the man I was being solicited to talk or write about was none other than Charles Spencer Chaplin. I turned them all down on the ground that I had written, in a book, just about everything I should want to say about him. Most of the telephone callers were amazed to hear this. One knowledgeable girl said, 'But we understand in this office that you once worked with him on a movie about Napoleon?' 'That's right, it's all in the book,' I said. 'Thanks for thinking of me, but goodbye.'

However, in reading just now the reams of tributes, potted biographies, critiques of every film, from the Essanay shorts to the final, dreadful *Countess of Hong Kong*, it struck me that everybody I read was picking up stories they'd heard, or read, or making a big deal out of a single meeting. Why? Were they being devious, dishonest? Not at all. They were doing what I should do, what I do regularly if I'm writing about Disraeli or Lloyd

George or Jack Hobbs or anyone else who was in his glory days when I was a tot, or not yet born. All the writers, even the greybeards of film criticism, were—the awful truth dawned—too young to have known him. And their knowledge, too, of practically every film up to *Modern Times* had come from reverent little pilgrimages to film clubs or Motion Picture Museums, which, in Britain and America, are growing like mushrooms.

So, I thought, maybe I should, here and now, and only here and now, have a last word about this extraordinary, irascible, generous, conscienceless, thoughtful, mischievous, overwhelmingly charming man about whose work the young and the old generations, I gather, now agree to differ. At my end of the calendar, it is now established as gospel that Chaplin was the first genius of film comedy, its inventor, and that nobody has touched him for weaving together slapstick and pathos in artful ways. (I ought to say that way back there in my twenties I had a friend, a sly unfooled Irishman, who enjoyed Max Linder and Buster Keaton and the Marx Brothers, but found Chaplin from the beginning arch, self-conscious and nauseatingly sentimental. But old Heb Davidson, still, I hope, of Donard Demesne, County Wicklow, was always an exception, a wicked dissenter from all conventional wisdom.) Now I gather—from the young critics who have paused to celebrate the anniversary— that Buster Keaton is the resurrected god and that Chaplin, as comedian, is sorry stuff. I have not seen any writing of this kind about him here, but it appears to me a standard view in Britain, among, that is, the intelligentsia, who were, sixty years ago, the first people to rescue the early Chaplin from the masses who adored him and suggest he was almost too good for them. The new view, surprising to me, was put crisply last week by *The Economist*, which—remarking correctly that Chaplin's comedy was rooted in the Victorian music hall, both in its slapstick and its maudlin sentimental songs— concluded that this is why today his comedy 'is so unfunny and manipulative'.

Well, that's all that need or can be said about the comedian. For although it is possible—indeed, it happens all the time—that people can be taught to enjoy a composer, a painter, a writer (what are our arts schools for?), there is absolutely no way that anyone can be instructed, beguiled, persuaded, to find someone funny whom they find unfunny. The most useless arguments between friends are about which writer or performer is or is not funny, and which food is or is not delicious.

But how about this man, who one day in 1934 wrote to me (a miracle, that: he rarely wrote to anyone) asking me to go out to Hollywood and help him with the script of a projected film on Napoleon? I have written at length on how I got to know him—that the previous year, as a graduate student cruising around the United States, I had a commission from a London paper to interview him, that I went to his studio to meet him; that he took me up to his house; and that the rest of the summer I was up there most days and many evenings. He was then 44, a tiny, dapper man, a graceful golliwog in an angora sweater, topped by a remarkably handsome face of almost sculptural bone structure. I was 24, lean and gabby, hipped on the movies and certainly, at first, dazzled to be taken up by the most famous man in the world—an obvious title

99

when you remember that, since his movies were silent, the natives of about a hundred and fifty countries had seen and laughed at him. The old cowboy philosopher Will Rogers put it in a nutshell: 'The Zulus knew Chaplin better than Arkansas knew Garbo.'

So in the second year, 1934, I drove off across the country, landed in Hollywood and reported to his funny little rundown bungalow studio. Next day, we retired to a small workroom, a shabby place (he always said he was uncomfortable working in lavish surroundings) with peeling wallpaper, worn oilcloth on the floor, three straight-backed chairs, a plain table, an upright piano out of tune. The room was a shock, an interesting reflection of something noticed about other rich men who had been born in dire poverty. It was not there to recall the poverty, but to remind you that perhaps the new money was not there for keeps. It explained, too, I think his habit of never carrying money. He either signed restaurant bills or got his assistant director or another employee to pay for him.

Most days I spent the afternoons in the local library, boning up on books about Napoleon's life in exile on St Helena. Next morning we would go over the stuff, and Chaplin would start to create scenes, in mime: a row with his British doctor, a complaint dictated back to Britain, daydreams about a battle or Josephine, or an imperial attack of indigestion. That latter bit could have come straight out of *The Immigrant* or *The Gold Rush*. In fact, I think I knew then the project would never work. Mostly he would stomp or slouch around the room mumbling incomprehensible dialogue, and look thoughtful or indignant or sombre, and he had

100

an astonishing gift to look more like Napoleon than Napoleon (or, for that matter, more like any of the many real people he mimicked). But he instinctively couldn't help making the point, in dumb show, that an emperor with a hiccup or a burp is just as helpless as a baby. Several times, in the weeks we worked on this rough script, a serious scene—Napoleon rewriting his will—would gradually turn into a piece of comic pantomime that had us helpless. The third member, brought in as the public stand-in to try things out on, was the old shambling Swede, Henry Bergman, who had played in practically every Chaplin comedy. We'd give up, and go chuckling off to lunch. One day, I went up to the house to dinner. We sat and played, as a duet, the song 'Titine', which he was to use in *Modern Times*. He broke off for a telephone call and when he came back, I remember, he had a toothpick. He sat back on a sofa and picked away. 'By the way,' he said, 'the Napoleon thing. It's a beautiful idea—for somebody else.' We didn't discuss it. Nobody discussed a personal decision made by Charles Spencer Chaplin. On the way out to dinner, he said, 'Nobody pays to see Chaplin do an artistic experiment. They go to see the little man.' Nothing more was said, ever. A week or two later, I packed and took off East. I'm sure he was right, as some later impersonations proved.

This is not the place to go into his exile to Switzerland. It had little to do with his politics. He was never more than what in those days was called 'a parlour pink' though he was accused of every radical crime in the book by malicious gossip columnists who resented his holding on to his British citizenship. It had much to do with paternity suits and his cavalier way of ignoring subpoenas on other womanly matters, and the instructions of the courts. The administration hounded him, and found nothing indictable, but when they rescinded his re-entry permit as he was on the Atlantic on his way to Europe, he had had enough, and abruptly decided to stay in Switzerland for life. It was a sad end to his long American adventure. He loved this country, but he never forgave the Truman administration's final, abrupt and shabby treatment of him.

Those paranoid years are long gone, and luckily the generation that doesn't know much about him will know even less of his old age. He remains, as W. C. Fields described him, better than he meant, 'A ballet dancer', the universal homeless waif, over-sentimental at times, certainly, endlessly inventive, as Fred Astaire was inventive, often touching, and to some of us still uniquely—funny.

San Francisco Earthquake

20 October 1989

Sometime in the middle of the First World War—it must have been towards the end of the dreadful year of 1916, after the nightmare slaughter of the Somme—an aunt of mine, whose husband was a soldier in France, announced that she didn't believe a word of what she read in the papers. She was going to write to her husband to find out for real what was going on on the Western Front. This showed, first, a touching ignorance of the censorship of letters, both ways. But eventually he replied. All he could tell her about the way the war was going was what life was like in a muddied trench he'd been living in for a month or two. And what a blasted 200 yards looked like between him and the German trenches. The whole war for him shrank to dampness, lice, chilblains, rats, bully beef, the sight of two ruined trees, and would she please send him some chocolate and cigarettes.

On Tuesday night and Wednesday of this past week, it struck me that the constant irony of the San Francisco earthquake, in this, the wonderful age of worldwide communication was that—compared with the people of Europe, Australia, India, wherever—the only people who hadn't a clue to what was going on were the people of San Francisco and other neighbouring cities, without power. From the first rumble and shudder of those wracking fifteen seconds, and on for a couple of days, they had no power, no television, no radio, no newspapers. A reporter who had flown in from the East on Wednesday wrote that it was a strange, embarrassing feeling to stand in almost any part of the city and tell these gaping natives about Candlestick Park, the Nimitz Freeway, the damage in the Mission district, the collapsed shopping mall ninety miles away in Santa Cruz, the buckled highways, the astonishing range of pictures she'd seen on television overnight. Mainly transmitted from that station in Atlanta, Georgia—CNN—which the irrepressible Ted Turner started years ago and which pulls in through innumerable saucers live coverage from everywhere on earth, and broadcasts without a pause, twenty-four hours a day. On Tuesday night in the East, when the

103

scene jumped to President Bush at a dinner to give us the latest word, the CNN anchor people charitably left him as soon as possible: he was already well behind the times. He had not been at home watching CNN Atlanta.

It was an eerie break for millions of Americans settling down across the country at 5:00 Pacific time, 8 p.m., in the East, that they were about to have the privilege of getting a vast panorama of the scene below, of the course, the baseball stadium, and the surrounding city, as seen by a blimp that is always on hand, on high, for such sporting occasions. All these fans were settling in, as I was, with a friend and a beer, to watch the third game of the baseball championship of the World Series. It was 5 o'clock, and we'd seen the 62,000 rustling away down there, and inevitably, they always like to set the stage, long panning shots of the enchanting bay and the great bridges glistening in the falling sun. We saw the pitchers warming up in the bullpen, the managers and teams chewing away, gum, perhaps, more often tobacco, in the dugout. We were ready for the introductions, the national anthem, then all but one of the batting team would trot back to the dugout, and the fielding team would spread for the first pitch, and there'd be a raucous roar of the Oakland fans who had come to see the Christians, the Giants that is, mauled.

Back to three anchormen in their booth. They chatter. One of them looks behind him and down, as if a friend had called. Then he looks up. Then the second deck of the stadium at Candlestick Park—well, the camera must have been clumsily handled, the deck seemed to sway and sag a little. I don't believe we knew this as a fact till it was over.

104

And, providentially, the huge crowd didn't seem to catch on either. In fact, after the first rolling wave there was a cheer, and a big cry of 'Play Ball'. And then a stranger wave, of a vast human sigh or gasp. And then the players broke up, their wives appeared on the field, and soon they were cradling bewildered children or walking quietly off with arms around their wives. To this day, the blessed, the unexplained truth is the absence of panic, I thought for a time the umpires had not turned up, some other failure of the usual arrangements. And then we heard. And in no time, the great blimp took off, and as the night came on soared and was seeing the incredible sight of a collapsed span of the Bay Bridge over the huge blacked-out city with smoke plumes rising there down toward the bay, and then the plumes turning into flames and the beginning of the fire. The pictures, picked up now from all around the bay, swam with menacing slowness all through the night, till at daybreak we saw, as I'm sure you did, wherever you were, the collapsed upper deck of the Nimitz Freeway on the Oakland side, the sudden ghastly appearance of what somebody called the concrete sandwich. Hasty guesses were made about the numbers of cars and people trapped in there, and overseas papers grabbed at a figure—250—which the police here first deplored, saying that after many hours only seven bodies had been dragged out. But on Thursday morning a reporter close by pointed to the compression of the upper deck of the highway on the lower and banished any hope of survivors by remarking that the visible space between the two decks was at most 18 inches high.

Apart from the strange, almost casual, departure

of the 60,000 baseball fans, it must be said that the other great and unanticipated blessing was the comparatively minute damage done to the city of San Francisco itself, accordingly, little loss of life, compared, that is, with April 1906. This reading on the Richter scale, as you'll have heard, was 6.9, exactly the measurement of last year's earthquake in Armenia, which took 25,000 lives. That difference is easily explained. Since 1906, California, northern California especially, has lived always with the prospect in mind of another great quake, and in 1907 drafted its first new building code, devised for the first time by structural engineers working with architects. It required bracing systems and reinforced masonry. And until the Second World War, the city withstood innumerable shocks, minor by Tuesday's reckoning. In 1946, another, tougher code went into effect. By 1965 we had a wealth of new building materials and by then, also, San Francisco was, lamentably, about to put up its first high-rises and downtown skyscrapers. So another more elaborate and stricter code was made to apply to all new building. In the early 1970s, by the way, they decided that the concrete decks on the two-tier bridges might, in an earthquake, be too heavy for the vertical supports. They reinforced them. The Golden Gate Bridge and two others across the Bay held firm this time, though engineers now suspect that the sustaining verticals on the Bay Bridge proved too skinny. One expert in earthquake engineering went so far—after the Nimitz disaster —as to doubt whether any more two-decker highways should be built.

What was most impressive was the speed and

harmony that marked the mobilization, within the hour, of the National Guard, the Army Corps of Engineers, the California state authorities, the city fathers, the police, engineers, the Red Cross, and a resource that San Francisco is unique in being able to call on: a permanent, steady earthquake medical team. Not to forget the heartening sight of thousands of ordinary citizens up from their beds in the middle of the night helping the teams at the collapsed highways or forming human ladders with buckets at the Marina fire, before they were able to rig up the system of pumping water from the Bay itself. All these volunteers, in San Francisco, were warned to go home and stay there, the great fear, once the fire started from burst gas mains was the fear that was devastatingly fulfilled in 1906, the gas leaks from other mains and the eruption of hundreds of other fires. When I first went to San Francisco, fifty-six years ago, and for several decades thereafter, old San Franciscans would wince at a gaffe regularly committed by visitors: to any mention of the Earthquake. It was always, the fire—the great fire. And it's true that while immense damage was done by the initial shock—8 points—on that April morning, the ravaging of the heart of the city was done by fire. So insatiable was the fire's appetite, raging over four square miles, that to save the northwestern part of the city, the army was called out from the Presidio, dynamited the whole cross avenue of Van Ness and held the fire.

Well, this time, there were no aftershocks to burst other mains (aftershocks can happen days or weeks or months after the first jolt). And all these helpers, expert and amateur, came together under

107

the government's central authority: the Federal Emergency Management Agency, which it so happens held a simulated earthquake drill throughout the city only two months ago. FEMA's main job is the granting of low-cost loans to people who have suffered loss of property or injury. FEMA just now suffers from a cruel disability; most of its national team is off in Puerto Rico, the Virgin Islands and South Carolina, working sixteen hours a day helping to repair the wrecked lives of over quarter of a million victims of Hurricane Hugo. A disaster insurance expert with FEMA brought us a timely, if grisly, reminder on Wednesday, that Hugo is a far greater human catastrophe than the earthquake. At this moment, FEMA is trying to handle 20,000 applications for help in the Virgin Islands, 45,000 in and around Charleston, South Carolina and 200,000 in Puerto Rico. FEMA's resources have touched bottom, and the man stressed for all of us who feel compassionate about San Francisco that cash—for Hugo, from people, anywhere—is still the main burden of their appeal.

The 1990s

Presidential Ghosts

23 February 1990

Of course, the most moving event of the week was the appearance, and the speech, of President Havel of Czechoslovakia before a joint session of both houses of Congress. Time and again, cries of 'Bravo' went up, and five times he was accorded something that happens to a Presidential address only once, at the end of it: namely a standing ovation. An extraordinary thing about the speech was noted in press and television reports of it. He wrote it himself!

This astounding fact was mentioned only a day or two before the publication of a book by the young woman who is more responsible than either President Reagan or President Bush for the popular view of their characters. She is Peggy Noonan, a witty, lyrical Irish troll, who wrote the speeches through which we came to believe we were seeing the true, the charming, the inspiring Ronald Reagan and George Bush. In fact, there is an alarming discovery available in Miss Noonan's book. It is that practically all the most famous, the most winning, the most characteristic utterances of both Presidents—were composed by her. From 'You ain't seen nothing yet' and 'Make my day!' to 'Read my lips' and 'a kinder, gentler, nation'.

For Mr Bush, especially, Miss Noonan was the alchemist who at a stroke, in the nomination acceptance speech at New Orleans in the summer of 1988, transformed our picture of George Bush

111

from that of an intense wimp, a rather awkward speaker, into a generous, kind and surprisingly eloquent practitioner of English prose. There was never a poll directly charting the effect of that speech on the voters, but there were two polls that parallel the remarkable change in the popular view of Mr Bush's character. Before the New Orleans speech, Mr Bush was running a few points behind Mr Dukakis as the general choice of President. After it, Mr Bush went ahead in comparative popularity and never looked back. And even when Miss Noonan left him and the White House, the remaining speech-writers, who had questioned and hounded the style she had composed for him, adopted it as best they could and maintained the character she had created. So that, or perhaps not so that, but either by accident or more likely as one natural consequence, Mr Bush today finds himself approved by a solid 70 per cent of the nation, a lovable peak achieved in our time only by John F. Kennedy in his first term. President Kennedy, I ought to say, also had his Henry Higgins. His immortal, incessantly quoted Inaugural speech, was written by Mr Theodore Sorensen, who stayed with him and on all formal occasions, impressed ever deeper on our ears and our consciousness the figure of a young, gallant and moving orator.

I emerged from Miss Noonan's book with mixed feelings—of wonder and distress. The distress arises from the growing discovery that I'm not sure I know, even now, the true character of either Ronald Reagan or George Bush. As a famous journalist once asked about a dozen celebrities he tracked down for private interviews, 'Are they the same at home?'

So, it was a shock, and a pleasant one, to realize during the hour that the Mr Havel who spoke here was both the private and the public man we were listening to. At one go, the first time we ever heard him, he provided the sort of rare satisfaction that must have come to people listening, for the first time, to Abraham Lincoln or Winston Churchill.

Which reminds me of a time, less than a month after the United States came into the Second World War, when, at Christmas time, Prime Minister Churchill arrived suddenly (his voyage was, of course, unannounced) in Washington to stay with President Roosevelt. These two had met, incidentally for the first time, to survey the theatres of war and sketch out a common strategy. Towards the end of this now famous visit, the two leaders agreed that, within a few days of Mr Churchill's safe return to London, each of them would go on air and broadcast to the peoples of the new transatlantic alliance his own inspiring version of their discussions. There was a firm but unwritten agreement that the two broadcasts, on radio of course, would fall on the same evening. The American radio networks were made privy to the arrangement, and while Churchill was flying home, Roosevelt wasted no time in summoning three of his most dependable and gifted ghosts, Judge Sam Rosenman, the poet Archibald MacLeish, and the playwright, Robert Sherwood, to compose as soon as possible (and in view of the formidable competition, no less than Churchill himself) a piece of memorable prose. They were, next morning, not much further along than a first draft when they had a telephone call from London, to the effect that Mr Churchill was safe at home and was going on the

BBC that very evening. He was requesting the President to have the American networks clear a circuit for simultaneous broadcast. Roosevelt was appalled at this cunning betrayal. It seemed that during the boisterous thirteen-hour homeward flight, Mr Churchill—bouncing through murky weather (with no jets in those days) and sometimes while taking over the controls of the bomber—the traitor Churchill, with no other points of reference than a map of the world, had dictated a masterly conspectus of the global battlefronts. The tapes, or cylinders, were delivered to a secretary in Downing Street, typed up, the BBC was alerted, and the Prime Minister went on the air with his rumbling, majestic cadences.

In Washington, there were at least four despondent listeners. 'How,' moaned President Roosevelt to his slaving ghosts, 'how can he do it? How *did* he do it?' It was the playwright Sherwood who gave the melancholy answer. 'I'm afraid, Mr President,' he said, 'he rolls his own.' It was nothing but the truth.

Well, the rare, if not unique, pleasure of listening to President Havel sprang from the knowledge that 'he rolls his own'. It is a pleasure that was bound to be felt most acutely by writers, by actors, by voters who have a prejudice in favour of men who have a way with words. On the other hand, speech-writers in the White House are known—half enviously, half contemptibly—as 'wordsmiths'. Once the writer's draft has been submitted to fifty government departments (fifty!), and questioned and torn apart, and returned, it is assumed that the body of the speech, the substance, the right stuff, is all there, like the structure of a

114

new house. Now it is up to the wordsmith to perform his or her particular function, which is that of a decorator. No wonder Miss Noonan lasted less than four years. The record of the corrections, rejections, of her originals, the stuffing of them with clumsy jargon, all the pretentious buzzwords that hang like a cloud of bees over the Pentagon, the State Department, the Office of Management and Budget, the almost paranoid fear by government types of simple idiom, homely phrases, natural humour, pungent lines. Once this long agony has been endured, the writer submits a final draft. Then the chief of staff must look it over and then, at least, hand it to the speaker, the puppet, the President, no less. And then the writer, Miss Noonan, sits with her fingers and her talents crossed, and listens to the speech itself, and hopes and sighs (so *that* had to go) or hugs a friend (they left it in, they left it in!). And next week, the Challenger shuttle will explode in mid-air, and she must begin again—and did—to compose that most touching and poignant of all President Reagan's eulogies to American dead.

Mr Havel spoke sometimes in English, warm, resonant, simple English; more often, he spoke in his native language followed, paragraph by paragraph, by the translation. I just said now that writers, people who enjoy words and the handling of them, are the ones most likely to have enjoyed Lincoln, Churchill and now President Havel. There is a catch here, and Mr Havel made us know that he is aware of it. People with a fondness for writing and eloquence always vote for a candidate who seems to have the gift of words over one who doesn't. Hence the deep disappointment of legions when Adlai Stevenson lost to General Eisenhower. Intellectuals tend to vote for intellectuals, whenever they appear as political candidates. Mr Havel noted that the men who declared American independence and wrote the Constitution and the Bill of Rights—Jefferson most of all—were intellectuals. He noted this fact almost wistfully. He must know that, apart from that astonishing and unique generation, intellectuals have a very poor record as politicians. He himself, a playwright, made quite clear that he is not a politician and does not mean to be.

The End of the Eighties—
Great or Greedy?

27 April 1990

Tuesday morning, a brilliant spring day, saw an extraordinary scene in downtown Manhattan that was variously described by newspaper reporters as the curtain call on the 1980s and, in a paper long known for its good, grey prose, as the last public appearance of 'the premier financial swindler of all time'.

There was a big restless crowd already on the sidewalk outside the Federal District Court when a black car slid up. The man himself, a very tall slim man in a dark suit, an affable-looking man with a tumble of black hair, unwound himself out of the car and had a rough time getting through the crowd, which was now surging and bubbling around him as it might for a movie star. In a way he is a

116

movie star, for at the same moment on a sidewalk in the mid-1970s on the East Side, there was another crowd, watching the filming of a character of which our man entering the courthouse was the prototype. The movie that is being shot here is an adaptation of Tom Wolfe's *Bonfire of the Vanities*, a Balzacian coroner's inquest on the life and death of the 1980s. And the character the cameras were training on was Sherman McCoy, who thought of himself as the King of the Jungle (the Wall Street jungle, that is) and who would, before the movie ended, get his cruel but just reward. At the same time, down in Federal Court, the original of Sherman McCoy was being asked how he pleaded to six felony counts: of conspiracy; filing false information with the Securities and Exchange Commission (which polices the stock market); securities fraud; violating the Commission's reporting requirements; mail fraud; and aiding and abetting in the filing of a false tax return. It has taken the United States Attorney General's office years to track through a jungle of documents and letters and memos and audits in order to present the case at Tuesday's hearing. In a simpler world, they might have been spared their sweat. For in no time at all in the courtroom, the tall man, all his affability dissolved, was sobbing: 'I realize by my acts I have hurt those who are closest to me. I am truly sorry.' The judge allowed him to dry his tears and then asked him, 'Mr Millken, how do you plead?' Through a cracking tone of voice, Michael Millken replied, 'Guilty, your Honour.'

Mr Millken has been known as the King of the Junk Bond, which may be very starkly defined as a perilously high-risk but (if it works) high-yield security. Junk bonds have undoubtedly helped many small firms through generous grants of credit, to survive and prosper. But more often than not, they have paper-financed giant takeovers, pushed them at once on to preposterous levels of debt and ruined them, along with legions of investors. However, none of the crimes to which Mr Millken pleaded guilty involved the junk bond market. He was charged with other crimes on that count, but the charges were dropped when he agreed to pay $200 million in fines, and set aside another $400 million to satisfy civil claims filed against him—a remarkable break for a big-time swindler. The crimes he admitted were, in general, illegal acts performed with accomplices which were intended to enrich Mr Millken's enormously prestigious firm, Drexel Burnham Lambert, whose prestige, whose existence, vanished with the wind with its collapse into bankruptcy less than three months ago. Mr Millken will be sentenced on 1 October. So he will have five months to enjoy himself at large. It is not likely to be a greatly restricted, or impoverished, life. After paying out those $600 million, he is reliably reported to be left with a little over $1 billion.

The exposure and ruination of a banker or other prominently wealthy man is always a fascinating story and—let's admit it—to most of us a meanly satisfying story. In a Depression, there are scores of them. They come, they excite us, they go. But every so often, the sudden decline and fall of one man sounds more like a general warning, a fire alarm, than a personal calamity, whenever the fallen man is seen as a symbol of a system that has gone awry. In the depth of the Great Depression, in early

1932, it is hackneyed to say that most ordinary people had lost faith in the bankers and the banking system. But of the big men that we thought had let us down, the financiers and statesmen who promised us that 'prosperity was just around the corner'—most were guilty of bad judgement, of myopic foresight. Their misdeeds were well within the law. Then on a March day in that year, a Swedish financier, one Ivar Kreuger, known as the Swedish match king, put a bullet through his chest. The news rocked the newspapers of the world. Kreuger had been celebrated, in awesome prose, by some of the most astute and serious journals in many countries. *Time* magazine called him a 'Titan' of finance. When his story came out, what we had to confront was an unbelievable record of financial crookery on a splendid international scale. I doubt that the columnist in last Wednesday's *New York Times*, if he had stopped to look over the story of Ivar Kreuger, would have called Michael Millken 'the premier financial swindler of all time'. Kreuger, in his grave, must be registering a vigorous dissent.

But Millken is in the same league with Kreuger, certainly as a symbol, as a symbol of what has been called 'the me decade', of what Tom Wolfe called 'the burning itch to grab it now'. The sentencing of Michael Millken will drive the last nail in the coffin of the junk bond and send a shudder through the millions of ordinary citizens who lost their shirts in the mass bankruptcy of the savings and loans, the building societies.

The day that Michael Millken came to court, a headline in a newspaper literary section read, 'In Books, Greed Is Out'. It topped a survey of the

119

best-seller lists and revealed that a trend in public taste that we guessed would soon be on its way out was already dead and gone. Throughout the 1980s, the non-fiction lists were headed by the autobiographies of self-made men, by titans like Lee Iacocca, the phoenix of the automobile, by Donald Trump, the young, bouncy, blond tycoon whose aspirations to take over hotels, casinos, airlines, resorts, cities—why not the country?—appear to be boundless. Along with these confessions of success, the non-fiction best-seller list was for many years filled out by 'How To' books, but mostly *How to Make a Million*, *How to Gain Comfort and Luxury in Early Retirement*, *How to Live the American Dream in Two Years Flat*. There has been a general retreat of such stuff from the stores and from the publishers' lists. A whole raft of the spring offerings suggest almost a concerted act of penance for the Reagan years we once so loved to praise. How about—*The Politics of Rich and Poor: Wealth and the American Electorate in the Reagan Aftermath*? And *Disorder and Decline: Crime and the Spiral of Decay in American Neighborhoods*. And *The Worst Years of Our Lives: An Outsider's View of the '80s*. Notice that these titles all carry emphatic subtitles, just to drive home the point that the author was never deceived and is about to indulge a full-throated lamentation for the fool's paradise of the 1980s. One publisher, who—I should guess—didn't anticipate the new trend and probably has several self-made heroes lined up for public exposure, sighed: 'What businessmen as heroes have we left?'

Well! What happened to the measured but shining tributes to Ronald Reagan the day he left

120

office? Or the long eulogy of George Will, the sharpest and most thoughtful of conservative commentators? Listen: 'Reagan's aim has been to restore the plain language of right and wrong, good and evil for the purpose of enabling people to make the most of freedom . . . The world seems less dangerous than it did in 1980, and Reagan is partly responsible . . . By knocking the budget into radical imbalance, he has placed a restraining hand on the 1990s, but it will not restrain the growth of the Welfare State . . . in 1981, America needed reassurance. It needed to recover confidence in its health and goodness. It needed to recover what was lost in the 1960s and '70s, the sense that it has a competence commensurate with its nobility and responsibilities. Reagan, like Roosevelt, has been a great reassurer, a steadying captain who calmed the passengers and, to some extent, the sea.'

And now, the community song has turned into a song of lamentation, a dirge and an indictment, of Greed and Decline and Disorder and Corruption. Reagan is now, suddenly, not a second Roosevelt but a second Harding, another very popular President in a prosperous time, who is now chiefly remembered for the shady financial shenanigans of his Cabinet. I wonder how the old man feels; sitting up there in his office tower in Beverly Hills, to hear and read from the sprightly new 1990s authors that he was presiding over a corrupt administration and a failing country. Surely the verdict of history, even in the short run, won't be so damning, or so lyrical. It all depends on which events stick in the public memory: the lowest unemployment rate and lowest inflation, or Iran-Contra and Michael Millken. There's no rule, no formula to guarantee the

121

remembrance of the good things. President Herbert Hoover was—for one—a remarkable American in many ways, not simply an engineer of international repute, but the man who saved Europe, after the First World War, from mass starvation. John Maynard Keynes said of him at the Versailles Peace Conference: 'He imported into the Councils of Paris . . . precisely that atmosphere of reality, knowledge, magnanimity and disinterestedness which, if they had been found in other quarters also, would have given us the Good Peace.' But Wall Street crashed during Hoover's reign and he is remembered cruelly as the author of the Depression.

Mr Reagan claims to know the American people well. I hope he knows that their frantic affection for every new crooner is only matched by their impatience for the next one. At the moment, he is the victim of an associated American trait: the yearning to anoint a new President as a Moses, and when he turns out not to be Moses, to dump him and look around for another one.

Fighting in What?

30 November 1990

Well, we've had four months of haphazard debate over Saddam Hussein, of amateur prophesying, of fuzzy Presidential rhetoric, of snatched analogies with Vietnam and Hitler, and of—compared with the 1960s—surprisingly little mockery from the colleges. At last what was always serious and relevant from the beginning has come out into the open. It has to be said that one of the obstacles to defining and arguing the real issue or issues in the Gulf has been President Bush's variety of explanations as to why the American troops had been dispatched there in the first place. Almost as if his advisers had set up a bargain basement of reasons, and he had wandered through it trying this one out for size on the American consumer, next day trying another one, or two.

At first, right at the beginning of August, Mr Bush said the United States had responded so promptly with the first big wave of troops because Saudi Arabia was at imminent risk of being invaded. So it was, and both parties in Congress and a national poll gave the President a thumping 85 per cent approval. At the same time, in the very early days Mr Bush told the people—that's you and me—that Mr Hussein had performed an act of 'naked aggression', and the day was long gone when we could permit dictators to do such things. Mrs Thatcher, who was over here at the time, prompted him and stiffened him, and echoed him in the same language. So now we knew, to our temporary satisfaction, that the United States was not going to tolerate—anywhere, it was implied— tinpot dictators marching into little countries, even though we had not jumped into Ethiopia, Angola, Cambodia.

It was at that time, in August, that we heard the first mention of Hitler again—a crude analogy with a tyrant who gobbled up little countries. There was a brief flurry of debate (between old historians for the most part) about Hitler and Mr Hussein: some saying Hussein was, if anything, more evil, more ruthless, and a tyrant with frightening ambitions to dominate, first the Middle East and after that, what? And their antagonists who said the comparison was ridiculous, that Saddam Hussein was, as a world threat, a midget compared with Hitler, not a man with a great nation in thrall.

Then people, country people, college students, professional cynics, began to say: the whole thing's about oil. Are we going to die for the oil companies? The administration jibbed at that one, and, it seemed to me, missed a great opportunity. Mr Cheney, the Secretary of Defense, did, I recall, on his first mission to the Gulf come out bluntly and say, yes, it's about oil, repeating a figure much banded about at the time: that, if Mr Hussein invaded Saudi Arabia and overran its shoreline, he would, could, control 42 per cent of the world's oil supply. But the President, though mentioning oil from time to time as almost an embarrassing necessity, didn't stress it or ever say, 'You bet, it's about oil.'

Neither he nor anyone else in or out of the administration, that I heard of, recalled what had been the one, great, persisting fear, that the Soviet Union would eventually, one day, soon or late, march south, bestride the Mediterranean, control the countries that border the Persian Gulf: in a word, control the source of Western Europe's energy, and, therefore, of its economies, its prosperity, and, very soon, of its survival as a continent of sovereign nations. I remember a hot argument with an old friend—this must have been twenty-five years ago—who had a strong but blinkered vision of the Soviet Union solely as a direct military threat to Western Europe; and a third party saying that if the Soviet Union did come to control the Gulf and patrol the Mediterranean, there would be no need for one Soviet bomb to drop on Western Europe: the Kremlin, having strangled their economies, could simply indicate to Britain, France, West Germany, all the NATO partners, that they had better get themselves governments agreeable to Moscow, and all would be well. I believe this nightmare was always present throughout the Cold War.

So, what I'm saying in accusing the Bush administration of missing a great opportunity for popular education was its failure to take up the jeering view of the oil threat and point out how many great wars in history start, if you like, with the Egyptians' chronic lack of wood, the whole of Western Europe's lack of spices to make food palatable, how often wars have been fought precisely because of the lack or denial of the raw materials by which you can live and prosper. Perhaps Mr Bush and his spokesmen ducked the vital question of access to Middle Eastern oil, maybe because people began to remind him how much less dependent the United States was than Western Europe and Japan on Middle Eastern oil.

At any rate, by that time we were now, I'd say, in September, October. People, the Congress, the pollsters, were saying that the President's support was slipping because he had not come out in public with one strong, clear explanation of why the United States was there, in such huge numbers, in the Gulf. The President did speak out from time to time, with that earnest hesitancy of his, which suggests that any minute now he's going to come up with the real reason. By then we were in the

125

Gulf, the President assured us, to maintain American values, to sustain our way of life. Some of these random, additional reasons puzzled people: it was surely a little risky to go on about championing American values. How about democracy, free speech, representative government? Because everybody knew by then that Kuwait was a medieval kingdom run by sheiks, and so were an Arab ally or two.

There were never, as with Vietnam, two strong opposing sides to what we call the national debate—never a rigid body of hawks, a dogged body of doves. Most people still seemed to agree that something had to be done about Mr Hussein in Kuwait, but they disputed under what provocation, and when force (war) should be used. Surprisingly few people (judging from the national polls) were against fighting Saddam Hussein under any circumstances. As the fall came on, the regular snippets of television interviews with the men and women 'out there' had been put on, I suppose, as morale builders, these interviews or little pep talks to the folks back home. They began to turn testy, grumbling. The commanders of the forces in the desert must have groaned many times at the decision of the networks to start these bright, chirpy interviews. But, there you are, it's a democracy, isn't it? We can't go back to the frontline censorship of the First and Second World Wars—of all wars before Vietnam, when, once for all, I imagine, microphones and cameras were allowed in foxholes; and troops who cursed the war in the morning were seen by the whole country in the evening.

The grumbling among the men in the desert was

126

an inevitable consequence, I believe, of America's long innocence of war on the home front (one hundred and twenty-five years) but also, in the short run, of the peculiar experience of war instilled by the Reagan and Bush administrations. Libya. Grenada. Panama. No debate, no angry appeals to the exclusive right of Congress to declare war. The decision was made in the White House one day, and next day the announcement of the bombing, of the swift invasion, of Grenada, of Panama. Then an anxious day or two, perhaps, but in a week, two at most, the war's all over, and most of the boys are on their way home.

I called these experiences 'peculiar' just now. They are certainly atypical of the experience of war by any great nation you can think of. The great, the dreadful, exception was, of course, Vietnam. And I believe the rising impatience of the American desert troops, the reported decline in morale, is due to the view—in the minds of the young men who may have to fight this war—that there are only two kinds of war: the quick, manageable Grenada–Panama war that they watched or followed in their teens, and the ghastly, prolonged, failing war of Vietnam that they have only read about or seen in the movies.

So it would be a natural puzzle in the minds of the men hunkered down there in the desert that, since this is plainly not Grenada or Panama, what is it? Mostly, we are told, they want action or they want out. A former Chairman of the Joint Chiefs of Staff, Admiral Crowe, remarked the other day: 'It's curious that some expect our military to train soldiers to stand up to hostile fire but doubt its ability to train them to occupy ground and wait

127

patiently.' Well, I'm pretty sure that most of the men who've been dispatched to the Gulf in the past four months did not expect to occupy the desert and wait patiently.

The last opinion anticipates the change, or movement, of opinion. The big change in the mixture of opinion, the hardening of attitudes barely arrived at, came with the President's decision, two weeks ago, to send another 150,000 American troops, at a time when we were being told that the economic sanctions were working, and that the United Nations Security Council was moving towards a resolution setting a deadline for Saddam Hussein to get out of Kuwait, and permitting the member nations to use other 'necessary means' to make him ('necessary means' being taken by everybody to mean 'go to war'). The President's boosting of American forces to a staggering 400,000 (just short of the total forces deployed in the Korean War) gave many, perhaps most Americans the idea, the fear, that the President was hell-bent on war, now or very soon. The shock of his action immediately precipitated, in the chemical sense, attitudes that had been invisible, wet, in solution. A cry goes up in Congress to have the President call Congress in special session. There are loud reminders to the President that, under the Constitution, only the Congress can declare war. (Nobody has yet mentioned the fact that the last time Congress declared war was forty-nine years ago!—the declaration against Italy in December 1941.) The Senate Armed Services Committee is called into a series of hearings (which are going on now), and every expert and former defence official and pundit and his brother is called to testify. The upshot, the loud, important upshot is that two of America's former military chiefs (chairmen of the Joint Chiefs of Staff), Admiral Crowe and General David Johns, have urged the President to pause in his belligerent rush, to give sanctions at least a year to work. The other attitude that has come out of these hearings is a body of opinion, in the Senate, to persuade the President to institute a rotation system for the dispatch and maintenance of American troops in the desert. Four months' duty, six at the most, is being suggested.

So this is where we were as the Security Council sat down on Thursday to vote on the resolution, sanctioning further 'necessary measures'.

But, there is one big, nasty fact that has at last emerged from the writings of one or two columnists who were ignored or declared to be alarmists way back there in August, when they suggested that Saddam Hussein was on the way to building a nuclear weapon and might have it within two or three years. That was what led some lonely conservatives to say that the choice was to fight Saddam Hussein now, or fight a stronger, nuclear-equipped Saddam Hussein two, three years from now. That suggested a, for once, *relevant* Hitler analogy.

Even President Bush has picked up the omen of this threat in recent speeches and remarks, which has led some 'experts' to say nonsense—it will be ten years before Mr Hussein has a destructive nuclear capability. This denial roused the dozing nuclear missile experts from their many think tanks. The President said the other day that the first Iraqi bomb could be months away. Senator

Edward Kennedy, the arch-liberal who, if there was only one dove in Washington would be it, spoke in the Senate Armed Services Committee hearings. His followers and idolaters surely expected him to say what we all want to believe, that Saddam Hussein is years, maybe ten years, away from a nuclear capability. Senator Kennedy said, 'The best estimates, I imagine, are eight or nine months'!

So, we are back to where we came in, in the middle of August, when I first reported this minority, almost secret fear of Saddam Hussein's nuclear potential. Reduced to a stark, practical alternative, the choice is in fact, a dilemma—a choice of two courses of action, either of which is unsatisfactory: (1) to give the sanctions a year or more to work, by which time he may have the bomb or, (2) to fight him now—with, ahead of us, unpredictable possibilities of massive casualties, the break-up of the United Nations alliance, civil war in the Middle East—at best a long, long war.

Riots in Los Angeles

1 May 1992

It was one of those evenings, last Wednesday, when you or I take a break from the world and its woes: out to dinner with a friend, talk golf and tennis mostly, and marvel at the news of that 10-year-old shrimp of a Russian girl who has boggled the experience of the veteran Florida teachers, is aching to turn professional and go out and slaughter Seles, Capriati, and any other young genius who thinks she's a prodigy.

And then home, and, as I always do just before turning in, to flip through thirty-two television channels—it's now fifty—and light briefly on Channel 24, which is Atlanta's CNN, the television world news station that is most often there, as the general said, 'fastest with the mostest'. I see a helicopter shot of a street intersection and stalled truck, and what looks like a man sprawled on the ground—one or two other men running around, making gestures. They are all so tiny, seen from the air. It's probably a random shooting somewhere, most likely in Harlem or Los Angeles, maybe. We see at least one every night. Something's hurriedly spoken about a verdict. So to bed, to read a new book which claims, and for once maybe rightly, to have solved after a hundred and four years the identity of Jack the Ripper. So to sleep.

Thursday morning, and—the first words I heard from an announcer in Los Angeles were, 'worse, much worse, than Watts'. Because we can now see it was historically the forerunner of dreadful things to come two, three years later, we had better look back to Watts. Watts was that frowsy but not slummy suburb of Los Angeles where a white policeman's arrest of a black youth started a rumour that the black man had been shot. The rumour grew: he'd been wounded, no, killed, in cold blood. Within an hour, a full-scale riot was thriving in that black neighbourhood, and within twenty-four hours the whole suburb was ablaze, loud with guns and happy looters. There was a time when it appeared the chaos might not be controlled by the ten thousand men of the National Guard, who'd been ordered in by the Governor of

California. The National Guard is the civilian reserve militia which every state has on call, and which can, in a war or other emergency, be mobilized as regular army under the regular military command. I try to clarify the function of the misleadingly named National Guard because we'll come to look at their part in this week's riots. By the end of that dreadful week in 1965, Watts was a large, gutted suburb. And it was mentioned the other night that after twenty-seven years, it is not wholly recovered or rebuilt.

Well, if the horror of Watts was triggered by a tiny casual arrest and a ballooning false rumour, what triggered the rage of south central Los Angeles last Wednesday night? Let's go back as calmly as we can and look at what started it all.

On the night of 3 March 1991, a black motorist was seen by a police car whizzing along a boulevard at a breakneck pace and the police pursued him. It took quite a time to catch up with him, by which time other police cars and many other policemen had come to form almost an impromptu posse, twenty-three in all. When they did catch him, two other men in the car gave themselves up without resistance; they were handcuffed and taken off into custody. The driver remained defiant and aggressive, so freewheeling with arms and legs that one of the policemen said he assumed the man was high on some drug.

Anyway, what came next would doubtless have been buried in the police records but for a unique accident that made what happened on that night-time street something for all the world to see. A man who lived in an apartment overlooking what was now a scene on the street was aroused by the

132

noise of the police siren and the following scuffle. He picked up his video camera, stood (on his porch, I imagine) and cranked away. His film lasted for eighty-one seconds, and horrified everybody who subsequently saw it, and saw it, and saw it, on television. Four police officers were flailing their batons and flogging the driver, writhing and squirming on the ground. It's true he wasn't going to lie down and take it—he wriggled, but his body also jerked in reflexes, of pain, surely, from the beating he was taking. In eighty-one seconds, almost a minute and a half, there were fifty-six counted beatings.

Eleven days later, a Los Angeles grand jury indicted one police sergeant and three police officers. They pleaded not guilty. The Attorney General of the United States responded by ordering an immediate review of complaints of brutality against the Los Angeles police. The review expanded to cover the whole nation—that was thirteen months ago—and the report has not been published. The Mayor of Los Angeles, a black man who's been in office for an unprecedented twenty years, appointed a commission to investigate the Los Angeles police department. There was for a time a wrangle over the chief of police, a white man, who was charged with insensitivity and condoning bad police behaviour. A month or two later, he promised to retire this spring. He was still there this week. A month or so after the beating, the driver, Rodney King, and his wife, filed a federal civil rights suit against the city of Los Angeles. Three weeks later, Mr King was discovered in a parked car with a transvestite prostitute. He failed to get away but after two months all charges were dropped.

Meanwhile, the grand jury brought no charges against the nineteen police officers who were bystanders. But the four men who were seen to do the beating eventually, after many legal manoeuvres, came to trial a year to the day after the event. By the way, on the motion of the defence which maintained that the four policemen could not get a fair trial in the black-dominated quarter where the incident took place, the trial was moved to another suburb (which, it's important to remark, is almost entirely white and is called home by about two thousand policemen and their families). Although one or two blacks were called for jury duty, they were quizzed and excused by the defence, which is its privilege. The sitting jury consisted of ten whites, one Hispanic, one Asian. On 23 April the case went to the jury. We gather from the jurors themselves that their verdict was arrived at within an hour or two (an astonishing feat for an American jury, which can battle it out for days and weeks) but took another three days to argue, and was eventually hung, on one count against one officer.

So it was this past Wednesday evening when the stunning verdict came—actually over the television, for the trial was televised throughout. The four had been found not guilty, of brutality and of excessive force (that is, going beyond the needs of the cause). In interviews after the result, the jurors willing to speak said the amateur motion picture was crude (so it was, it was filming a very crude event), did not express the physical threat Mr King posed, and that much of the flailing was into the thin night air.

It's fair to say that a vast majority of the country

will refuse to believe a word of it. That first shot I saw, of a stalled truck and a prone man and one or two running around, was the beginning: a white truck driver dragged to the pavement and beaten up by blacks. I'd better say at once that in all the following burnings and lootings were done by blacks and poor whites, who now had what everybody told them was just cause to vent their long-suppressed rage and disillusion in the equality that wasn't there, and the jobs that weren't forthcoming.

In the beginning, what we saw were the flaming suburbs by night, and black people complaining that it had taken the fire department twenty minutes to answer their call. On any night, the average calls to the Los Angeles fire department are ten. Last Wednesday night, over a hundred and twenty fires blazed in central and south central Los Angeles, and then beyond. And the firemen were being attacked, along with the police and the paramedics. Los Angeles is not a skyscraper city but a huge collection, connection, of ninety suburbs over five hundred and fifty square miles. Sunset Boulevard alone runs for twenty-two miles— through sections that could be in Hong Kong, in Mexico, in Korea, in Kansas City. On Thursday night forty fires burned, out beyond by miles, up into the rich and by now—I should guess—terrified habitat of the film and television folk: the designers, the yuppies, who mean no harm.

By Friday noon, the President had sent a light infantry battalion into a 'staging area' near Los Angeles, to be used if the National Guard and the police cannot control things. By Friday, the worst we feared had happened: the rioting, looting

135

contagion had spread to San Francisco, to Atlanta, to Seattle, and in a smaller way to other towns thousands of miles apart. There were peaceable black demonstrations in Kansas City and on the campus of a college in Baton Rouge, Louisiana.

In Watts, before the end, there was the awful fear that ten thousand of the National Guard might not be enough. If the violence from the poor and the hoodlum packs and the juvenile gangs takes over many cities, the President and his generals may have to worry whether there'll be enough troops to contain what could become a race rebellion.

There's one discernible piece of good news in all this. Now that the State of California has exhausted its legal procedure (the verdict is the end), the federal government can move in, and it could institute a new trial but not on the same grounds. That would run the risk of double jeopardy. The Justice Department, through the Attorney General, has revived a criminal investigation into the incident of the beating to see if the constitutional civil rights of Mr King were violated. It's the ground on which, just a year ago, the Kings filed their suit against the city of Los Angeles.

White House Style

6 November 1992

When I became the chief American correspondent of a paper whose mission, way back then, was to prompt and protect the thinking of one city, Manchester, I was disturbed at the thought that I was going to have to move myself and my family from New York to Washington. Washington of course was where all the chief foreign correspondents were based. To my great relief, I soon had a letter from my editor—a small, canny, spiky-haired, bespectacled imp of a Lancashireman. He wrote quite simply: 'No, I don't want you to move to Washington. I don't want you to report Washington, except from time to time. I want you, *all* the time, to report America. New York is the best news base, and the best home base for travel.'

That wise and wily sentence is one that might not only be passed on to editors of papers around the world. It would serve a useful purpose if it could be engraved or done up in needlework, framed and hung in the Oval Office of the White House. It would remind every President of a truth which every President, especially in his second term, is in danger of forgetting: that the White House is not home or anything remotely like the homes of the two hundred million people he is there to represent. The White House is a temporary Versailles and not the best place in which to maintain what Teddy Roosevelt called 'a

137

sense of the continent'.

You have to have been in the White House as a guest to appreciate its elegance and patrician comfort, and to have been treated like some venerated old monarch in luxurious exile, in order to feel the benign truth behind the phrase coined by the historian Arthur Schlesinger, 'the Imperial Presidency'. He was referring to the White House—I almost said the court—of Richard M. Nixon. And certainly there's been no Presidency in our time, or perhaps in any time, when the White House more resembled a royal palace. Mrs Kennedy had done the place over into an eighteenth-century French mansion more exquisite than most royal palaces. Mr Nixon added some folderols of a monarch's office as imagined by Hollywood. He summoned for ceremonial occasions a row of trumpeters in uniform with tight white pumps and knee breeches, looking for all the world like the wedding guard of honour designed for King Rudolf of Ruritania (Ronald Colman) and Princess Flavia (Madeleine Carroll).

The television pictures of this absurdity evoked such hilarity and mirth (not least in the British Royal Family) that these yeomen of the guard were soon disbanded. But what Mr Nixon had revealed, in exaggeration, was a perception of himself to which a President after a year or two is in danger of succumbing: that he is in charge of—that he rules—a nation and that the word is handed down from the White House, not up from the people. It may be said that every Prime Minister probably feels the same in his official residence. I doubt it. Once, at a White House dinner, I sat next to the son of the British Prime Minister, who was at that moment the President's guest of honour. The son had been received, as everyone is, by a young Marine officer in a spanking dress uniform. His lady companion took the Marine's proffered arm. They were led through a small suite with a small orchestra playing waltzes by Strauss. Other beautiful rooms or galleries they passed through were ablaze with gilt and glass. On into the main reception room; more Marines, more impeccable manners—the reception line—the shaking hands with the king—I mean the President—and the First Lady. Cocktails and smiling chatter. And on into two linked dining rooms, and a splendid banquet sparkling with a hundred candles. A soothing fountain of music showered from another room. 'Home', said the Prime Minister's son, 'was never like this.' And, in truth, by comparison, No. 10 Downing Street is a modest upper-middle-class town house.

Apart from this beautiful protective shell in which the President lives, there is the constant human situation, in which he is surrounded by people who defer to him and who pass on to him every day their own view (which might be as blinkered as his) of what is happening, what is being felt and thought, on the Great Outside. The outside is the United States and its people. Only in the past month or so did Mr Bush attempt to listen to their troubles, to emerge from his cocoon of complacency ('yes, there are people having a bad time but the economy's growing, ninety-three million at work—things are getting better all the time'). This reminded me of the fatal 1932 assurance Herbert Hoover issued from the White House to millions shivering in tar-paper shacks

139

down by the rivers, and to the quarter of the working people of America who had no work: 'Prosperity is just around the corner.'

Some of you may have expected me to talk about the failures of the Bush campaign, for, only two days after the election, the papers are full of reasons and excuses and explanations by Republicans about failures of technique: he should have had sharper figures, he should have been more insulting earlier, he should have used more women, he should have hired as mean a man as the one who invented the infamous Willie Horton television commercial last time. (He was the Massachusetts black man who, given parole by Governor Dukakis, promptly raped a woman.) One bitter intimate who could enjoy the frankness of having left the administration came a little closer to the central truth when he moaned: 'He surrounded himself with second-rate talent and clones. He was only comfortable with a white-bread crowd, a bunch of white male Protestants and number-crunchers.' I can sympathize with that man's view. I and my generation *are* probably more comfortable with WASPs (and a Catholic friend or two) than with the polyglot, white—black—Latino—brown—Asian, multi-cultural society that America has increasingly become. But Clinton has reached out to it, and listened to it, is at home with it, his generation is a link with it.

This was never clearer than on Thursday morning, when the *New York Times* carried a front-page photograph of the President-elect with his mother and pals at a friend's house. Clinton in threadbare jeans, a check wool shirt, unzipped windbreaker, bulging Reeboks. Mostly young pals

140

in laughing bunches similarly dressed, or undressed. Not a suit, not a necktie, not a button-down shirt in sight. 'Well,' I said to my wife, 'can you believe this? There is the next President of the United States and his buddies.' I wasn't suggesting that Mr Clinton was putting on an act, as poor Mr Bush had to do when he wolfed a hamburger at the local lunch counter and said, 'Gee whillikins, this is great.' 'Clinton', said my wife sternly, 'is the President of those people and he dresses like them.' Quite right. Unbuttoned, one way or another, is his natural style. Along with the passing of George Bush, we shall see, I fear, the passing of the blue blazer.

The Irish in New York City

19 March 1993

A year or two ago, the brouhaha about the St Patrick's Day parade began—as many other social conflicts have done—with the coming out (their term) of homosexuals. I suppose that means it's been about twenty years since men and women in large numbers asserted that homosexuality was a lifestyle of choice, not, as for many centuries it had been, 'the sin that dare not speak its name'.

To the Catholic Church, however, whether or not it speaks its name, it is still a sin. And that belief is at the root of the never-ending wrangle in this city, between the Church and the homosexuals who claim to be good Catholics. The City of New York, its government, its laws and ordinances, theoretically stands in between, though, according to who's Mayor, it goes along with one side or the other. Last year, our first black Mayor, Mr David Dinkins, marched in the parade under the banner of the so-proclaimed Gays and Lesbians. He was often booed along the way, and he had several kinds of refuse thrown at him. He has survived. This year he stayed home, respecting a decision of the courts—which came only on the eve of the parade—that denied the homosexual group a permit to mount their own separate parade.

I'd better stop talking about homosexuals in general because they are not, as such, a party to the dispute, any more than are all New York's Irish. The adversaries in this contest are the ILGO—the Irish Lesbian and Gay Organization—and the most venerable of Irish Catholic societies in this city, the Ancient Order of Hibernians. The Gays and Lesbians, whom from now on we shall call the ILGOs, were organized only a few years ago and are said to have one hundred and twenty paid-up members. The Ancient Hibernians and their order go back to 1836, to a time when the prevailing Anglo-Americans began to be alarmed at the thousands of Irish immigrants pouring into New York from Liverpool and Cobh (only twelve years later the flood would arrive, the starving refugees from the Irish potato famine). The Anglo-Americans were greatly bothered by the noisy and effective Irish entry into local politics. In 1835 Irishmen had organized to drive the local Whigs from the polls, and when the Mayor and a sheriff's posse tumbled along to restore law and order, they were put to flight with blinding showers of green confetti and the threat of a brawl. The city fathers consequently retaliated with ordinances, just short of laws, that sharply discriminated against the Irish in housing and employment. The year after that Keystone Kops chase between the Irish and the Mayor and his henchmen, 1836, the Ancient Order of Hibernians was founded.

They have always been the sponsors of the St Patrick's Day parade here. And, after the disruption of last year's parade by angry onlookers resenting the marching homosexuals, the Hibernians were first in line to claim an exclusive right to sponsor and organize this parade, but also announced they would not tolerate a homosexual group. The city granted the Hibernians a permit but ignored their threat to ban the ILGOs. Whereupon, the ILGOs appealed to the city to declare that the Hibernians had no constitutional right to ban them. Everything, you'll notice, from playing a radio in public to selling films of close-up sexual intercourse comes down, sooner or later, to the First Amendment—the free press—right of the Constitution. Well, the city couldn't at that point take on the Constitution. In the end, the whole row went to the courts. The ILGOs had thought up what they took to be an even-handed, fair solution: they asked for a permit to hold a separate parade, an hour or two before the big one. The judge said no, too big a risk of a literal meeting of the minds and bodies, what we call a confrontation, especially if, as the ILGOs wanted, they marched south and, at the end, met the oncoming Hibernians.

So, now denied any legal right to march in the big parade or to stage one of their own, what were they to do? On the eve of the great day, they announced that they would defy the court and the

Mayor and the city and—most of all—Cardinal O'Connor, the head of this diocese, who always, except last year, stands under a canopy outside St Patrick's cathedral nodding and blessing all the groups, the marching bands, the societies, the local units, the drum majorettes, all the emerald-tinged bodies that go by: 198 units, 120,000 paraders.

Not surprisingly, when the nasty, grey, drenching day dawned there were over four thousand police at the ready, more than eight hundred more than last year. As the Hibernians were assembling down at 42nd Street and Fifth Avenue, the ILGOs set up in marching order and waving banners ('Cardinal O'Connor Is a Bigot in a Dress', 'ILGOs Against Bigotry and Intolerance', 'Freedom for ILGOs'), and they marched in triumph. Exactly one block. At 43rd Street they approached a wall of policemen who, like trainers routinely leading the horses into their stalls, quietly arrested over two hundred, which was just about the total muster of the ILGOs brigade. There wasn't a truncheon, a flailing of a stick or a visible bully. The ILGOs, whatever their words said, kept to the promised deed: they practised civil, not to say deferential, disobedience. In about fifteen minutes, the homosexual rebellion was all over. The big parade began and for four, five hours, the endless troops of the faithful plodded through rain coming down, as they say, like stair rods. On the sidewalk outside St Patrick's cathedral, were onlookers under umbrellas still roused by the Cardinal's stinging peroration at the early Mass: 'Neither respectability nor political correctness is worth one comma of the Apostle's Creed.' There were some present at the Mass who, however, had other sinners in mind. 'A pity', grumbled a Republican and Hibernian, 'the day doesn't focus on the key issue: the British presence in Ireland.'

This tremendous argument—about the Hibernians and the ILGOs—has been going on for months, and debated with eloquence, with absurdity, with—on both sides—bigoted charges of bigotry, in the City Council, in the pubs and clubs, on television endlessly. But it strikes me: two points were never made, not anyway in my hearing or reading. One is ironic and not likely to be made much of by the faithful. It is: who was St Patrick? He was a Scot, kidnapped at the age of 17 by the brutal Romans in one of their press-gang raids, whipped off to Ireland to be made a pig-keeper, which he hated, but, being an apprentice saint, endured for six years until he yearned to get back to his native land, and did so. But at some point he had a dream in which he was urged, by the Almighty, to fulfil his true mission, to return to Ireland and preach the gospel. He did. He made himself a bishop, he baptized converts, and he ordained priests and allowed them to marry (how about that, Cardinal O'Connor?). So, his mission in life was not to glorify the Irish but to save them from perdition.

The other point is the legal decision of the judge, which was no more and no less than to approve the Ancient Order of Hibernians' constitutional right to bar the ILGOs. The propriety of this ruling was never gone into by the ILGOs, who stayed with heated protests against bigotry, homophobia, fascism and the like. One angry man brought up the analogy of McSorley's Tavern, an old Irish pub downtown that, in the

145

discrimination battles of the 1960s, had at last to let in women, two women, as it happened, who were determined to invade any public place where men liked to be with men. But note the word 'public'. McSorley's Tavern is public—so is any land or property owned by the city or the state. In such places, you may not, under the law, bar anyone on account of race or religion. But, the judge pointed out, the Ancient Order of Hibernians is a private society. Like any other private club or society owning its own premises, it can legally keep its membership to men, to women, to whites, to blacks. It can bar anybody it likes, bachelors, Italians, Englishmen, left-handed people. This is the simple truth in the law the ILGOs couldn't bear to face.

In spite of the Hibernians' announcement that they welcomed open homosexuals in the parade but not marching under a banner that proclaimed them as something special and different, the ILGOs didn't want that. They wanted to use the parade not as a celebration of St Patrick but as an advertisement for open homosexuality.

Why do the Irish—Irish-Americans (perhaps most immigrants)—get so much more inflamed about such issues than their relatives in the homeland? Well, for the Irish, there's the long history of discrimination against them. Mainly, though, I think that when any immigrant or ethnic group comes into the welter of this seething, polyglot city, they make an extra effort to show they're different and to water, or exaggerate, their roots. An old Irish friend of mine, whom I've known for over sixty years, wrote to me the other day. His letter arrived coincidentally on the morning of our parade. He wrote: 'As soon as an Irishman leaves home and enters America, he ceases to be whatever he was but behaves rather more so.'

'Give me your tired, your poor . . .'

25 June 1993

There can hardly be an American born here who cannot recite the five thundering lines inscribed on the Statue of Liberty: the hectoring command— 'Give me your tired, your poor, /Your huddled masses yearning to breathe free, /The wretched refuse of your teeming shore.—/Send these, the homeless tempest-tossed, to me: /I lift my lamp beside the golden door.' Generous words, almost arrogant in their bravery. Whether they constitute fine poetry or doggerel, they touched the hearts and minds of millions of Europeans—always the poor, often the persecuted, very often the fugitives from military service. They were spurred to pack a few belongings, often no more than a blanket, a cooking pot, a prayer book, a corset, to climb aboard box cars deep inside Russia or Hungary or Lithuania or Germany and be carried to the great ports: Constantinople, Piraeus, Antwerp, Bremen, and then put aboard. There, in enclosures outside the embarkation city, they were bathed, de-loused, fed, their baggage and clothes fumigated. They were prepared for the land of the free.

We are talking about the routine procedures employed with the fourteen and a half million immigrants who arrived here, mainly New York or Boston, in the first two decades of the twentieth century. Looking up in awe to the bosom of the colossal lady peering out towards Europe, they would very soon find out that the physical routine of getting into the United States was not quite what a poor foundling might expect of a new, compassionate mother.

Coming across the Atlantic, they were not so much allotted space as stowed aboard, as many as nine hundred in steerage. Sailing slowly up the lower bay of New York City, they would spot their first Americans climbing aboard from a Coast Guard cutter, two men and a woman: immigration inspectors, whose first job was to look over the ship's manifest and see if the captain had recorded cases of contagious disease. Considering the frequency and unpredictability at the time of ravaging epidemics across the continent of Europe, they looked out first for signs of cholera, typhoid, tuberculosis. If you showed any sign of these fearsome diseases, you were at once taken off to quarantine on an island in the bay and got ready for early deportation.

Once the newcomers had been herded into a large reception hall, they would be tagged with numbers and grouped according to their native tongue, which for the vast majority of them was the only one they spoke. They moved, shadowed by interpreters, in lines past a doctor in a blue uniform, a man with a chalk in his hand—an instant diagnostician. He was certainly a fast one and had the confidence that comes from not knowing anything about CT scans, or MRIs, or PSAs. He saw an ageing man with purple lips and chalked on his back: H—possible heart disease. Separate this man! Children in arms stood down to see if they betrayed the limp of rickets. T on the back was the expulsion sign of tuberculosis. Two other doctors dipped into a bowl of disinfectant and folded a suspect eyelid back with a buttonhook. Trachoma—very prevalent in Southern and Eastern Europe and a sure harbinger of blindness. You, too, were on your way back home.

We won't follow the release of most of the healthy rest to railroad agents, con men, honest bosses and sweatshop owners looking for, and getting in luscious numbers, an army of cheap labourers, for most of whom the prospect was better than life in the homeland.

The expectation, among the mass of the settled population, was that these strangers would settle in too. But with every wave of new immigrants there was always a booming counterwave of protest, from the people who'd been here a long time, two, three or more generations of what we now call the Anglos and their collateral Nordics—Swedes, Norwegians, Germans. They had run the country, its government, its institutions for a hundred years or more. So every breaking wave of new immigrants made a rude sound to the residents, and they protested, then they discriminated. Often Washington legislated, as it did in the 1920s and again in the 1950s against what were called 'undesirable types', meaning Orientals, Southern and Eastern Europeans. Even as late as the time I first came here, in the early 1930s, there were still pasted on shop windows and employment agencies stickers left over from early in the century: 'No Irish Need Apply.' But now, equally new to me, just

149

outside the entrance to an apartment building was a sign: a wooden post surmounted by a rectangle, a sort of mahogany plaque, very handsome, a meticulously printed sign of gold lettering on a black background. It said 'Apartments To Let, Three To Six Rooms. Restricted.' That last word was not put in as an afterthought. It was printed in the same fine style as the rest of the announcement. 'Restricted', I discovered, was shorthand for 'No Jews Need Apply'. This was standard practice here in New York, in Manhattan especially; the other four boroughs, getting most of their business and work from the legions of incoming Jews, could not afford to be so particular. That rather callous sign vanished. It came to be made illegal in the late 1940s, when a Republican Governor of New York, Thomas E. Dewey (who had two failing shots at the Presidency against Franklin Roosevelt), pushed through the state legislature the first (in this country) fair employment and fair housing Act. (The practice of exclusion was not totally abandoned. It continued in parts of the Upper East Side, unofficially, without the dreaded word, discreetly, on tiptoe, in the English manner.) Today there are no signs, except scurrilous ones painted by hooligans. But in the teeming boroughs, in Queens, Staten Island, the Bronx, Brooklyn, blacks glare at the successful Korean fruiterers, the pious religious Jewish sects watch their step, people who once went to Chinatown for entertainment and exquisite cheap sandals now stay away, after hearing of boatloads of smuggled Chinese brought in here to swell the active army of gangsters. It is news to most of us that there have been for some time ruthless and

150

very active Chinese gangs working profitably in—what else?—drugs.

But at the moment the victim, the scapegoat, everybody's feared interloper, is the Haitian. I mentioned lately the drastically changed ethnic composition of the fleet of New York's taxi drivers. Where once taxi drivers were first- or second-generation Irishmen, Italians, Germans, now, they are Puerto Ricans, Haitians, Russians, Israelis. Why should the arrivals from Haiti be so feared?

Well, since the Haitian military overthrew President Aristide almost two years ago, about forty thousand Haitians have fled from what is quite plainly a particularly brutal tyranny. They came floating in across the Caribbean and on to Florida, and hundreds, perhaps many thousands, of them never made it. Simply fell off their miserable little boats or sank with all hands. President Bush decided to apply the existing immigration laws which offer legal haven if you can prove that you are a political refugee escaping likely persecution. If you simply sought a better life, but could give no proof of past or pending persecution, you were returned to Haiti.

During the Presidential campaign, Mr Clinton called this policy illegal and cruel and swore to reverse it and let in the Haitian masses huddled in their leaky boats. Tremendous joy throughout Haiti! At once, over a hundred thousand people helped to build more leaky boats. In the face of this totally unpredicted tidal wave, President Clinton reverted to the Bush policy. A national howl of pain from Haiti and cries of outrage from American liberals.

Last Monday the Supreme Court, nodding

regretfully at the mention of the word cruelty, nevertheless ruled by 8 to 1 that this policy, intercepting the unpersecuted ones, was constitutional. Just before this ruling was handed down, a hundred and twenty-five refugees from Haiti, who had been judged to be true political refugees, were released from the American naval base in Cuba and flown to Miami—some to New York—there to be allowed to be absorbed into the American way of life. They were designated a 'special group'. What was so special about them— apart from an unconscionable long time they had been detained, is that they were all HIV positive, infected with the virus that causes AIDS.

So, in one action, freedom is available to diseased people who will at once be entitled to free medical care, to a home, to an interpreter, to daily maintenance. But in the more sweeping action, affecting all the boat people, the Supreme Court has added a phrase to Emma Lazarus's soaring invitation: 'Give me your tired, your poor, your huddled masses yearning to breathe free—but see they carry a return ticket.'

Thirtieth Anniversary of Kennedy Assassination

26 November 1993

I've always thought of 'anniversary'—the turn of the year, or literally the return of the year—as a happy word. But there've been one or two lately that considerably bruised the idea of anniversary as a festive time. I'd say that ten years ago—less—most Americans, asked to respond offhand to the prospect of 1992, the five hundredth anniversary of Christopher Columbus limping ashore on this hemisphere, would have looked forward to it as an all-American fiesta. But in the meantime, a literature of disillusion had been spawned, and when October 1992 arrived there were very few fireworks and—from one end of the Americas to the other, many memorial parades, many trooping Indian tribes observing 12 October as a day of mourning.

What they were mourning was their experience, the native experience of the conquistadors. The very name says 'conquest', and in the fifteenth century the conquest by any European nation of a native society meant subjection, enslavement, rapine, often torture and suppression of the native religion. It took about four centuries for intending conquerors (the French and the British are the best examples) to have the sense to let the subject peoples keep many of the mores and all of their religions.

The sudden revelation of all this, last year, in books and in magazine and newspaper pieces can only mean that for a couple of centuries or so the white man's settlement, the conquest of the Americas, must have been very badly taught in schools. The 'truths' revealed last year were always true but quietly relegated to the shadows, while the big spotlight was turned on the European view of Columbus as a master sailor, an extremely courageous explorer, a remarkable commander, a visionary and a devout Catholic, all of which he was.

However, once the brutal side of the Spanish conquests became common knowledge, became in the past two years something of a publishing industry, it was not possible to say, 'well, too bad, let's forget that part', and on the great October day enjoy, as John Adams recommended for the Fourth of July: 'fireworks, parades, bands, and general rejoicing'. In fact, when Columbus Day was over, the Governors and Mayors, not to mention the members of Congress, expressed sighs of relief that the few riots and eruptions of violence happened in only three or four countries and they were in Central and South America.

Well, I have to say that I believe very many Americans young and old will be greatly relieved that 22 November is over, not from any fear this time of protest marches or riots, but relief from the sheer din of morbid nostalgia. Thirty years ago, 22 November 1963, was, as surely everyone listening now must know, was the assassination of President Kennedy. If disillusion with Columbus was a publishing industry, *two* industries based on the life of John Kennedy have flourished and overwhelmed us this past month or so. One is what you might call the Camelot industry, the perpetuation and embroidering of the beautiful myth taken from Tennyson—of an ideal, small nation whose 'shining hour' was the time it was presided over by a brave young king. The other, a growth industry that gives no sign of stopping growing, is the Kennedy conspiracy industry.

To say much about it would only massage the sales representatives of this feverish speciality. Let me just say that I have no peculiar or privileged knowledge of the affair. I have fairly creditable credentials: I was there at the time. I practically wrote the next day's issue of the English newspaper for which I was at the time the chief American correspondent. I read every word of the Warren Commission's report (which, by the way, was a Commission of able, inquisitive and honourable men, none of them, so far as I know, crippled by a hobby horse). Subsequently, I read the early books and a summary of the—was it 1974?—House Committee's renewed inquiry. And of course, like everybody who was at the time a sentient adult, I have paid attention to most of the later reports and theories and revised versions. I do not believe that the President was killed on the orders of the Kremlin, Fidel Castro, Lyndon Johnson, J. Edgar Hoover, Mao Tse-tung, Generalissimo Francisco Franco, Carrie Nation or Dr Crippen. I lean to the belief that a very forlorn, agitated, lonely psychopath named Lee Harvey Oswald did it, without help or coaching. And as for the maze of motives that the conspiracy boys and girls would have you thread through, it seems to me that the likeliest is one small enough to seem trivial to the big apocalyptic revisionists but big enough to have inspired some of the world's greatest literature— including *Othello* and *Madame Bovary*,—namely, Oswald's suspicion, which his widow says plagued him at the time, that she adored Kennedy and was at the same time, sleeping with an FBI agent. So far as I'm concerned, there is no more to say.

About the mythical kingdom of Camelot, which during the run of the fanciful musical of the same name came to be merged with the fact of the Kennedy Presidency, we can only say now, it must show that nations, like individuals, have a constant yearning for leaders who are larger, more heroic, than life. And John Kennedy and his wife arrived as something quite new in the history of the Presidency: a beautiful young couple. So what was wrong about having a handsome young President with a beautiful wife? Nothing, except we went on from there to romanticize their public lives (the private life seemed blissfully right—a delusion that was not shared by the White House press corps, but in those days one of the taboos that was observed and never discussed was against writing about the sexual peccadilloes of the President, if any). A White House butler, who wrote—fifty years ago—a memoir of the Presidents he'd served, described President Harding as 'a ladies' man' but only in the opposite sense to his characterization of Teddy Roosevelt as 'a man's man'. Fortunately for John Kennedy, the taboo against writing about or publicly disclosing sexual habits of the public man was still in force. If it had not been so, I doubt he'd ever have been able to run for public office.

As it was, after the grim years of the Second World War, and the unexpectedly bitter ordeal of the Korean War, and a stretch of government by a late-middle-aged man, it was a tonic to see a young handsome President up there on his brilliant, frosty inauguration day saying, 'the torch has been passed to a new generation', even though all the equals he had to deal with were the old men of the recent wars. We readily embraced the glitter and charm and promise of a kind of chivalry in the Presidency. This romantic hunger was so strong that when the ill-conceived and wretchedly executed invasion of Cuba failed miserably, and Kennedy said he was sorry for it, his popular standing in the polls went soaring.

A journalist I know wrote movingly the other day about his boyhood view of Kennedy as a magical 'little guy on a black and white television set, who, although he was a rich politician from Boston, I believed represented me and understood me. This boy enjoyed chanting over what he called the sing-song aphorisms of Ted Sorensen—he was the author of the Kennedy Inaugural speech. "Ask not what your country can do for you; ask rather what you can do for your country."' The same journalist—now, I guess, crowding 50—wrote on this 22nd: 'Kennedy was the first great fraud of the post-modern era. He was the surprised and grateful object of a mass delusion, he came from a state where electing Irish politicians by fraud was an art form. His father was a bandit and a profiteer . . . JFK never won a majority in a national election; it seems likely that the election of 1960 was stolen for him by the Daley machine in Chicago.' That is, I think, almost certainly true. But as for the other judgements, they are too brutal; they are the cynical outcries of a disappointed sentimentalist. We should not now blame Kennedy for our misplaced romanticism. He brought to the Presidency the energy of an optimistic spirit. On the initiative of a Congressman from Wisconsin, he invented the Peace Corps. He got us deeply involved in Vietnam. In the early assertion of the civil rights of blacks, he did use the National Guard with, as he would have said, 'vigah' where Eisenhower had used it with reluctance. He had wit and a low-key gift for Irish blarney. He was disorganized and acted too often on impulse. He had no gift for cajoling and nudging and

157

arm-twisting the Congress. He once called Congress 'the enemy'. When he died, there were something like ninety bills that were dead or dying. Luckily, he was succeeded by Lyndon Johnson, no charmer but the best con man ever to convert an enemy, who got more than two-thirds of those bills through the Congress in the following six months.

It has been remarked that when an American President dies, a halo descends on him and stays there with his memory. This is not true of McKinley. It's very true of Lincoln and Kennedy. The debates about their true worth still go on, or, perhaps, only about Kennedy. Lincoln has almost been sanctified, and the bad and arbitrary things about him are buried in his grave. Let it be so, once and for all, with John Fitzgerald Kennedy.

Boston

11 March 1994

'The Bostonians, almost without [an] exception, are derived from one country and a single stock. They are all descendants of Englishmen and, of course, are united by all the great bonds of society—language, religion, government, manners and interest.' That was written by the President of Yale (then known as Yale College) in 1796. Quoting that sentence in a federal guidebook in 1936, the writer says, as for this 'legend of ethnic homogeneity, it is so much pernicious twaddle'.

I lived across the river from Boston just sixty years ago and it could be truly said way back then that 'five minutes' walk from the State House will take the visitor to any one of several sections of the city where English is a foreign language . . . every third person you meet on the street is foreign-born, and three out of four are of other than English descent'. This guidebook, again, mind, quoting the census figures of 1930, begins with another bit of demolition prose, to wit: 'The modern fable that Boston is now an "Irish city" is no better founded than the English Puritan myth. Of Boston's quarter of a million foreign born, the largest number come from Canada—45,000. Ireland, 43,000. Italy, 36,000. Russia (mainly Jews), 31,000. From the UK, 22,000. The rest come from Poland, Norway, Denmark, Germany, Greece and Lithuania.'

I bring up that accounting of sixty years ago in order to add a note which Americans of English origin, no matter how distant, tend to believe is still true or ought to be, namely, 'The old New England stock still largely controls leading banks, business enterprises, museums, hospitals and universities, but numerically is insignificant.' Today no minority but a spread of minorities controls the banks and businesses. When I was there, the Irish, though powerful in local politics, had hardly begun to challenge, on the national political scene, the Cabots and Saltonstalls and Lodges and Forbeses. Today the three main federal, that's to say United States government, buildings (employing 35,000) are called the Thomas O'Neill Federal Building, the J. W. McCormack Building and the John Fitzgerald Kennedy Federal Building.

There is, so far as I know, no James Michael Curley Building, an extraordinary oversight because, more than any other man this century,

Curley marked the political triumph of the immigrant Irish over the entrenched old Yankees. A tall, dapper, handsome Irishman with, for those days, longish grey locks and flashing eyes, a black Irishman if ever there was one, he spent over a quarter of a century in politics, eight years in Congress, two as Governor, sixteen as Mayor, two spells in jail, during the second of which he was still Mayor and ran the city competently from his cell. The knowledge of all this, which dropped on me like a thunderbolt at the beginning of my year in Boston, was something that Bostonians, I mean the old Yankees, were almost proud to show you, through the example of Curley and later the recently dead Speaker O'Neill (of the United States House of Representatives), that Boston could still produce men of sap and mischief. The corollary is also true: that the Anglo-Saxon minority of Boston, no longer calling themselves the old Brahmins (Curley called them 'our Brahmin overlords'), are pale, respectable shadows of the originals.

What sparked these thoughts about Boston and what we'd now call its ethnic composition was an item reported the other day in a quiet nook of my newspaper: that in one state alone, California, there was a sudden flurry of lawsuits from Hispanic children protesting that they are not receiving a bilingual education. Ten years ago, there was something of a national debate on whether any school should teach in two languages. Now there's a move, throughout all the Southern border states, Florida, Louisiana, Texas, Arizona, California, to make it illegal *not* to have bilingual education. In two ways Hispanic (or what we're now supposed to

160

call Latino) children are suing to be taught basic subjects in their native Spanish, and English as a second language. Meanwhile, English-speaking children are protesting that the basic education at their school is given in Spanish, which they don't understand, so they want basics in English, and Spanish as a second language. This is plainly a movement that will, in time, overtake all elementary and secondary education. A freakish offshoot of this movement (I think it was in Chicago) was where black children—who at home, on the streets, at play, speak their own brand of Black English—are beginning, through their parents and the nearest lawyer at the ready, to demand that in school, the basics should be taught in Black English, and that Formal English, or what you and I call English, should be taught as a second language.

It used to be the case, before and after the Second World War, that immigrants from any country were, willing or not, tossed into the ocean of English speakers, the immersion method. They learned, pretty soon, that so long as they spoke only the language they'd arrived with they would be doomed to swell the pool of cheap labour. Learn English, and you are already on your way from what today is called your 'entry profession', meaning first humble job, janitor, dustman, trucker or messenger. What has happened throughout the second half of the century is that the immigrant, especially the Spanish-speaking immigrant, has acquired a new self-respect as a special type of independent American. Many of them don't want to mix in, though I think these lawsuits will reflect a truth which sooner than later they panic to discover: that the only way you can rise into the middle class over most of the country is by way of the English language.

I find it striking that, so far anyway, we've not read of this kind of lawsuit coming from the Asians. Very conspicuously, more than any other type, they come, they flounder for a while with the new language, but, whether or not their parents pick up any rudimentary English, the children are at the grindstone every minute of every school day, and in a year or two are fluent and—it's a byword by now—markedly superior in learning to other nationals. They bloom sooner than anybody into clerks, office workers, then businessmen, doctors, lawyers, most notably as scientists and medical researchers. They are, naturally, greatly resented for the palpable superiority. And in some cities, New York is one, there has always been—in neighbourhoods where blacks and Asians live side by side—the prospect of boycotts (of Asian merchants) and, as you'd sadly guess, of riots.

My trip to Boston, in the first place, was not, however, meant to be mainly about immigrant tensions. It was about a remarkable model of a fish, up above the Speaker's chair in the House, known as the Hall of Representatives. There stands, or hangs, or gapes against the wall what is known as the Sacred Cod. It is the emblem of the item that saved the economy, and hence the foundation of the state—the Commonwealth of Massachusetts. Boston is still known to lisping children as 'the home of the bean and the cod'. Last week, the Governor of Massachusetts put in a plea to Washington—help!—a plea for emergency financial aid from the federal government for the industry that kept Massachusetts on the map. This is only one chapter of a story that takes in the whole country, from the far northwest, Seattle, in the state of Washington, across to New England and down all the East Coast to the Gulf of Mexico. A friend of mind—a Bostonian by the way—called me in horror the other day, alarmed to hear that the cod are dying in the polluted ocean. Polluted ocean? Yes, that's what we are only now beginning to accept as a true fact of life. She asked me if I'd read the long scare story in the *New York Times* and complained, rightly, that some government department, after saying nothing for years, suddenly spews at us a flood of statistics that proclaim a national crisis.

Quite simply, the fact is that—take New England first, and its principal port of Boston—after three hundred and fifty years, the oldest American fishing ground is almost barren of the fish it caught and sold and traded and lived by: haddock, cod, flounder. Last week, on one day, the fishermen in Boston Harbor tooted their boat horns. They wanted as much government help as they might get after an earthquake. Somebody said that the honking of the horns sounded like a funeral dirge. But down three hundred miles to Chesapeake Bay, what native son Mencken called 'the vast protein factory of Chesapeake Bay', and on and all the way down to New Orleans, there are few groupers, and no more red snappers, which were the main catch of the southern East Coast. On the Pacific Coast, where I started, the great port of Seattle reports that the decline of the famous Pacific salmon is 'catastrophic . . . threatening to wipe out not only whole industries but also cultures and communities that depend on the catch'. The fishermen, both commercial and sporting, have been warned that unless there's a dramatic improvement from some unknown source, there may be a ban on all salmon fishing along the—what? Fifteen hundred miles of the American Pacific Coast. Now they tell us! 'Government officials', it says here, 'say that most of the commercial fishing grounds outside Alaska are in trouble, and that of the world's [not America's, but the *world's*] seventeen principal fishing zones, thirteen are in trouble.'

This widespread shortage is not something the normal fish-eater has begun to notice. Here in the East, we wish we saw more of the noble striped bass, our finest eating fish. But I get splendid salmon. Of course, I realize, on second thoughts, that it's Norwegian. Both Norway and several South American countries are making a killing here with imported farmed fish, raised in pens. The killing of course forces down the cost of the local article.

It occurs to me that if New England is losing the thing that helped the first settlers survive, Virginia and the Carolinas are fighting to keep the thing that helped *them* survive after a false start with glassmaking. And what was that? The tobacco leaf. That's another story, hilarious or tragic, according to your interest.

Trick or Treat

4 November 1994

On the evening of Monday, 31 October, millions of doors were knocked on and opened in response to the cry: Trick or Treat? If there is one Irish institution, other than the practice of charm, or blarney, that came into the United States and conquered, it is the secular festival of Hallowe'en. I stress secular because, so far as I can discover, few secular, or, if you like, pagan festivals passed so solidly into Christian practice.

It was originally a Celtic festival called Samhain, and Celtic scholars or crossword buffs, perhaps, will no doubt be eager to translate it for me. Samhain was the Celtic harvest festival, but also thought of as the time when the spirits of the dead came back to their old haunts, I suppose is the proper word. Until the ninth century, it seems people were content to accept these visitations as the return, from the underworld, of demons and goblins and other monsters. How and why the Roman Catholic Church managed in eight hundred and something AD to introduce this weird festival and its usages into the Christian liturgy is to me a remarkable mystery, and must remain one pending an explanatory fax from Rome.

Anyway, the original pagan festival became All Saints Day (now it was saints and not demons that came back) and 31 October became All-Hallows Eve.

I believe there is no record of daubing faces with

165

soot or red dye, mask-wearing, tricking and treating in this country until the middle of the nineteenth century and the arrival, in lively multitudes, of the Irish. The interesting switch here is that apparently right from the start, except among the extremely devout, they cast off the religious elements and turned it into a children's holiday, as somebody said, of trick or treating and general mischief-making. If so, the mischief-making was pretty innocent. And, wherever they settled, the Irish, for a generation or two, were always the poorest people in town. No wonder they sent children off (very often their own) to knock on the doors of the comfortable and say 'trick or treat'—in the full expectation that nobody wants to have a scary trick practised on them, and would willingly cough up a cake, a pie, a candy bar or some such.

So last Monday, inside the lift in our building, there was posted a sheet of paper, with two parallel lists written on it. On the left, a list of tenants willing to subject themselves to the knockings and giggling of children in the building and to provide them with a treat. On the right was a list of children willing to offer themselves up for the reception of these goodies.

You'll have noticed the phrase, 'children in the building'. It's the first sinister change in the once general custom of kissing your tots goodbye and good luck and sending them out into the night to roam and knock and garner a cornucopia of treats. Kids used to love to do this the way we, when a little older and in another country, set out into the darkness of Christmas Eve with four or five other songsters and jogged around the town till all hours, carolling outside houses that were well lit, and looked prosperous, and might—did—have you in for a mince pie.

But to send your—and anybody else's—children out on the town without a protective adult these nights would be taken in some quarters as a heartless form of child neglect punishable in the courts. For more years now than I care to count— ten, twenty—the last thing on any parent's mind is to send small children, or, for that matter, young teenagers, out at night for any purpose, secular or holy. And as you no doubt know, in some cities, there are curfews for people under 18. I don't need to tell you that the painful restriction of Hallowe'en to one apartment building in cities, or one street block under adult patrol in the countryside, is yet another response to the growing and seemingly incurable affliction of random public crime. Most crime, as you've no doubt heard, is committed between members of the same family (most homicides, at any rate), or between close friends or members of one family feuding with another. And always, and dependably swelling the homicides in Los Angeles, Miami, Detroit and half a dozen cities we'd never guess at, are the ritual murders of teenage gangs who have replaced life, liberty and the pursuit of happiness with the triple pledge: respect, reputation and retaliation. Which means, pitifully, once you're initiated into a gang, you earn respect by a serious mugging or attempted shooting, reputation by clocking up a record of shootings, and retaliation by avenging the wounds, or murders, of your own gangsters by another murder, on the principle of an eye for an eye.

167

But in spite of this remarkable closed circuit of crime, which eats away at the decent community life of this country, there is a great deal of random street crime. And what could be more appetizing, likely to be safer, than a swift assault on a gaggle of small children? There's been enough of it in the recent past to have some cities post warnings, in the week before Hallowe'en, urging parents to forgo Hallowe'en altogether; a cruel blow, surely, to the aspirations, pleasures, of the young. Such parents are, usually, fundamentalist Christians, who dislike very much, or detest, the clause in the Bill of Rights First Amendment that dictates the separation of Church and State. The extremist wing of them longs to make this nation a Christian nation, against the lively presence of so many other religions here, and against the unwavering rulings of the United States Supreme Court. They take every opportunity of introducing Christian customs, symbols, feasts into public places; and just as resolutely, and just as tiresomely, the civil liberties maniacs (not just civil liberties upholders) grimly fight and oppose the militant Christians—and usually win. As, for instance, whenever a church or any Christian religious group mounts a Christmas crib in, say, a village square, up jumps the American Civil Liberties Union, goes to court and is conceded yet another victory by pointing out that the crib is on display on public property, maintained and paid for with the taxes of Muslims, Jews, agnostics and heathens.

But now Hallowe'en, the latest bait to the religious right. In at least five states, they have this year begged or urged or tried to order families to abandon Hallowe'en or change its rituals

168

drastically and celebrate it as a sacred Christian festival. Because, they insist, they've just discovered, perhaps, that all these years, for a century and a half, America has been practising without shame a purely pagan festival and perpetuating, in the innocent young, a belief in the most wicked and primitive superstitions. Black cats. Witches. Ghosts. Scary monsters. Death's heads made out of pumpkins, that healthy, pure, Puritan fruit, if ever there was one. So in Maryland, New York, Ohio, Georgia, California, only of course in certain places bouncing with Christian fundamentalists, the public-elementary schools, fearing the prospect of litigation, have reluctantly told children to come to school in their normal dress and forgo the innumerable comic or ghastly masks available. Of course, the first protests have come from the manufacturers and retailers, in hot Republican territory, of masks, lifelike but in this context sinister, of Bill Clinton. I myself was about to appear as Madonna if we had stayed in New York, but we were flying off to family. Still, I was cheered to arrive at the airport and duck under a great sweeping sheet of something swaying slightly in the atmosphere, like a giant cobweb. It *was* a giant cobweb, reaching, without explanation, from one shining pillar to another squeaky clean wall or counter. Candle-lit pumpkins everywhere; one or two small passengers who plainly, from their scarred or deformed faces, had just arrived, or were on their way, to the underworld. It was very rousing. And, I must mention, on the last day of the American golf tour championship in San Francisco, marching up the eighteenth fairway was a very athletic figure with a skeleton's head. It was the

169

super-golfer Greg Norman, doing his bit to defy the hysterical Christian right. In some cities, the brethren announced that Hallowe'en night would be replaced by 'Hallelujah night' and prizes would be given—to tots, mind you—for the best biblical costume. Not much public sympathy, I'm afraid, for the prim little one who chose to come as David instead of Dracula. The way around this, in some wicked places, was to appear as a ferocious Goliath or, so defying the parents too, as one or other of the more disreputable inhabitants of Sodom and Gomorrah.

The television stations, I'm happy to say, paid no attention whatever to the reformers. Of our seventy-two operating channels, I'd guess that at least forty were drenched with blood last Monday night: every horror film ever made, an actual revival of such old Saturday night series—serieses—as Chiller Theater, and the more vivid films of Hammer Productions and the Japanese company that gave us the incomparable Godzilla. Also, a public station notable for its nightly one-hour profiles, biographies, of the famous (and very well done, from Julius Caesar to Sigmund Freud and Humphrey Bogart, Charles Darwin and Charles Laughton), came out with a piece that drained the previous horrors away with a documentary life proving—and it was quite true—the essential lovability of Vincent Price. It was a kind of final purge of pity and terror, worthy of the Greeks.

Fiftieth Anniversary of VE Day

5 May 1995

This weekend, I suppose every nation that fought in the Second World War will be recalling 7–8 May 1945 and the general jubilation that greeted the end of the fighting in what an American Navy commander I knew called 'the European sector'. It's a phrase, I imagine, that could never have occurred to the armies and the people of Europe. But it's an oddity worth mentioning, because although it is a touch stilted, it spoke volumes for the American view—here on the Pacific Coast—of VE Day, as distinct from a European view. That sailor friend was in San Francisco at the time, and so was I. And, more to the point, so were thousands of soldiers, sailors and Marines having a brief final fling before shipping out through the Golden Gate and into the huge Pacific towards the Japanese islands, where most of them expected to be fighting or dying through the summer and fall. Indeed, given the Japanese's fanatical capacity for holding their ground till the last man—the expert guess was that we could not expect to invade the main islands before the spring of 1946. General Marshall debated with the Secretary of War and with General Omar Bradley whether the price to be exacted by that distant VJ Day would be one or two million lives.

When the certainty of VE Day was reported here (there'd been a false alarm two days before in a dispatch filed by an over-eager American agency reporter), when it really came, the whooping it up was muted but delayed here, because while Londoners were aswarm along the Mall, and New Yorkers, early risers anyway, were pouring into Times Square to watch the illuminated news ticker, we here in San Francisco (and we were the delegates of fifty-one nations and about three or four hundred press, and radio reporters, in the second week of the cumbersome, the immensely tedious business of setting up the various bodies of a new League of Nations, christened—before he died by Franklin Roosevelt—the United Nations), we and the rest of the San Francisco population, were in bed and snoozing at four in the morning. By the time we woke, there were small crowds out on Market Street. But by 9 o'clock, the delegates to the founding conference of the United Nations were assembled in plenary session in the Opera House here, chatting animatedly, brought to order by the gavel of the temporary Secretary General, and an announcement was made. The Nazis had surrendered. There was a short wave of polite applause, the generals and the statesmen all sat down, and the business was resumed of writing the UN charter to, as it says, 'save succeeding generations from the scourge of war'. A great and noble aim, and in the brilliant spring of 1945, it was, believe me, thought to be an achievable aim.

I sifted through the delegations and buttonholed many soldiers and politicians and civil servants from many countries. And I don't remember any one of them who made a wry face when that memorable phrase was recited or when we looked ahead to the prospect of a long peace. I don't believe the most cynical delegate present would

172

ever have guessed or predicted that by the fiftieth anniversary of the United Nations, the world would have endured, by the UN's own count, something like two hundred and forty wars, and, in this anniversary year, a half-dozen very active and murderous ones.

But even if idealism was rampant in San Francisco in 1945 (and it was), what was so markedly different about VE Day here and the rejoicings in the capitals of Europe was the looming prospect over the Pacific horizon, of worse to come. At the end of the celebratory week, I was sitting in a movie theatre with a Marine officer; the European and New York newsreels (of course, there was no television yet) had been flown out to the West Coast, so we saw the surging, reverberating crowds around Buckingham Palace, the Royal Family there on the balcony, and the squat, rosy-faced figure of Churchill making the V sign. My Marine officer said, no resentment intended, just casually, almost amused: 'You'd think the war was over.' And of course, to the peoples of Europe, so it was. But my Marine's offhand remark was one I would never forget. He shipped out within the week, and was soon fighting on the island of Okinawa, which was thought vital to take a hold as the first stepping stone, a launch pad for the mass bombing and invasion of Japan eight hundred miles away. One-third of all the American Marine casualties of the Second World War were counted in the taking of Okinawa. My Marine officer was one of them.

We have only just now, last month, celebrated the landing on Okinawa. I suppose 'celebrated' is the word, but the anniversary ceremony involved

173

most conspicuously the widows and family survivors of the dead. And this time, which marks the fiftieth anniversary of so many great events, the urge toward hilarity and joy is rebuked by the uncomfortable fact that the victory, the successful battles, the liberating of the Holocaust victims, coincided with so many other dreadful and humiliating events. So, in no more than a month or so, we've been commemorating some events we'd rather forget.

I have atop a bookcase in my study a postcard, about three times the normal length. I bought it in 1931 after I'd walked along a street of many children, walking skeletons with bulging bellies. (We'd never heard in Britain about the actual famine and deep despair of the famished, one plausible cause of Hitler.) I walked along and came to a marble arch, a high wall and steps going up to the entrance of the most breathtaking horizon of architecture I had ever seen then, or have ever seen since. It was a vast, far-reaching palace, with four majestic sides, *the* masterpiece of northern Baroque. I'm sorry I found this postcard—a few weeks ago—on the fiftieth anniversary of the fire-bombing of Dresden, when 120,000 (mostly civilians) were burned alive or drowned in the river they plunged into. British and American bombers pelted Dresden, in two waves, over a night and a day. Possibly our most ignoble act of the war, it was certainly nothing to celebrate.

Last weekend, there was no way for Americans to avoid the news of another mighty celebration in the city that we knew as Saigon, now Ho Chi Minh City, capital of a united Communist Vietnam. What was being celebrated (not by us) was the

174

twentieth anniversary of the surrender of South Vietnam in the long, eight-year war that America lost, after President Kennedy's military advisers and technicians turned into President Johnson's American soldiers and sailors and airmen, and in the end, into half a million fighting men. There's no need to go on, to stress what we've been saying throughout those twenty years, that Vietnam was a wound from which the United States has never wholly recovered. So this week's pictures and reports, all they did was turn the knife in the wound. Another twist of it was given by Lyndon Johnson's Secretary of Defense, who—throughout his service in that office—was the super-hawk, so much so, it was by many people called McNamara's War. Now he has written a tearful memoir saying he knew early on the war was wrong, the war should never have been fought. He stops short of the rueful verdict of another former hawk, the late Secretary of State Dean Acheson, who said at the end: 'Vietnam was worse than immoral—it was a mistake.'

Mr Robert McNamara has lit up a fiery controversy by his agonized confessional. He has been challenged by the obvious question: Why did he stay on? Why didn't he resign if that's the way he felt? Anthony Eden resigned when he couldn't square the government's policy with being Foreign Secretary. Mr Cyrus Vance resigned as President Carter's Secretary of State when his conscience wouldn't let him conceal from the allies Mr Carter's disastrous adventure in the desert to rescue the Iran hostages. Lord Carrington resigned as Foreign Secretary when Argentina invaded the Falklands, not because he was responsible, he said,

175

simply he ought to have seen it coming. Mr McNamara's excuse is his loyalty to President Johnson. It's exactly how Colonel Oliver North defended his running a secret, underground foreign policy in the Iran-Contra affair. It's a strange excuse. No Cabinet officer, nobody serving the government, takes an oath to the President. He or she takes an oath only to 'uphold the Constitution of the United States'.

So you see, this fiftieth anniversary, commemoration, has more properly justified the American word for commemoration: 'memorializing'. We're sorrier for more millions than we're happy for.

And now, the act of commemoration itself is being performed. Where? Amazingly, in Moscow, in the building where Stalin's man, Molotov, signed the treacherous pact with Hitler's man, Ribbentrop, that brought on all this woe and the devastation of Europe. There's one, only one, anniversary I now look forward to, one to *celebrate*. I hope I'm here for it: 5 June 1997, the fiftieth anniversary of another spring morning when General George Marshall, on the initiative of his successor, Dean Acheson, announced the breathtaking American plan to invest $17 billion in Europe, to do what Dean Acheson said it was meant to do, and which it did: 'to repair the fabric of European life'.

O.J.—the Verdict

6 October 1995

The Congress suspended business for fifteen minutes, airlines delayed flights, bank tellers stopped counting bills, empty streets were remarked on in the big cities across the country, as, just before ten in the morning in California, and 1 p.m. in New York, the television commentators started what one called 'the countdown' which was—this time—not a word clocking the launching of John Glenn's capsule through 81,000 miles, as thirty-three years ago, but the calling off of the minutes as they ticked away towards the verdict in the case of 'The People of California vs. O. J. Simpson', not so long ago a folk hero, sometime actor, the greatest running back in the history of American football. But, from the moment of his arrest almost sixteen months ago, the Los Angeles District Attorney's office, the prosecutor, chose rather to cast him as an American Othello, a man whipped by jealousy to the point of murdering the woman he loved not wisely but too well.

In the beginning, in June 1994 (seven months before the trial began), everything we heard that might be evidence in the trial ran against O. J. Simpson. Quite simply, here is an outline of the undisputed plot. After midnight of Sunday, 12 June 1994, Mrs Simpson was found savagely slaughtered with many stab wounds, outside her house in a posh section of Los Angeles. By her side was a young man, a waiter who had come to return some

177

eyeglasses Mrs Simpson's mother had left, the evening before, at his restaurant. About an hour before, a chauffeur had picked up Mr Simpson at *his* house (the Simpsons were separated) and driven him to the airport to keep a long-planned business date in Chicago. Of course, he flew back shortly after he arrived at the Chicago hotel. After the funeral, police charged him with the double murder. He agreed to turn himself in, but instead he disappeared, leaving behind a sad, rambling letter protesting his innocence, conceding he had had a good life, and saying goodbye. The police eventually tracked him in a white car speeding at a great rate along one of the Los Angeles highways. A friend who was driving him reported over a cellular phone that Simpson was holding a gun to his head and threatening suicide. The car followed a roundabout course and at last went back to Mr Simpson's home, where he stayed slumped in the car for an hour before police managed to coax him out. He was taken into custody and two days later pleaded not guilty and was held without bail.

The trial was set on the docket for late in the year, but it took for ever to choose a jury, and various other niceties of the California criminal code had to be observed (remember, this was not a federal trial)—a code that is in some ways more stringent than most, and stuffed with precedents which counsel are quick to cite on very fragile pretexts. (This meant, in the long run, that the trial itself would have a very long run.) Finally, in the middle of January this year, it started, and ended nine months later, by which time the court had lost ten jurors in all, through sickness, minor misbehaviour of some sort, admitted prejudice; one

In the studio, 1970s. AC was always relieved and relaxed once the recording was completed.

AC and President Eisenhower share a light moment during the
filming of 'General Eisenhower on the Military Churchill' at
Eisenhower's Gettysburg, Pennsylvania, home, August 1967.

AC on the dais with Attorney General Robert Kennedy speaking,
at a luncheon meeting of members of Congress in New York City,
February 1968.

Adlai Stevenson's 54th birthday: Stevenson receiving a cake
from the New Yorker book critic Clifton Fadiman, with AC on the right.

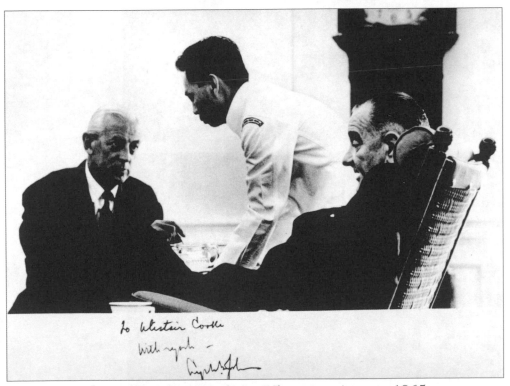

AC interviewing LBJ about Vietnam, August 1965,
photograph signed and dedicated to AC by LBJ.

AC at his
favourite 'twilight'
time of day –
when conversation
and whisky flowed.
Here, in his study
at 1150 Fifth
Avenue, in 1972.

AC putting in the long gallery at 1150 Fifth Avenue, where numerous carpets were replaced over the years owing to divots.

AC left the apartment, crossed Fifth Avenue and practised his swing in Central Park regardless of the time of year.

AC chipping out of a bunker at Island's End Golf & Country Club, Inc.

AC after a round with Bing Crosby and Robert Cameron (aerial photographer), June 1973.

On the roof of 1150 Fifth Avenue, overlooking the reservoir
– the view he saw from his desk every day. 1972.

In the living room of 1150 Fifth Avenue, adjacent
to a window providing the same parkside view. 1972.

Portrait by long-time friend Roddy McDowall, who captured AC as only a good friend could. This picture remains one of Jane's and Susie's favourites.

or two, I feel fairly certain, hadn't thought too deeply about the meaning of sequestration, and under whatever pretext, were silently crying, 'Let me out of here.'

Sequestration! In California, a judge may, and in this case did, order the jury's exile from normal life to a degree that a dictator held under house arrest would very likely protest before the International Court of Justice. The jury, after interminable challenges, queries and manufactured indignation from both sides, and subsequent excuses or dismissals, consisted of nine blacks, two whites and one Latino. They, along with the originals, had been told the trial might last three or four months. They must brace themselves to obey the rules. They would be sequestered in a hotel, separated from the other guests. They would be led to their meals. They were not allowed to read newspapers or magazines, listen to radio, or watch television. Movies were chosen for them, which they saw together. The married were from time to time allowed conjugal visits.

When at last the jury began their deliberations, at 9 o'clock last Monday morning, the commentators —shoals of them, mostly lawyers, legal scholars, former prosecutors, notable defence attorneys and so on—settled down to speculate and guess at the verdict. The overwhelming consensus was that the jury would take a week or two to declare itself a hung jury. Suddenly, in the middle of the day the word went to the judge: we have reached a verdict. That was a stunner for everybody. But the judge said the secret would remain sealed overnight.

This gave us all time to guess now what evidence had been decisive. The DNA analysis of the bloodstains? Although this excruciatingly complex stuff (which possibly a few hundred people alive understand) took four days to explain to the jury, my own sense was that, in general, juries distrust medical expertise, especially when there are conflicting theories, and that this jury might well have believed the defence's contention that the Los Angeles Police Department had been sloppy in analysing the blood samples, might have contaminated them.

The prosecution's main case was that Mr Simpson was the only villain, a known wife-beater who, once he knew for certain that he had lost her, and she was living her own life, couldn't bear the loss of his control over her. One June night, he went berserk, left his house, drove off to her house, murdered her and Mr Goldman, drove home, changed, buried or hid the clothes and the weapon, took a shower, dressed and packed for Chicago. (The defence said, by the way, that by the prosecution's estimate of time, he would have had to do all that in five minutes.) But the chauffeur had to wait forty-one minutes for him, and when he appeared, he said he'd overslept and had to take a shower. The prosecution maintained that nobody saw Simpson for over an hour, and he had ample time to commit the murders.

Since there were no witnesses, both sides had to stress the physical evidence, of which there were two items all agreed were crucial. One was a bloody glove, the other a bloody sock, both found by the police in Simpson's home. It was not disputed that the rescued droplets belonged to nobody in the world but Mr Simpson. And that, for the prosecution, was conclusive proof of his guilt.

But the defence lawyers touched the nerve of all doubt when they asked who found the glove, and when. The answer was, one Mark Fuhrman, a detective who, without a warrant, climbed over the fence to Simpson's home and later produced the glove, the blood still moist seven hours after Mr Simpson dropped it, if he did (a chemical impossibility, two doctors testified). And why did it take two months for the bloody sock to appear, after two months of exhaustive search of houses, gates, grass, cars, furniture, everything? The defence contention, which seemed very melodramatic when it was first launched, was that this same Fuhrman was a racist who chose, with one other detective, to frame Mr Simpson and actually planted the glove and smeared the sock. Mr Fuhrman was challenged on the stand as to his reputation as a racist. He denied any hint of it. In ten years he had never used the word 'nigger'. I must say he sounded plausible at the time, and the prosecution ridiculed the whole macabre nonsense of a conspiracy contrived by two or more of the Los Angeles Police Department which we should not forget—the jury didn't—has had an unsavoury reputation over many years for its powerful minority of race-hating cops.

Alas for the prosecution's ridicule. In a turn that marked the collapse of their case, a screenwriter was found who had, over three years, recorded many hours of taped interviews with Detective Fuhrman, in which he used 'nigger' forty-three times, in which he told of police initiatives in framing blacks. At one point he had wished all the blacks in America could be piled up and burned. (It seems to me very naive to say that these disclosures from a foul-mouthed bigot would not deeply affect a jury with nine black members, however high-minded their final discussion.) Off in retirement in the mountains of Idaho, former Detective Fuhrman was quoted as saying, 'If I go down, the case goes down.' And so it was.

All our analysing and judgements made in retrospect were swept away by the one item of evidence (out of 45,000 pages of it) that the jury had asked to be read over. It was the testimony of the chauffeur, who picked up Mr Simpson and drove him to the airport. It came out that in the first two minutes of their gathering, they voted 10 to 2 for acquittal. But they decided to take Ms Clark, the chief prosecutor, at her word, that the nub, the root, of the evidence was the time-line: the jury's decision whether or not Simpson had time to drive to Mrs Simpson's home, perform the double murder, get home, clean up, hide the clothes and the weapon, shower, dress and be ready for the waiting chauffeur.

The jury trooped back. They heard the chauffeur's testimony. He got the time of arrival at Simpson's house wrong by an hour, but corrected himself. He didn't see O.J.'s car (because the prosecution held he had not yet driven it back). The jury cut off the rest of the chauffeur's testimony. They had heard enough. They went back and reached a not-guilty verdict within the hour.

There is a point that worried some of us from the start who were inclined to believe in Simpson's guilt. It is the ferocity of the murder, calculated by both sides to have taken more than ten minutes: thirty-two stab wounds in Mr Goldman (did he put up a fight?) and Mrs Simpson practically decapitated. Yet Simpson revealed after his arrest not a bruise or a blemish on his body. And no blood on anything he subsequently wore. Altogether, the incriminating blood evidence was very sparse—the jury thought sparse enough to have been planted.

When the verdict was announced, and had travelled in seconds the length and breadth of the country, there was great and thunderous rejoicing among blacks everywhere, from the most famous black university to the seediest inner-city slum. There is one consolation for the people who think justice was denied. There were no riots, anywhere.

The Old Rocking Chair

3 May 1996

Early on a fine June morning, under a blue, blue sky, we took off from Point Mogu, a Coast Guard base in Southern California, and we clattered off in a small fleet of helicopters out on to the huge, sail-less Pacific. 'We' were the travelling White House press corps, which in those days consisted of no more than, say, fifteen or twenty correspondents, plus yours truly—the only foreign correspondent present. Not more than ten miles offshore, there loomed up a monster of a ship with a flat top comprising, it seemed, several football fields. It was the aircraft carrier, the USS *Kitty Hawk*.

We were to see a performance of missile-firing, both by day and by night, from the *Kitty Hawk*'s

183

yawning deck, an event that had been postponed, for one official reason and another. But now the Navy was ready, and the President, who had flown on ahead of us, was ready. And the day was perfection. What we were to see was how missiles from the carrier's deck swooshed at impossible speed off to the horizon to pinpoint drag targets— large, flying red banners (which looked to us no bigger than handkerchiefs). They were red to imply that they were Soviet targets. The daytime performance was brilliant indeed. Enormous, sleek missiles whooshed up from below. They were Phantoms, so called, and they skimmed across the bow and were lost to sight in a matter of seconds. Then, coming up on elevators like a sudden plague of wasps, was a fleet of little, manned jets, a hundred or more of them. They unfolded their wings and whizzed off over the blue water till they were recalled and came hurtling back at a hundred and fifty miles an hour to be retrieved with a jolt by their arresting cables.

But, for beauty and theatrical impressiveness, nothing could compare with the night show: the great ship immovable in this most motionless of oceans; the last, long, red streaks of the sun dissolving into the horizon; and the coming on of an eerie sort of darkness, an encompassing purple twilight; and a long silence, suddenly punctured by horns and buzzing sounds, punched up by coordinators on an immense console winking in several colours in the darkness of the upper bridge. What I was doing there will appear in good time. In response to these winking orders, small armies of figures in phosphorescent uniforms came running and advancing and retreating across the deck down

184

below, like bright clockwork toys. At intervals, there was a deep rumble, as of underground steam pressure, and a huge missile exploded out of the ship's belly, rose like a flying submarine, and could just be seen in pursuit of an illuminated flying target far away. There was a faint, tiny explosion, the target fell like a shot bird, the missile vanished like an expiring cinder, and we all clapped. We had hit the Soviet target! We hit all the targets that night (of course) and the President was well pleased.

Before the show started, we had been the guests of the officers at dinner, in an underground dining room about twice the size of the *Queen Mary*'s. Then we were led along many decks and corridors toward a lower bridge, where, we were told, we should have a privileged view of things. The most privileged view of all, of course, would be given to the President alone, sitting with the admiral on the topmost bridge. As the reporters were pattering on our way I felt a smart slap on my shoulder, an affectionate oath spoken from behind, and lo!—a friend from the very beginning of America's war in the Pacific, a young officer I'd known and had merry evenings with back in February 1942 when I was assigned as a correspondent to San Francisco, the Seventh Naval District, and, most secret, never to be written about, the Net, the underwater net across San Francisco Bay. The young officer had broadened and grizzled slightly (hadn't we all?) and was now vice admiral of the Pacific fleet. With a quick pull on my arm, he said, 'You don't want to go up there. Follow me!' We snaked up a narrow, winding stairway, came to a small door, knocked three times, and there appeared a junior officer with what Britons call a torch, and Americans, less frighteningly, a flashlight. He cupped it with one hand, so it would not disturb the surrounding blackness of the enclosed bridge. As we ducked in and crept into the only two seats in this tiny room, half of which was a semicircle of the console, there was one silhouetted figure that was as still and sharp as a cut-out—the back of the man's head resting against the high back of a most extraordinary chair to be in this tiny cockpit. It was a rocking chair, and the head was, of course, the head of President John F. Kennedy.

Later, I asked my old friend about it. I'd thought I knew everything about the physical condition of President Kennedy, and how much of it was, by an unspoken agreement in those days, kept secret. I recalled the brief uproar during the primary campaign, when Senator Lyndon Johnson was running against Kennedy, and the Johnson team put out the scurrilous news that Senator Kennedy had Addison's disease (so he had) which explained the yellowish pigment in his skin sometimes. He also occasionally appeared to have a hump (known, I discovered later, as a cortisone hump). We noticed these things at the time as, simply, on and off days of a very busy public man. Anyway, there was then a code, unwritten, never brought up, which would have made it tasteless to mention such things. As for Kennedy and Lyndon Johnson's foul accusation, the Kennedy camp promptly denied it, and no more was said.

So, as I say, after the brilliant and sombre missile show that June night in 1963 in the Pacific, I asked my old sailor friend, 'How about the rocking chair, where did you get it?' 'Oh,' he said, 'it's his, nobody else's. They fly it everywhere. Seems he has to have it. He can't walk for too long without either taking a bath or going to work in the rocking chair.' More than a year later when I was making a memorial album about President Kennedy, compiling many recorded interviews with every sort of person who'd known him, I mentioned to Mrs Kennedy that when he didn't have that slightly waxy complexion he always looked as if he'd just emerged from a hot bath. She said, 'So he had. He took them all the time. It was the only place, the only time he didn't feel the pain in his back.' (That was from his naval war wound.)

You can see now why the most vivid memory of that memorable night on the *Kitty Hawk* was not the magic of the soaring missiles, leaping like dolphins at play in the apocalypse, but—that rocking chair. First, it made me realize how drastically the conventions, you might almost say the courtesies, of reporting have changed in thirty years; some might say deteriorated. The first hint I had of a new—not a new convention but you might say a new feeling—a completely new emotion among a new generation of reporters, was in 1958, just five years before that night with Kennedy in the Pacific. There had been, I recall, a long debate in the United Nations Security Council. Mr John Foster Dulles, who was Eisenhower's Secretary of State, long after midnight finished a speech and went off home. He didn't go home. He went straight to a hospital. Within a day or two, there appeared as a banner headline, on the front page of the *New York Daily News* (a tabloid but then a good and responsible one): 'Dulles Has Inoperable Cancer.' I wrote for my paper next day, 'No

187

mention has been made in this country about the unique break with tradition implicit in the publication last Sunday of his doctor's bulletin.' We had come a long way since the case of President Grover Cleveland, more than a century ago, who woke up one morning with a sore throat which persisted. One of his doctors, smarter than the rest, correctly diagnosed cancer of the throat. So one day the Presidential yacht was commissioned for a weekend cruise. They went out to sea, the cancer was operated on, the President returned, convalesced for some days, a week or more in the White House. There were no press conferences in those days. He never had to see anyone he didn't choose to see. Nothing was put out, nothing was, in fact, known. About thirty years after he'd died, it came out.

And then in our own time, there is what I'm now told is the even more unbelievable press silence about Franklin Roosevelt. It is true that (I should guess) throughout thirteen years, 95 per cent of the American people never thought that their President was paralysed from the waist down. Maybe 60 per cent would have said they knew, if they'd been reminded that, way back in his fortieth year, when he was Governor of New York, he had had poliomyelitis. But what the people of every nation saw throughout his unprecedented long reign was the strong upper body, the bull-like stance, the hands gripping a lectern, the confident, inimitable tenor voice rousing and consoling the people. Nothing was ever said or written (and all photography was banned) of his being lifted into a chair, the wheelchair he lived his life in, the daily ordeal of simply getting out of bed. I think it was an admirable convention the press observed. Today, it would be thought an outrageous suppression of free speech.

And, last week, we saw that Kennedy rocking chair on the stage of an auction house in New York, not in a museum: an artefact of a President, and a time, and an affliction. Its historical value is beyond price. Its value at auction was—$453,000. Responding to this and other monstrous bids, an auctioneer's representative said: 'Well, they are buying pieces of history.' Not so; this audience were buying a faded vision, the myth of the first Presidency to be cast in Hollywood—the handsome, war-hero President, and the beautiful, delicate, elegant wife. Somebody called it Camelot —which is not history but myth. And people paid dearly to recover some symbols of the myth, and pretend it was a historical fact.

Silver Watergate

20 June 1997

Americans seems to be celebrating, or at least recalling, more anniversaries than anybody these days. And I think it must have much to do with the never-ending increase in television channels, and the constant problem of filling them with programmes throughout the day. Most stations, like most newspapers, employ somebody to consult every day one of those big books like the *Time Tables of History*, which record in parallel columns what was happening around the world in government, science, the arts, sport, literature, inventions, exploration, medicine and so on, from prehistory to Only Yesterday. But last Tuesday there fell an anniversary that all the networks seized on because they had whole libraries of tape, of film about it: the outstanding American scandal of our time, certainly the greatest constitutional crisis since the Civil War.

Like most viewers, I suppose, I hadn't noticed anything particularly significant about the date, 17 June 1997. It flashed on my retina with the opening shot of the evening news: a late-middle-aged man standing on aeroplane steps, swarthy, grinning, arms spreadeagled like a new dictator just arrived to a thunderous welcome. But this man wasn't coming. He was going. A student in his early twenties, watching, said, simply, the incredible sentence: 'Who *is* he?' He was Richard M. Nixon, the only President in American history to resign in disgrace. I suppose the young man might be forgiven. Tuesday was the twenty-fifth anniversary of the event that brought Mr Nixon down, a year or two before this young man was born. I myself at his age would have had a hard time recognizing General Botha, Britain's enemy in the Boer War, which had also happened—to me—in the very distant past, namely six years before I was born.

It occurred to me that since this otherwise bright young man didn't recognize the famous, the infamous, President Nixon, twenty-five years might also have dulled the memory of a lot of people who were alive and sentient at the time. The event was to be for ever known as Watergate; and this week many Americans dated their distrust in and cynicism about Washington and government itself from Watergate. So I think it's worth looking back and retelling as simply and clearly as possible the tale of the rather ridiculous burglary that began on 17 June 1972 and ended on 8 August 1974 with a heavily jowled and heavy-hearted Richard Nixon announcing over television that he was resigning the Presidency there and then, that his rather astonished Vice President, Mr Gerald Ford, would be sworn in next day, and he would fly home, once and for all, to California.

Two o'clock on a hot morning, then, in Washington. In June, at a large apartment complex known as the Watergate Building, a guard was making his nightly rounds. As he passed by the offices of the Democratic National Committee, he noticed a tape on the lock of their door. He thought this odd and he smelled a rat, five rats. He called the police and they hotfooted it over and caught, inside the Democrats' office, five men, two of them Cubans. They had cameras and electronic gear for bugging telephones. It looked like—it was—a clumsy attempt to bug the Democrats' phones.

It drew only comical attention in the papers, but naturally the press guessed that the raid must have been staged by the Republicans, maybe by enthusiastic Nixon fans. It was a Presidential year, and the campaign was hotting up. Next day, Wednesday, the White House announced that the burglars were 'operating neither on our behalf nor with our consent'. That word came from Mr Nixon's re-election campaign manager, his Attorney General, later a convicted felon sent to jail. For a week or two, facetious references continued to be made about what the papers called

191

'the Watergate caper'. Then the silly story was forgotten, but not by two reporters on the *Washington Post*, later to become nationally if not world-famous as a brilliant investigative team; two reporters in their late twenties, Woodward and Bernstein. After about six weeks of mooching around, digging into lots of apparently irrelevant documents, reports, memoranda, and interviewing all sorts of people (they worked on an average about sixteen hours a day), on 1 August they published a piece in their paper asserting that the Watergate break-in was not, as everybody had come to take for granted, a wild partisan escapade by a couple of loony Cubans and helpers who feared that, if Mr Nixon's Democratic opponent was elected in November, Fidel Castro and the Communists would take over the United States. The break-in, they said, was linked financially with a Committee to Re-elect the President, known later as CREEP—which of course, was a proper legitimate organization.

Political parties must report the source of their campaign contributions. But the Democrats, and the two reporters, discovered that $114,000 was missing from President Nixon's reported contributions. It was, the reporters said, the exact amount paid out by CREEP's finance chairman to—guess who?—the leader of the burglars' gang. They went on to reveal it as a down payment of what was meant to be a massive campaign of espionage and sabotage against the Democrats (and even against reporters secretly listed as 'Nixon enemies'). The day after the discovery of the secret fund, President Nixon denounced the *Washington Post* for 'mudslinging' and 'shabby journalism'. But

192

Woodward and Bernstein had picked up a scent which led from the break-in and the secret fund and the laundering of great sums of money in Miami and other places. And the trail led nearer and nearer to the President's men in the White House. By the spring of 1973, a former CIA official and several Republican Party officials had pleaded guilty, and co-conspirators in this whole plot and the President's two senior advisers (who by now must have known that Woodward and Bernstein had their number) decided to resign. We would hear much more from them at a special Senate investigating committee set up as the Woodward–Bernstein plot grew thicker and murkier. The chairman of that committee was a courtly old Southern lawyer (Senator Ervin) but his roguish charm did not soften his legal jabs or his curiosity in wondering 'What did the President know and when did he know it?' At one of these hearings, a minor White House official, testifying in answer to a question, said, 'Oh, that was all on the tapes'. The tapes? What tapes? Oh, didn't they know? The President secretly taped all and every conversation in his White House office. The Committee at first gasped and then rejoiced. They requested the tapes from the White House. Mr Nixon claimed 'executive privilege'. Senator Ervin retorted, 'Executive poppycock! I could send the Sergeant-at-Arms up to the White House, and say, with Shakespeare, what meat doth this Caesar eat that he grows so fat?' The Supreme Court ordered the tapes to be surrendered. First, a batch that Mr Nixon had edited. Then another batch, unedited. The tapes were an appalling revelation. Apart from showing up Mr Nixon as a remarkable practitioner

193

of foul language, there were masses of conversations about the secret fund, about first paying off the burglars so they wouldn't blow the whistle on the White House people involved.

But in all the thousands of discussions and private plotting and arguing about the whole smelly business, there was no single speech or confession from the President's own mouth that he had known about the raid early on and tried to cover up the consequences. By the spring of 1974, the Watergate scandal had grown so serious and Mr Nixon's part in it so conspicuous, if still not specific, that the House Judiciary Committee met to consider Articles of Impeachment against him. At the beginning of August 1974 Mr Nixon was forced by the Supreme Court to release one last, very early, tape. There, as gross as a manacle, was the missing link: the President himself telling an aide to get busy at once and stop the CIA and FBI from investigating the break-in. That sentence was spoken only six days after the break-in itself. It showed that Nixon had known all along, had relentlessly covered up, and lied steadily and unblinkingly to the Congress, the press, the people, for two years. The Committee voted for his impeachment, mainly on the charge of obstruction of justice. On 8 August, he resigned, rather than stand trial before the Senate.

Looking back on it now, through all the tortuous complexity of the conspiracy, I believe there were two fateful moments fatal for the conspirators. One was the moment the Watergate guard saw the Democratic National Committee office's door-lock taped. The other was the offhand remark of that minor White House official that the President

194

taped everything talked about in his office—and forgot to turn off the machine! The guard's name was Frank Kelly. The White House official was one Alexander Butterfield. Kelly and Butterfield will have their names permanently inscribed as footnotes to the historical record.

The only other consequence of the whole business that strikes me as having had a lasting influence on journalism is the fame of Woodward and Bernstein. They were pioneers of investigative reporting: diligent, serious and extremely careful. Unfortunately, they have inspired a whole generation of reporters in the English-speaking countries who take very little interest in the movers and shakers of their time, but are brought up on the idea that unveiling a personal (preferably a sexual) scandal is the whole purpose of good journalism. It's true, and it's awful.

The End of Civilization

25 July 1997

I don't know which cliché to avoid and which to fall back upon. The end of an era, shopworn for centuries. During the Second War, we used to be told: 'If we don't fight Hitler, it will be the end of civilization as we know it.' Well, last Friday the bell tolled, and it sounded the end of civilization as I, and I'm sure many of you, came to know it. In a simple, brutal phrase: last Friday, F. W. Woolworth's announced it was closing down all its four hundred stores in the United States. Whether

195

the paralysis is to spread to Europe, it didn't say.

For once, some older people may be shocked to notice, I am able to use a trade name without the risk of a scolding from the powers above. To younger people that sentence will probably be double Dutch. But I went into journalism when— and for many years thereafter—it was forbidden to use a trade name in an ordinary descriptive piece, either in your newspaper (if it was a serious paper and not a rag) or, over the air—when the BBC *was* the air. An example or two. Once, I covered the very rare event of a cricket match got up between Yale and Harvard. There were three spectators in a field till there bounced on to the scene, just to show that some corner of a foreign field is for ever England, a parson carrying (it was a chilly day) a thermos. It never crossed my mind that in the very upright (in those days) *Manchester Guardian*, you could not outrage the readers by writing a trade name. I frankly had forgotten, if I ever knew, that 'thermos' was one. The alert A. P. Wadsworth, an editor never to be caught napping, saw that it was changed. In the published piece, what the parson was carrying was a 'vacuumatic container'. I must say, my sentence sort of lost its swing. Another time, I innocently wrote that someone applied for some good reason, a smear of 'Vaseline'. Old A.P. was again on the alert. What the man smeared, in print, was a dollop of 'petroleum jelly'.

Happily, for some of us, that austere custom has died. Anyway, I would not be able to do this talk at all if I were forbidden to use trade names. So, again, I remark to everybody over, say, 45, 'the bell tolls and it tolls for thee'. No more Woolworth's!

They are closing those ancient, incomparable

196

discount stores for the most obvious reason: they've been losing money for years. Last year, they reported an operating loss of $37 million. Anyway, one hundred and seventeen years was a long life for any institution, and, considering the revolution that's happened to the business of making and marketing household necessities, it's astounding that Woolworth's survived so long: during a half-century in which discount stores were absorbed by larger chains, by shopping malls, by huge stores built not in town, since an actual majority of the population ceased to live in cities, but on the highways close to thriving suburbs. The same thing happened even to Woolworth's bigger competitors, not to mention what one writer memorably dubs as 'hundreds of local chains that have faded into the collective memory of a nation warmly nostalgic for old stores but not willing to shop in them any more'.

However, this is not to be a nostalgic piece. It's to recall a special American impulse of which Woolworth's was a prime example. Let's recall something of the world in the year that Woolworth and several other bright boys started something new in 1879! I'm skipping, if you'll excuse me, the enormous events recorded by all historians: like the war between Chile and Bolivia; the founding of the Irish Land League to campaign for independence from Britain; the founding of Christian Science; the collapse of the Firth of Tay bridge in a winter storm. I'm thinking of America only, and of smaller things that would have a bigger influence on more people everywhere.

In 1879 a Scottish-American immigrant, Robert Gair, a paper-bag maker, invented a machine to produce cheap cardboard cartons already cut and creased and folded. It raised Robert Gair's normal production of 50 paper bags an hour to 7,500 cartons.

A saloon keeper in Dayton, Ohio, Jake Ritty, took a sea voyage for his health, noticed a device on the steamship that recorded the revolutions of the propeller, and so gave an accurate daily record of the ship's speed. Hmm, he thought, it gave him an idea. He patented it as 'Ritty's Incomparable Cashier', the first cash register to keep a cumulative record of the day's transactions which later elevated a plate so both the clerk and the customer could see the figure.

An early electrical engineer thought the telephone shouldn't remain a company luxury. A company switchboard: that would do it, first in New Haven, Connecticut. It would make the telephone available to small stores, to families, perhaps soon to everybody. In 1879 there were fifty thousand American telephones; by 1890, a quarter of a million. Also in 1879, in Brooklyn, New York, a dairy company delivered milk in bottles instead of measuring it from barrels into housewives' jugs. Wow! It took thirty years for the practice to start in England. In December, one Thomas Edison announced he had invented a light bulb that would burn for one thousand hours. To the jeers of the gas lighting experts and the intelligentsia, he said electric lighting would become so cheap that only the rich would be able to afford candles.

And in 1879, in a small town in upstate New York, a shop assistant, 27, urged his boss to install a single counter, at which all the goods were to be priced at five cents each. To pacify this lunatic, the shopkeeper agreed. Then this young Frank Woolworth borrowed from a businessman the vast sum of $400. He opened his own store, in which everything was priced at five cents. His store failed. But the same lender liked Frank's courage and staked him a store in a Pennsylvania small town which would, however, have two divisions of goods: one at five cents, another at ten cents. It was the first of its kind. It worked. Young Mr Woolworth had one ambition: to build a chain of stores where poor and working people could find open-shelf self-service, and everything to buy for a nickel or a dime. It came to be called the Five and Ten. It started with a five-cent fire shovel, and went on to egg-whisks, pie-plates, moustache cups, puzzles, clothes, locks, keys, galoshes, a soda fountain, chirping household pets, full meals, everything. In 1913 Frank built the world's tallest building, sixty storeys high. He died in 1919, leaving over a thousand Woolworth's stores in the United States and hundreds more in other countries. He thought, as everybody did, it would go on for ever.

What these half-dozen men had in common was not merely an inventive spirit. What I called a common 'impulse' was the idea of enlarging the possessions that working people could afford. The thirty-five years after the end of the Civil War, that's to say from 1865 to 1900, were the golden time of American inventiveness. Half a million patents were granted. But it's true to say that many if not most of them, successful or not, were attempts to do something that half a century later was best summed up in a sentence by a poor boy from Indiana who ran for President, and lost, against Roosevelt, Wendell Willkie. 'It is the destiny of America', he said, 'to turn the luxuries of the rich into conveniences for the many.' So, George Eastman didn't want to invent a camera that would make the Germans envious. He wanted to make a cheap, family camera, and did it; and everywhere, in many languages, it was known as Ein Kodak. There was Singer's cheap, home sewing machine. The typewriter was so tricky and impersonal. Authors thought it took the soul out of writing. It took fifty years, after it was invented, to catch on.

It's worth remarking that most of these—what you might call popular inventors—were originally poor. A one-room schoolhouse, or none. Edison's total education was three months in an elementary school. They knew in the flesh what it was like to lack the finer necessities, so there was a special pride in, as Woolworth put it, 'applying democracy to human needs and desires'. Automobiles were for the rich. Is that so? Henry Ford invented the assembly line and made the first *volkswagens*— cheap cars for everybody. An American clockmaker was just as appreciative as you are of the delicate workmanship of a Swiss watch. But what he wanted to do was to make a *dollar* watch. 'But does it work?' facetious Europeans would ask. It did. Just as today, hearing that most Americans can tap, on cable, sixty or seventy television channels, 'But is there anything you can watch on them, tee hee?' The answer is yes; in my case, I tap over forty channels and wish I had more than five hours every evening to give over to the magic tube. Hotels were for the rich. So, how about motor courts, later motels? Same with paper and napkins and, with half the workforce now women, frozen dinners, take-out food, etc., etc., etc.

So, what were first known as variety stores gave birth to Woolworth's and bigger chains still, and more mail-order catalogues offering more and cheaper goods than, if possible, the blessed Sears Roebuck catalogue, another casualty. And the deep freeze in every home eventually killed off the beloved soda fountain: you could make your own sundaes, parfaits, milk shakes. And now the huge shopping malls on the highway are beginning to tremble. Computer systems are leading at a breathless rate to computer shopping. Soon, tedious grandfathers will bore their kin with tearful memories of the days when they got in the car and drove off to the supermarket in the shopping mall on Highway 58.

In the meantime, there is no pause in the unstoppable movement to, as Woolworth said, 'apply democracy to people's desires'. This is a prospect that doesn't alarm me, for one. What I have called the American impulse lifted more millions out of a threadbare living, and gave them a better material life than all the generations before them. So, on the demise of a famous business, I say, let's hear it for Frank W. Woolworth and Robert Gair and Jack Ritty and George Eastman— and remember what the teacher said: 'Never forget, children, that if it hadn't been for Thomas Edison, you'd be watching television by candlelight.'

The Kennedy Missile Tapes

24 October 1997

Thirty-five years ago this Sunday, 26 October, I woke up here in New York City, and looked out of the window at a sparkling and, I felt then, a god-given scene. A dazzling, crystalline day in late fall, looking over Central Park's forest of light green, yellow-golden foliage to the West Side skyline and, above it, a cloudless sky. The forest ends down to the left, and gives way to a large blue lake, a city reservoir. And, on that shining morning, a seagull came winging in from the ocean and soared high over the reservoir and the park and was gone off to the northern horizon to tell its marvellous story. Did I say a seagull? Of course, but for a happy split second it seemed to be a dove, to announce the blessed tidings: that we had overnight emerged unscathed from a prospect which, the previous night, the President of the United States thought would be avoided only by the mercy of God, or what we call Luck: the prospect, in a day or two, of a nuclear war.

Even people—temperamental scaremongers and bloodshot journalists—who are given to the most lurid view of any event may recoil, I think, at such a grandiose sentence. But we have only now become privy to the taped private discussions of President Kennedy and his advisers, and the desperate communications with the Soviet leader Khrushchev. I'm sure that blood-chilling sentence is nothing but the truth. I say 'only now' made privy, because there has just been published, for all to read, the transcript of the tapes recorded in the White House of the two weeks of discussion between President Kennedy and his advisers on what to do about the alarming discovery by American reconnaissance planes of nuclear missile bases and launching sites in Cuba that could have been planted there only by the Soviet Union.

Some listeners may still be reeling in disbelief at the simple mention of 'the Kennedy Tapes'. Wasn't it Mr Nixon who taped conversations in the White House, a record that eventually proved he had covered up the Watergate scandal and bribed participants to stay mum about it? Yes, but lately it turns out other Presidents taped conversations with cronies and visitors and only *they* knew they were doing it. Lyndon Johnson's most private thoughts and pep talks are now available. We hear that Franklin Roosevelt had a crude taping system, entirely at the touch of his own inclination. And only last week, President Clinton released tapes—videotapes, talking pictures, no less—of meetings with foreigners and one or two shady characters, many of whom gave large sums of money to the Democratic Party.

It's enough to make you, in retrospect, feel actually sympathetic towards President Nixon. His big mistake, not made by his predecessors or successors, was that he forgot to turn the machine off. The way our experience of Presidential shenanigans is going, it may soon be that the big act of 'obstruction of justice' (a ground for impeachment) will be turning off the tape recorder in the White House. I ought to say, after these disheartening revelations, that President

203

Truman didn't make secret recordings. Neither did Eisenhower. And a former Clinton aide who is now free to feel relieved, said chucklingly the other Sunday, 'Nobody in the White House today dare scribble a date in his appointment book, let alone write a memo.'

But you'll have guessed that, in this unexpected and unpredicted flood of Presidential tapes, the now-released 'Kennedy Tapes' (the two weeks of secret talks in the White House between Monday, 15 October and Saturday, 27 October) are at once the most historic and most blood-curdling. For they record an event that has been called, without melodrama or exaggeration, 'the single most dangerous episode in the history of mankind'.

It began for me on—I can't swear to the date but it must have been—the Saturday before Monday, 15 October 1962, in an aeroplane: the press plane that goes on ahead of the Presidential plane, wherever he's off to. He was going off to Chicago to give a needed lift to a Democratic Senator, I believe, who was up for re-election in a few days' time. Nineteen sixty-two was what they call an 'off year'—not a Presidential but a Congressional election year. We were winging along when suddenly there came striding in from the cockpit the President's press secretary, Pierre Salinger. He had serious news for us. He had just been in radio touch with the President's plane. The President was showing symptoms of the flu, and we were all going to turn around and go back to Washington.

I don't know how many days we, the press, enquired about the flu or how soon we came to know better. But we now know—it must have been while the President was heading west to Chicago—

204

that he heard from the CIA the thundering news that an army reconnaissance plane had taken pictures over Cuba, that the pictures had been developed, and, clear as a flower petal, were missiles and launch pads and all the paraphernalia of missile launching grounds.

On Monday the 15th Kennedy put together a committee of the Secretary of State, Secretary of Defense, Chairman of the Joint Chiefs of Staff, National Security advisers, and one or two other men who'd been close to the conduct of foreign affairs. That first meeting is the first recorded session of the two weeks' discussions about the developing crisis. And I ought to say now that the tapes were technically infinitely inferior to the Nixon tapes of a decade later: a low-pitched drone of hissing, crackling sounds, not to mention the overlapping voices that you get in any recorded conversation of a roomful of people. It took two Harvard professors more than a year, with the help of expert court reporters, to improve the sounds and make all but a fraction of the dialogue understandable.

At the start you may wonder why Mr Khrushchev was able to install such hugely visible technology without being spotted. At the time, the White House was absorbed, even obsessed, with the likelihood that the Soviets were going to seize Berlin, and Cuba was not being routinely patrolled by reconnaissance planes. Mr Khrushchev's mistake (it now appears) was not to know that American reconnaissance had got to the point where photographs taken from 30,000 feet could count the leaves on a tree. The Soviet ambassador was called in and assured the President to his face that whatever his planes saw, they could not be missiles or missile pads, since the Soviet Union was quite innocent of such a plot. President Kennedy didn't contradict him, just bowed out and went back to his committee meetings.

The problem of what to do with these installations was not complex. It was very stark and simple, and so were the responses the committee batted back and forth. From the start, there was no general agreement on a course of action, but in the beginning it was agreed that one of three things could be done: a sudden, unannounced air strike to 'take out' (destroy) the weapons; a wide aerial attack, covering airfields and storage areas; thirdly, to mount as soon as possible a full-scale invasion of Cuba.

Kennedy heard all alternatives, tapped his pencil, made only one positive assertion: 'We're certainly going to do number one, we're going to take out those missiles.' Through the next six days and nights, the discussions probed all the likely Soviet responses to any and all military action. To delay, or tip the Soviets off to a chosen form of action, would hasten their building work and probably make them move the missiles underground somewhere. To delay while making martial sounds in Khrushchev's direction might make him come out more defiantly in support of Fidel Castro, a position from which he could not then retreat. It took a week for a fourth alternative to grow and become one favoured by the President: a proclaimed naval blockade of Cuba—this too was ferociously debated. It's remarkable that the Senate's king of the doves (when later it came to Vietnam), Senator William Fulbright, was dead against the blockade because it would announce a direct confrontation with Khrushchev. Kennedy's brother called it a slow form of death. Fulbright, like the top military, was all for 'an all-out invasion'.

After the President announced the blockade over national television, everybody waited for Russian ships on the way to Cuba to turn back or risk attack. Khrushchev offered to remove the missiles if the United States would promise not to invade. Then he suggested removing the Cuban missiles in exchange for the American removal of allied missiles in Turkey. To do that, Kennedy thought, would invite the outrage of the NATO allies and perhaps mark the end of NATO itself. All this while, new photographs showed the Russians were hectically installing missiles. At the end of the second week Kennedy, having gone ahead with the blockade and secretly amassed in Florida an invasion force larger than anything since D-Day, called in the Congressional leaders of both parties and wearily told them not to expect a peaceful solution. 'If we stop one Russian ship, it means war. If we invade Cuba, it means war. There's no telling.' He went to bed on the Saturday night fairly convinced in his own mind that a war was imminent, and that it would begin with the Russians firing tactical nuclear weapons on Florida. He said goodnight to the committee, the machine was turned off, and he hoped he'd see them tomorrow. 'None of us might ever see each other. Now it's up to luck.'

At dawn, the marvellous news came in that the Russians' lead ship, the *Grozny*, had turned back from the blockade. That was the Sunday morning that, against a clear blue sky, the seagull flew in from the ocean looking like a dove.

The Evolution of the Grand Jury

31 July 1998

A few weeks ago, I realized that I had spoken a sentence that must have been totally incomprehensible to most listeners—in the United Kingdom, anyway. I don't know about India, Australia, New Zealand and other countries that inherit the tradition of the common law from England. What I'm saying is that it occurred to me, rather late in the day, that when I said, 'so far, in the case of the President and Miss Lewinsky, so far seventy witnesses have appeared before the grand jury', it's unlikely, to be polite, that one British listener in a hundred under the age of say, 85 or 90, has any precise idea what a grand jury is, since the institution was abandoned in the United Kingdom in 1913 and formally abolished in 1933.

I'd better start and say how the grand jury came about in England, centuries ago, how and why it was so eagerly taken up by colonial America, how in fact it was used as an opening wedge in the War of Independence, and how it has developed here since.

One of the greatest English lawyers called the grand jury 'the glory and the greatest invention of English law'. It took about four hundred years from its rude birth to turn into its modern form. Edward III was the inventor and 1368 the crucial date. He decided to choose twenty-four men in each of the English counties to form a board that would report on and watch out for crimes in the county: a sort of clearing house or detention centre for criminals who might then go to trial. From the beginning, it was an accusatory body. It took another three hundred years for the grand jury to perform the function it performs today. First in England, the grand jury turned into, usually, sixteen neighbours who knew the man accused of a crime. Judges, riding 'on circuit' coming into town, would collect the sixteen and say, 'John Doe is accused of stealing ten pounds. Is he the sort of man who might steal money?' The neighbours, men who knew him well, would say, 'Not the sort' or 'Well, perhaps'. They'd vote, and if a majority said 'Yes, possibly', then John Doe would go to trial. Otherwise, no case. This all sounds very simple and artless. But the grand jury was the first protection the citizen had against gossip, malicious charges, hearsay, political prosecutions.

Of course, the grand jury crossed the Atlantic with the first English settlers and took root in American law. It was greatly prized, especially by the colonists who were growing more and more outraged by the arbitrary behaviour of the king's ministers here. It was the Governor of each colony (or his underlings) who charged people with crimes and mounted prosecutions in the king's name. There came a time, about forty-odd years before the Revolution broke out, when one grand jury had the nerve to refuse to accept the charges brought against an editor by the king's prosecutor. And thereafter the rebellious colonials used the grand jury as an instrument of resistance to the over-reaching authority of the English governors. A twentieth-century American judge called the grand jury, in retrospect, 'the first arm of democratic self-government'. And the blessing of this protection was not forgotten when they came to write the Constitution, or rather the Amendments called the Bill of Rights. The Fifth says, 'no person shall be held to answer for a capital or otherwise infamous crime, unless on a presentment of indictment by a grand jury'.

By now, in all federal courts, the grand jury is compulsory, but only about half the states stick with the system as a preliminary hearing. The other states authorize a magistrate, which, inevitably, brings us to England, what happened there, and why it fell into disuse and was abolished. If there is one man who was more responsible than another for killing off the grand jury, it was a young Lancastrian—a Liverpudlian, son of an army sergeant major—who got a scholarship to Oxford, dazzled every examiner he ran into, became a devastatingly brilliant, witty and arrogant barrister, and at the age of 46 became Lord Chancellor: F. E. 'Freddy' Smith, subsequently the first Earl of Birkenhead.

He it was who mounted the case against the grand jury in its present form and wrote a devastating attack on it. First, he said, since grand juries were recruited from people on the voting registers, it was preposterous in a city of seven million to keep up the pretence that the chosen jurors would know the man well enough to say if he was likely to have committed a crime. Next, an institution which had been the protector of the liberties of an accused person was now a prosecutor's weapon with which to beat a jury into the conviction that the accused was guilty before he could be tried. Today, in America, this is truer than ever. The public prosecutor (the District Attorney, or in our present crisis, the special prosecutor) can come before the grand jury with a team of lawyers (which Mr Starr has done) and call all the prosecution witnesses he wants, which he has done. Mr Starr has already had over seventy accusers of President Clinton appear. But the accused is not permitted a lawyer or any witnesses. Birkenhead maintained, with his own savagely wounding sarcasm, that this protector of a citizen's liberty began the protective process by recruiting every accuser, every gossip-monger, every hearsay miscreant (to this day, hearsay is allowed), to trap the accused in a machinery of guilt and then invite him to wriggle his way out. In other words, it's become a preliminary trial in which the accused is to be proved guilty before he has a legal chance to prove himself innocent.

Birkenhead wound up by saying that the grand jury system, once the genuine guardian of a citizen's innocence, had turned into an inquisition —the creature of the prosecutor—which was authoritarian, undemocratic and a monstrous anachronism. His argument was so compelling that the grand jury was, to everybody's relief, formally abolished in 1933. Better leave it, the consensus became, to a magistrate or a tribunal of magistrates, with their knowledge of the law and of human beings. They might be, some of them, blinkered, but they would, on the whole, do better at deciding whether an accused man ought to go to trial.

To this day, in America, all that a grand jury is meant to do is to decide if there is a case, if the accused ought to be tried. Yet I assure you I've been saddened down the years to discover how many Americans, and I'm thinking of educated people as well as illiterates, see a headline in the paper: 'John Doe Indicted For Fraud', and at once register the emotion that John Doe has been found halfway guilty, as if a grand jury indictment was a preliminary trial.

The thing which sticks in the throat of libertarians is the curious old fact that the accused is not allowed a lawyer or any witnesses. So, this brings us to the serious, possibly dire, condition in which, suddenly, the President finds himself. Mr Starr, the special prosecutor, had the gall, or the courage, to issue a subpoena on the President to appear before the grand jury that has been looking (till it's almost blind) into the relations between Miss Monica Lewinsky and the President.

This act, of subpoenaing the President, happened only once before, way back when a man was being tried for treason. Thomas Jefferson was subpoenaed. He didn't appear but he delivered relevant documents, as did Nixon. Other Presidents —Ford and Reagan—have videotaped evidence. But in none of these was the President the accused. In the Lewinsky case, the target is President Clinton. And the question of whether a sitting President can be prosecuted before or after Articles of Impeachment had gone to the House of Representatives, whether simply, a sitting President can be subject to criminal prosecution, is a question that last week had constitutional lawyers arguing furiously pro and con. Happily, the problem became irrelevant. Mr Clinton did not accept or reject the subpoena. Mr Starr, the special prosecutor, exercised a unique gesture of magnanimity, and agreed to withdraw the subpoena if the President would testify on videotape in the White House before his (Starr's) lawyers. And, breaking the most baffling, some say the most undemocratic provision of the grand jury system, the President will be allowed to have a lawyer present.

So, two weeks from now, the leakers are going to discover whether the President will go on stoutly denying he ever had a sexual relationship with Miss Lewinsky. But she has suddenly been given immunity from prosecution by Mr Starr, so she can tell the truth without fear or favour, leaving us in stark fact to decide which of them is lying. (She's already said yes, they had sex. She can prove it with a stained dress.) The root question is not whether Mr Clinton had sex with Miss Lewinsky (amazingly about 65 per cent of the country thinks so, while the same number think he's being a good President!), which Mr Starr has been aching for six months to have answered, but: Did the President try to persuade Miss Lewinsky to lie if she ever appeared before the grand jury? As you'll see, her grant of immunity gives her the freedom to tell a truth that could bring the President down. Because if the grand jury finds that the President did take part in a cosy conspiracy to withhold the truth, then he could be guilty of one of the high crimes stated in the Constitution that provide grounds for impeachment: obstruction of justice.

This is the perilous position the President finds himself in as he mingles this weekend with his jet-set supporters on the south (the fashionable) shore of Long Island. In the meantime, and as Hamlet said, 'looking before and after', there is a case to be made, that so far as I know has never been made or is likely to be made in this country, against the *existence* of the grand jury system.

213

The President Will Address the Nation

21 August 1998

'The President will address the nation at 10 p.m. this evening, Eastern Daylight Time, 9 Central, 7 Pacific.'

Of all the times a similar announcement has come over the radio or the television I can't recall a time when more Americans mentally made this date with history—as they did last Monday, this time, more than sixty millions of them. Whatever the outcome from that four-minute speech of the President, Monday, 17 August 1998 will be remembered as long as there is a television station with an unfaded videotape, not to mention a living American with a memory of the time.

Looking back on the days before the fateful hour, it strikes me now that, semi-consciously, vast numbers of people had the feeling, the hope too, that this would mark the end of the affair. This only showed how much we've been brainwashed by the movies. In the real drama, of Prosecutor Starr versus President Clinton, it was at best only the beginning of the end.

I ought to say, though, why even some veteran politicians of both parties hoped that the President's address to the nation would put an early end to things. The chairman of the Senate Judiciary Committee, who would be the man to arrange the trial of the President (if the House voted articles of impeachment), an old hand at such hearings and a political opponent, said just before the address that if the President made an outright, from-the-heart, candid confession of his relationship with Miss Lewinsky, and gave convincing word that he had not conspired or cajoled anybody into covering it up or otherwise lying about it, if he then threw himself on the mercy of the American people, he could most likely be forgiven because, as the Senator put it, for the good of the nation and our form of government, nobody wants to impeach him.

When the President had finished, the Senator, that same Judiciary Committee chairman, was—like many members of both parties—aghast with anger and disappointment. They felt, as the overwhelming editorial opinion of the country expressed it, that he had spoken from a legally contrived script, that as a confession it was feeble and inadequate. Several of Mr Clinton's Cabinet rallied with urgent pleas to move on and carry out the nation's business. But the President's leaders of his own party were as dispirited as the press. The House Democratic leader: 'I am very disappointed in his personal conduct.' The Democrats' Senate leader: 'A more complete explanation of his relationship should have come earlier.' One of the senior Senators of the two most populous states, California and New York, both Democrats, Senator Moynihan of New York, remarked that he had made no adequate apology to 'an awful lot of people he has put through terrible times'. These 'people' must have referred mainly to his loyal staff—not least to Mrs Clinton whom, the President said, he had 'misled', which turned out to mean that only last Sunday, the night before his address, did he tell his wife that he had lied about the Lewinsky affair. Then the senior Senator from California, the most politically powerful of all the states with an essential mass of votes to offer in any election, Senator Dianne Feinstein—who stood at the President's side on the famous, or infamous, day in January when he wagged his finger at us and swore to the nation he had had no sexual relationship with Miss Lewinsky—after Monday night, Senator Feinstein said she was blazing with anger. 'I believed him. I felt betrayed.'

So, if finally so many influential people, papers, Democrats, have changed their mind and lost their loyalty, why does the great body of the Democrats in Congress stay mum so far? Because of the puzzling fact that while 70 per cent of the voters believed the President had lied before Monday evening, over 60 per cent say he's been a good President and shouldn't be impeached. This contradiction is, especially for the politicians of both parties who are running for re-election in November, the great, awkward stumbling block to the free exercise of their conscience.

What was it about the speech, apart from its brevity, and lack of open-hearted candour, that left so many with the complaining word 'inadequate'? Well, before it was written, and finally transcribed to a teleprompter, the substance and style of the speech had been fought over, we are told, up to the last hour on Monday evening, by two factions: the President's White House political cronies, and his legal advisers. The polls told him his one chance of redemption was a heartfelt, complete confession, an apology to many supporters, with no mention of the special prosecutor or the length of the investigation; then throw himself on the people's mercy. The politicians lost. The lawyers had convinced themselves that his best chance of survival was to contrive a careful legal evasion of the whole truth. So the speech was a lawyer's extra-delicate exercise in weasel words. I cannot think whom these characters imagined they would fool by having the President go back to his deposition (in the Paula Jones case), after which he gave that little speech to the press and said, 'I swear to you I did not have a sexual relationship with that woman, Miss Lewinsky.' So on Monday night he says that phrase in January was 'legally correct', but in the next sentence, his lawyers had him say: 'Indeed I did have a relationship with Miss Lewinsky that was not appropriate.' Mr Clinton left it to the sixty-odd million viewers to figure out the difference between a sexual relationship and an inappropriate one. Incidentally, and very much incident to Presidential crises, 'inappropriate' has become (since Mr Nixon used it frequently twenty-five years ago) the adjective of choice for defendants, for men accused of practically any crime in the book. Nixon, till the day he abdicated, never said he did wrong; he left office because he did not have 'sufficient political backing in the Congress'. His actions had been, he feared, 'inappropriate'.

Once Monday's speech was over, the first effect that the sharpest White House reporters noticed was on the faces of the staff, the close advisers who could be seen next morning. One who used to be there, and very close indeed to the President, said it was heartbreaking to see these aides, and to the end fervent supporters, loyalists of the President, restraining their disappointment and humiliation. They had forgiven him Gennifer Flowers, with

217

whom he'd sworn he'd never had any sex, then said months later, sorry, sorry, just once. She said, with hours of taped telephone calls to give weight to her claim, that they had been lovers for twelve years. All forgiven. Paula Jones and the self-exposure incident in the hotel, long ago, which even the judge in the Paula Jones case said was, if true, gross behaviour: the judge threw the case out, not for disbelieving Miss Jones, but for finding no evidence that she had suffered grievous harm, professionally and privately.

But over Miss Lewinsky, they trusted him, as did many, many more. It came out in the past few days that Mr Clinton, before a grand jury, refused to answer most questions on the Lewinsky matter, about which, we reliably hear, he was amazed to discover how much detail Mr Starr knew—presumably from the grand jury testimony recently of Miss Lewinsky. Accordingly, Miss Lewinsky was called back to the grand jury this Thursday.

Well, having waded through this welter and foam of cross-currents of opinion, whatever the final consensus, we have to confront the root question of self-government: what is meant by moral authority and does a leader need it? At the bland, the non-caring end of the political spectrum are modern, secular so-called 'progressives' of several generations, who say the President's sexual habits are none of our business, and if they don't interfere with his policies, then everything is hunky-dory. A lot of people feel this way.

Moral authority in a leader, as old man Aristotle pointed out two thousand and more years ago, resides in a leader because he is a better-than-average character. Moral authority does not mean

218

sexual behaviour. It means the capacity for being trusted, to have the people believe the word of the leader in many things and be ready to follow him when he judges what is the right thing to do. It means Lincoln declaring that a civil war had to be fought not to free an enslaved race but to preserve the Union. It meant Franklin Roosevelt taking the United States into the war against Hitler and Japan, not because it was legal (he did something that brought cries for *his* impeachment) but because it was right. It was Harry Truman declaring that since the League of Nations failed because the Western Europeans were too cowardly to stop Mussolini in Ethiopia, the United States had a moral duty to save the United Nations by going into South Korea to stem the Communist invasion from the North. It is the pattern of lying in Mr Clinton that the prosecutor is investigating, and that has offended and bewildered the country.

This may still leave unexplained the discrepancy between the 60 per cent of the country who believed he lied about his sexual relations with Miss Lewinsky, as with Paula Jones, as with Gennifer Flowers, and the 60 per cent who say still he's a good President and shouldn't go. There is one pungent voice that is worth at least listening to: an old politician from Connecticut, not a party man, a maverick and a retired governor who now teaches politics at the University of Virginia. Asked how it comes about that about 60 per cent think Clinton lied, and about 60 per cent want him to stay, Governor Lowell Weicker, implying that this reflects the sad moral climate of our time, said: 'That 60 per cent—those people are equally to be condemned with the President' as having no sense of the moral side of leadership.

So, after the four-minute confessional on Monday, there are only two opinions that are shared by the great majority of the people. One, that this investigation is by no means over, that the President's troubles reach forward certainly to the day of Mr Starr's delivery of an impeachment report to the House. The other consensus, which sympathetic and even forgiving people are reluctant to come to, is that if he survives, Mr Clinton will be a limping leader through the remaining two years of his Presidency.

New Words for Objects New and Old

16 October 1998

An old friend of mine, an Englishman, was saying how close British English and American English have come together compared with the days, say, of my boyhood when nobody in Britain, except kings, statesmen, ambassadors and bankers had ever heard an American speak. I was 21 when sound (what we called 'talking pictures') came in, and I remember the shock to all of us when we heard the weird sounds coming out of the mouths of the people on the screen.

And of course, quite apart from becoming familiar with the odd pronunciations of Americans of all sorts, we began to notice differences in the usage of words; we became aware for the first time of the great changes and unknown additions to the language that had been made by Englishmen who had been settling in America for three hundred years. It occurred to most of us rather late that this was bound to happen when Englishmen arrived on a new continent, saw a new landscape which had to be described with different words (tidewater, creek), new foods, new habits of life and work, not to mention the adoption, first from the Dutch, of new words for objects new and old: Englishmen who'd eaten buns found themselves eating crullers, and sitting out on the stoops of their houses. If you want to follow the impress of Spanish, Russian, German, Italian, Hungarian, Czech and the other European languages on the English of America, all you have to do is go to the library and take out the 2,400 finely printed pages of Mr H. L. Mencken's massive work, *The American Language*. And that will take you only as far as 1950.

The point my old friend was making was that after almost seventy years of talking pictures, and with the radio and television now becoming universal media, nothing in American speech or writing surprises us any more and the two languages have rubbed together so closely for so long that they are practically indistinguishable.

Well, there's much in this. But there are still little signs in any given piece of American prose playing a mischievous devil's advocate. One time last year I wrote a piece of English prose, quite guileless stuff, a page of fiction about a single mild adventure of a young man in New York. I asked this same old Englishman to go over it and strike out words which proved that, though the locale of the story was New York City, and the presumption of the story and all the fixings was that it had been written by an American, there were lots of little

221

signs which showed it could not have been written by anyone but an Englishman. I'll just say two things: that my friend missed them, and that most Englishmen would have, too.

Just last week there was printed in the *New Yorker* magazine a phrase about Californian wines, proving that the writer or the copy editor was English. No American talks or writes about Californian wines. California wines. 'California' is the adjective. 'Californian' is a noun: a native or resident of California. The other most gross and most frequent trick which not one Englishman in a thousand ever seems to notice is this: I say or write, 'I have a friend in England called Alan Owen.' That is an immediate giveaway. No American could say or write it unless they'd been corrupted by long close association with the Brits. Americans write and say, 'I have a friend in England *named* Alan Owen.' Maybe he's *called* Al. 'Called' would refer to a nickname. 'Named' is used where the English use 'called'. In other words, a President named William Jefferson Clinton is called Bill Clinton. 'Named' always for the baptismal name . . . right?

We went on to discuss American words, phrases, usually slang, that are picked up in England (E. B. White said it usually took fifteen years) and there go wrong, quite often assuming an opposite meaning. A beauty close to home is the word 'bomb'. When a book, a play, a movie flops with a sickly thud, it is said to have bombed. 'It ran a year in London, but bombed in New York.' Inexplicably, it got to England and took on the opposite meaning. I shall never, you'll appreciate, forget a telephone call from my daughter in England when a book of mine, a history of America carrying the succinct title *America*, had just come out. 'Daddy,' she shouted across the Atlantic, 'your book is a bomb!' I very much prayed it wasn't so. Indeed, the fact it wasn't is one reason why I'm sitting here talking to you at this late date—in comfort.

All this amiable light talk sprang from a darker happening: the passing of a great American writer, who received a large, worthy obituary in the *New York Times* but, to my surprise and dismay, did not rate a mention in the news magazines. I'm afraid it's because the writers of literary obituaries are too young to have remembered the splendid prime and great popularity of the man. His name was Jerome Weidman, and, if we were living in the 1930s, 1940s or 1950s and he had died, you would no more have been ignorant of his name than today you would say, Who is John Updike, Martin Amis? (Who, asked a contemporary of a grandson of mine, who was Ernest Hemingway?) There you have it, the frailty, the treachery, of fame. Jerome Weidman was not just a popular novelist, in the sense that James Michener or Dorothy Sayers were popular novelists. Jerome Weidman was a popular novelist who greatly impressed the literary world of New York with his first novel. He was 24 years old and earning $11 a week as an office boy and starting secretary, when in the spring of 1937, he published *I Can Get It For You Wholesale*.

Here was a story mining a new vein by a young man who, even at that tender age, knew the subject, the terrain and the people inside out. It was about Manhattan's garment centre—the hub and vortex of maybe half a million New Yorkers who whirled every day around the making of pants and coats; a mainly Jewish industry, because so many immigrant tailors originally had set it up.

Jerome Weidman's mother was Hungarian, and his father a young Austrian who, like George Gershwin's Russian father, was alerted to the prospect of America and the immigrant ships by hearing the sound of a bugle, the call to fight for the Austrian emperor, which didn't mean a year or two of military service but a semi-life sentence. He hopped it to New York City and went at once, on the Lower East Side, back to his only trade: he made trousers, pants. His son Jerome maintained against all comers that his father's unique genius was for making better pants pockets than any other tailor on earth.

Jerome was brought up on the Lower East Side, with the sights and sounds and idiom of the garment men and their families. That first book created a character, Harry Bogen, a shrewd, quicksilver scamp who in several disguises was to appear in his later books. All the best ones were about this life he knew as well as Dickens knew the East End of London. What was new and liberated the American novel from gentility (or the Hemingway flat protest against it) was the running talk, the exact sound and sense of these lowly characters—the first-generation immigrant sons striving to be free.

Now you'll see why such a man, such a writer, prompted our whole talk about the American language. Jerome Weidman was the first American street-smart novelist. (There—there's another one, turned in England often into 'street-wise'; nobody's wise on the streets, but Jerome Weidman and his swarming characters are nothing if not street-

224

smart.) He never adopted this language, but it came so naturally that when he chose titles for his subsequent works he fell as naturally as Ira and George Gershwin did into simply taking over some prevailing bit of American idiom slang. After *I Can Get It For You Wholesale* came *What's In It For Me?* and *The Price Is Right*—marvellously constructed short novels that made guessing the next turn of character as tense as tracking down a murderer. His last book, written in 1987, was a memoir, and the then senior book editor of the *New Yorker* magazine headed his review with the single, simple word: Pro. So he was, the complete professional, as Balzac was a pro, and Dickens. Indeed, it's not reaching too far to say that Jerome Weidman was the Dickens of the Lower East Side (throw in the Bronx, too). He never started out with an ambition to be a writer. He was going into the garment business, and then, he thought, law school. Then he read Mark Twain and saw how he made literature out of the humblest material. All you needed was insight into character and an ear for the character's speech. 'Life for me on East Fourth Street', Weidman once wrote, 'when I was a boy was not unlike what life on the banks of the Mississippi had been for young Sam Clemens of Hannibal, Missouri. Guileless, untrained and unselfconscious, I put the stories down on paper the way I learned to walk.'

After a fine rollicking success as a novelist, he wrote a musical play about the incomparable, cocky, little Italianate reform Mayor of New York City, Fiorello La Guardia. It was called simply *Fiorello*. The most prestigious theatre prize in this country (as also for fiction, history, whatever) is the

225

Pulitzer Prize. On a spring day in 1960, in his forty-eighth year, Jerome Weidman was deliciously thunderstruck to hear he had won it with *Fiorello*. I should tell you that if another famous novelist had lived on a year or two longer, you may be sure that one of the first calls of congratulation would have come from him: Jerome's old friend, the late W. Somerset Maugham. As it was, the first call came from his mother. Neither Jerome's father nor mother was comfortable with English. They were of that generation that was forever wary of the outside world they'd moved into—the world of America and Americans. Jerome Weidman recalled with pride, and typical exactness, what his mother said to him in that telephone call: 'Mr Mawgham was right. That a college like Columbia University, when they decided to give you a price like this should go and pick a day to do it that it's the twelfth anniversary of the founding of the State of Israel. If you listened to me and became a lawyer a wonderful thing like this could never have happened.'

He will be rediscovered, and revived, and read, when many, more famous and fashionable American writers, big guns today, are dead and gone for ever.

Jerome Weidman, born Lower East Side, New York City, 1913. Died Upper East Side, New York City, October 1998. RIP. Jerome, Harry Bogen, and Momma and Poppa Weidman.

Loneliness, Male Companionship and the Hunt

30 July 1999

Here are the opening sentences of two novels, both published in 1933.

> They drove uncertainly along the avenue that led to the house . . . The navy-blue car was built high off the ground and the name on its bonnet recalled a bankrupt, forgotten firm of motor-makers. Inside, the car was done up in a material like grey corduroy, with folding seats in unexpected places, constructed liberally to accommodate some Edwardian Swiss Family Robinson.

Here is the opening of the second novel, written the same year:

> You know how it is there early in the morning in Havana with the bums still asleep against the walls of the buildings, before even the ice wagons come by with ice for the bars. Well, we came across the square from the dock to the café to get coffee and there was only one beggar awake in the square and he was getting a drink out of the fountain. But when we got inside the café and sat down, there were the three of them waiting for us.

The first passage is a piece of considered literary prose that could have been written in 1923 or even 1913. It was written for an audience rather like the writer: literary, sensitive, leisured. The second passage has all the leisure of a ticking time bomb. And in 1933 it was a shocker. The reader is addressed as an equal but there is no suggestion of a literary man anywhere. It's more like an anecdote a travelling salesman is telling to a buddy sitting up at a bar.

What shocked most literary folk, both in Britain and America, in 1933 was the baldness of the writing. Not an adjective or an adverb in sight. Just plain nouns hitting plainer verbs. And yet, as one or two critics reluctantly admitted, in no more than a sentence or two a picture has been painted that is vivid, arresting, of a time and a feel for a place. And a note of suspense is struck at once: 'There were the three of them waiting for us.'

Well, it had taken most of twenty years for the author to be able to fashion such a sentence to his own satisfaction. The writer was Ernest Miller Hemingway, who was born a hundred years ago this past week in a Chicago suburb. In his teens, he already had the itch to write and skipped college to work on a newspaper in Kansas City, Missouri. He'd hardly got his hand in at reporting when America was in the First World War, and the 18-year-old Hemingway joined an ambulance unit attached to the Italian infantry. He was badly wounded four months before the Armistice, and when that happened he was still convalescing in a hospital in Milan. In little more than a year, a Toronto paper took him on as a foreign correspondent—the dashing life he'd hardly dreamed would ever come his way. He travelled far and wide in France, Italy, Spain, Switzerland and Germany. Two years after the signing of the peace treaty, he was on the road in and around Greece, following a surging population of refugees much like the beaten families we saw deserting Kosovo. One dispatch reported: 'In a staggering march, the Christian population of Eastern Thrace is jamming the roads towards Macedonia . . . An old man marches bent under a young pig, a scythe and a gun, with a chicken tied to his scythe. A husband spreads a blanket over a woman in labor in one of the carts to keep off the driving rain. She is the only person making a sound. Then his little daughter looks at her in horror and begins to cry. And the procession keeps moving.'

The oddest thing about him was a descriptive gift, expressed with such plainness and simplicity. It was something he worked on consciously while he was still a newspaper reporter. Based, in his early twenties, in a room over a sawmill in Paris, he appeared to belong to the circle of newly arrived American expatriates. But, from the start, it has not been much remarked, he shrank from their dilettantism. He was a professional writer who meant to achieve something new in the American language. What moved him most in those early days were memories of the shooting trips he had taken with his father into the Michigan woods, and it cannot have been simply an amazing coincidence, rather an impulse welling up from his unconscious, that his first stories, about those boyhood excursions, contained the elements of the romantic situations to which, for the rest of his life, he would be most susceptible: loneliness, male

229

companionship and the hunt—especially the hunt —whether in the infantryman's first experience of hand-to-hand combat, or in stalking game amid *The Green Hills of Africa*, or in the bullring, with its tension between human mettle and an animal's courage.

However, it was not the themes that obsessed him, so much as how they were to be written about, the ambition he held for his writing: 'To put down what really happened in action, what the actual things were which made the emotion and which would be valid in a year or ten years.' He wrote hard and long, rarely more than two hundred words a day and spent the next day paring them down. He'd already found out that, for him, adjectives and adverbs, when they were describing action or emotion, were devices of delay, of tapping the teeth while getting ready to find the right word. His idol Mark Twain had had something to say about that. (I have to throw in a background note that in America what in England is known as a firefly is in America more familiarly 'a lightning bug'.) Mark Twain wrote: 'the difference between the right word and the nearly right word is the difference between lightning and a lightning bug.'

The critics did not take kindly to Hemingway's first books. They thought that here was an author who had for no discoverable reason created a self-conscious, tough-guy, no-nonsense style. That's probably because most of the influential critics lived in London and New York, in a metropolis, and didn't have in their childhood background the vernacular that Hemingway distilled and refined into a personal style. It was nothing more mysterious or synthetic than the ordinary speech of ordinary people of the Mississippi Valley, as bare as the prairie and as sinuous as the fifty-four rivers that feed it, just the speech you will hear all around you any day in the smallest spurts of conversation of farmers, garage mechanics, shopkeepers, salesmen, soldiers, gardeners, merchants, anywhere from Cairo, Illinois, to Duluth, Minnesota. But it was what the mass of Hemingway's readers, a new generation of young non-critics, recognized as themselves and their emotions nakedly and truly expressed. In time, even some of the intelligentsia came to concede that Hemingway had managed, in a very bare idiom, to show that the emotions of ordinary, even illiterate, people were just as fine and complex as their very own.

Like all true originals, Hemingway was too often judged by people who didn't know the difference between the true Midwestern vernacular and the crude imitations of it which were soon being practised—thanks to Hemingway—everywhere, from Glasgow to Hollywood. Striking proof that he had achieved 'the real thing', extracted from that Midwestern ore and passed on as something original and precious into literature, is suggested by the fact that in the Nobel country itself, which gave him its literature award, his example, they say, transformed Swedish fiction. As for the English-speaking world, it seems to me that no one since Dryden has so revolutionized the English narrative sentence of his time.

For myself, I would add a little to those three elements I said were at the root of his view of life: loneliness, male companionship, the hunt. I would add that he brings to relationships between the old

231

and the young a certain touch of tenderness. And there is always that strain of suspense.

The best way I can express my own admiration for Hemingway is to do an outrageous thing. Years ago, an American monthly magazine ran a competition for a parody of Hemingway. I entered it, and I did not win. I got a letter back from the judge saying, 'this is preposterous—this isn't a crude parody, which our readers would recognize—this is too true, this is essence of Hemingway. Which book did you steal it from? Sorry.' Maybe it will say more in fewer words than I have used to convey what to me is touching, dramatic, comically grave and suspenseful about his writing. This is a very short story about an old man and his grandson in Florida, stopping at a lunch counter to get a hamburger.

A FIRST TIME FOR EVERYTHING

The old man and the boy went in and sat down on the swivel stools and behind the counter there were two of them waiting. One was a black man in a white apron and the other was a big blonde with corn-colored locks. It was the boy's first time down there in Florida and his hands showed up on the counter like baby whitefish against the brown arms of the old man that were blotched with the benevolent skin cancer.

The old man nodded without speaking, and the black man who knew all the signs dropped on the shiny stove something that looked like a red coaster you'd put a drinking glass on, and later would look like a brown coaster. Then he lifted his arm high and snatched from a shelf a fat white roll between his

232

splayed thumb and little finger the way he would receive a throw cleanly like in the high school play-offs. The boy looked up at the old man.

'They are the rolls,' the old man said, 'first baked by Macdonald of the Isles, a Scottish chieftain who in the manner of the Scots called them baps with their floury but crisp outsides. But these are closer to what the English call buns, which are softer but not as soft and delicate as the good buns they made in the old days in the Basque country. Basque buns are best.'

'Will they come together to enclose it?' the boy asked.

'They will enclose it good,' said the old man.

The black man had finished now and scooped the coaster between the two halves of the bap and slid the whole onto a clean white plate. The big blonde extended her right hand and whisked the plate with a single turn of her buttocks in front of the boy. It reminded the old man of the way the great Manolete performed a veronica in the forgotten afternoons when the sun went low in the good times. The boy lifted the thing to his lips.

'Now,' said the old man, 'you are having your first Big Mac.'

'Truly?' asked the boy.

'Truly,' said the old man.

Park Avenue's Colourful Christmas

24 December 1999

The curious thing about a city that boasts extravagantly about its best features, as well as some of its worst, is that there is a never-mentioned little miracle in New York City. It is the railed-off plots of grass that for almost three miles run down the middle of Park Avenue and divide the uptown and downtown traffic. Along this whole stretch (fifty-four blocks from 96th to 42nd Street), what is a constant delight and surprise is the regularly changing character of these more than fifty little gardens. And they're not so little: each, one city block long and about fifteen feet wide.

You drive down this avenue one season of the year through a great ripple of crocuses. Another time, tulips from here to infinity. Sometimes you notice that at each end of each garden there is a new young tree, a hundred or so of them from the 96th Street entrance down to where the Avenue ends at Grand Central Station. Or maybe next time, they are locusts or London plane trees. At Christmas time, as now, they've been replaced by small firs.

I suppose we take it so easily for granted (and thousands of the true city types never notice the changes at all) because the very large workforce that performs these magical transformations works by night and by stealth. In fifty years of living round the corner from this long divide of Park Avenue I have never seen any of them at their remarkable labour of creating, along three miles, complete variations of miniature landscapes about, it seems, once every few weeks.

I know they're at it, because I once tactfully guessed at the fortune it requires to employ them and to maintain this city perquisite. I happened to know the possessor of the fortune, a lady named Mary Lasker (heiress of an advertising multi-millionaire, a self-effacing, absolutely non-socialite doer of many unadvertised good works of which the Park Avenue divider is the only conspicuous one). At Christmas time, especially, it makes me think again, with gratitude, of the late Mary Lasker. For now each tree, a hundred or so, is lit at twilight.

By Mrs Lasker's request, and, thank God, this confirming dictate of the Park Avenue property owners, the trees are not gaily decorated with red bulbs and green bulbs and purple bulbs and yellow bulbs—illuminations that make so many city squares and streets look like amusement arcades gone berserk. Each of the Park Avenue firs is decorated with about five hundred tiny oyster-white bulbs. So at twilight, you look down from the small eminence of 96th Street at this three-mile stretch of small, small fountains of light. All the way down, the only colours are the alternating reds and greens of the traffic lights at the fifty-odd intersections. Now, by day it used to be that the long canyon of Park Avenue was majestically closed at the southern end by the great gold dome of Grand Central Station. Then they built behind it a towering, flat monolith of a skyscraper which blotted out the dome (or indeed the outline) of Grand Central. This defiling obstacle tower has

235

been ingeniously made to evaporate by the night—
at Christmas time. As the dark comes on, and both
Grand Central and the monolith behind it fade into
the black sky, there appears by magic a great white
cross. This is achieved by leaving on the lights of so
many offices on one floor to form the horizontal
bar and many more offices to form the vertical bar.

Simple and sublime; but in the past year or two,
I'm afraid, it's been an object of sporadic
controversy. From whom? From that fervent bank
of First Amendment protestors who sometimes
sound as if there were no other clauses in the Bill
of Rights: 'Congress shall make no law respecting
an establishment of religion.' This has been taken
in many court appeals in many states to forbid
every expression of any religion—by word,
decorating, symbol—on *public* property. This
argument has been going on for years and years
and is effectively won, mainly in places where
agnostics or atheists speak louder and longer than
the true believers in any religion popular in a given
town. So far, by the way, there have been no
protests against the dozen performances of *Messiah*
and a half-dozen of Bach's *Christmas Oratorio*,
even done in public auditoriums or theatres. The
board of ACLU (the American Civil Liberties
Union) appears to be slipping.

There are some states, however, that can afford
to be more blasé or unintimidated by the First
Amendment fanatics, for an interesting *new*
reason. What is it that Florida, Texas and
California have in common that favourably affects
the practice of the Christian religion and, say, tends
to discourage the march of an army of atheists with
banners? The answer: they are the states

(Southwestern states) into which more South and Central American immigrants have arrived in the past quarter-century than in the rest of the country put together, the vast majority of them practising Roman Catholics. What they have brought to Christmas is a colourful and quite different tradition of Christmas decoration. Whereas most of the United States picked up the English nineteenth-century trimmings—Prince Albert's Christmas tree, holly and ivy, green and red and so forth, while Britain picked up from New York (via the Dutch settlers) the idea, the well-known figure, of Santa Claus—the Mexicans especially have given us the most colourful and original variations. This week, the Governor of Texas, one George W. Bush, gave a little television tour of the Governor's mansion and showed off a marvellous array of Christmas trees—cacti and pepper trees—hung with orange, and pink flowers and home-made Christmas cribs that looked as if they had been imported from that first Christian (Coptic) chapel outside Cairo, which has those primitive, comic-strip figures of Adam and Eve and a jolly snake. But here in Austin, Texas, were all the nativity figures: the Wise Men, Joseph and Mary, the shepherds, as marvellous little painted wooden figures which we (the civilized Anglo-European types who couldn't draw a broomstick) call 'primitives'.

Governor Bush, you may have heard, is running for President, and running very hard (the election is only nine months away). And he showed off the delightful Mexican decorations with understandable effusiveness, stopping from time to time to talk in Spanish to a passing child. The public, of course, can visit the Governor's mansion, just as the public makes daily tours of the White House. Incidentally, I ought to throw in that anyone running for public office, for state office anyway, in Florida, Texas, Nevada, Southern California nowadays had better speak Spanish as well as English if he/she holds any hope of being elected.

But whatever variations different immigrant groups may bring in, there is one symbolic expression of Christmas, one that dependably returns every year to appear in theatrical form in city theatres and centres, on national television in half a dozen versions, and is at the moment dazzling nightly audiences in New York City's vast Radio City Music Hall. It is Charles Dickens' *A Christmas Carol*. And the booksellers, including the titans online, indicate that every year the sales of *A Christmas Carol* go smartly up. (Poor Dickens, who lost £200 on the book, sued an outrageous couple who pirated his work and sold it cheaply. He was awarded £1,500 damages, so the couple declared bankruptcy, and Dickens got nothing but had to pay out £700 for his own court fees.)

I suppose that we, for most of the century, have thought of the *Carol* as the most vivid representation of an old English tradition of Christmas: the feasting and the carolling and Christmas cards and the parties with their particular customs, the tree, the pudding, the kissing and dancing and general merriment. Nothing could be more untrue. For centuries, Christmas was an annual street brawl with a reputation for debauchery and general rowdiness. The Church of England and the Puritans here

238

prohibited it as a religious ceremony (or a celebration of Christ's birth) until well into the eighteenth century. When Dickens published the *Carol* in 1843 nobody had ever seen a Christmas card or a Christmas tree, except at Windsor. The street brawl was still a fact, deplored by respectable people who by then had the custom of taking a half-day off on Christmas Day and holding a special mid-afternoon dinner: the turkey, which had long established himself after his long journey from America, and fowl (I mean game) and pastries, and many, many jellies, and Christmas punch.

When the *Carol* appeared, what delighted everybody was the entertaining, suspenseful plot. But Thackeray said it defied literary criticism. It was a work whose central idea was that Christmas was the paradox of a merry time that entailed duties and obligations, especially to the poor, and added the astonishing new notion that Christmas was a special time of the year for redemption—for everybody to take stock and begin to lead a better life.

It's impossible today to appreciate the shock of this idea disguised as brilliant entertainment. It's at the root of the custom of New Year resolutions. But the wish to make amends for the flaws in one's character is something that some people, a few, become conscious of as they grow old. One was the late, the recently late, actor George C. Scott. Not too long before he died, he gave an engaging, vibrant television interview. He was an engaging, vibrant man. There was much talk about his towering portrayal of General George Patton. When he was asked what his favourite role was, he

239

did not hesitate. George C. Scott was in private life a violent man. It was therefore a surprising and happy thing to hear him say that his favourite role of all was—Ebenezer Scrooge.

2000–2004

The Death of the Old Media

14 January 2000

In America at any rate, the twenty-first century came in with a bang, a sound so loud and so new that I'd guess most people over 60 suddenly felt they were living on a different planet or had, like Rip Van Winkle, been asleep for twenty years and come awake to discover that their world was beyond recognition.

I detect, by extra-sensory perception or a shudder in the radio signal, a slight attack in some listeners of shyness. So, I will cure it at once by going directly to the cause. Does anybody read Washington Irving any more? In blunter words, a question hovering on many lips: Who is Rip Van Winkle? Before oldsters smirk with impatience and roar, 'What nonsense! Of course we read Washington Irving when we were children,' let me remind you of my frequent researches in this matter of assuming that every young person around shares your cultural or folk background, and then adds his or her own. I asked a grandson of mine, in his twenties, very bright, also, better, very intelligent, 'Who was Charlie Chaplin?' 'Er,' he said, 'his name comes up in crossword puzzles.' So do (I learned from other twenty-something-year-olds) the names of Albert Schweitzer, Sigmund Freud and Winston Churchill. Winston Churchill?! A stunning item of disbelief till I recall an early Gallup poll, taken in England in the autumn of 1940. Note the year and the time, when—if the

243

besieged or surrendered free world had a hero—it was Churchill, standing with or for Britain alone against Hitler's armies eighteen miles away on the French shore. Dr Gallup took a poll of the general population of England (not Britain), asking the simple question: 'Who is Winston Churchill?' Dr Gallup, I remember, was scolded at the time for bad taste. But his distinction was to be the first man to want to find out what the people really felt and not what editors or public men told us they felt. His strength was to ask rude questions that went like a stake through the heart of preconceptions and popular false assumptions.

The result of Dr Gallup's poll was interesting. Of course, 96 per cent of the English knew all, or much, about him. But 4 per cent had never heard of him! They were farmers, most, if not all, had no radio, and they all lived in one county. Its identity was never published. So far as I know, it remained a secret known only to Dr Gallup, as the identity of the *Washington Post*'s 'Deep Throat' is locked still in the bosom of the editor of the *Post* at the time of Watergate.

Well, all this flowed naturally from my rude assumption that quite a lot of listeners don't know, or have forgotten, the incomparable tale of Rip Van Winkle and secretly would like to know it. In brief, here it is.

First, I should say, so nobody will be embarrassed from now on: Washington Irving was an American essayist and historian, born at the end of the eighteenth century and lived through the first half of the nineteenth. He wrote a comic *History of New York from the Beginning of the World to the End of the Dutch Dynasty*, supposedly written

244

by one Diedrich Knickerbocker. The book was so popular that the moniker 'Knickerbocker' became a synonym for a New Yorker. He was at one time American Minister to Spain, and wrote four volumes on its history. He retired up in the Hudson Valley and wrote true or invented folk tales about that part of the state.

The most famous of these was about a middle-aged Dutchman, Rip Van Winkle. His wife was described as a termagant. He himself was in no doubt that he was henpecked. (And maybe his popularity—you never know—was in his appearing as the champion of every henpecked husband throughout the Republic.) And Rip did what many of them had longed to do: one day he upped and left home with his dog and went wandering in the Catskill Mountains. This was just before the colonies rebelled and started the War of Independence. Rip met a dwarf carrying a large keg. Rip helped him with it and together they came into a valley where dwelt a group or tribe of dwarfs. Rip was invited to celebrate his arrival with these new friends, none of whom (so far as he could see) had a henpecking wife. He drank a long sustaining drink and fell asleep. He woke up twenty years later to find many bewildering changes. He himself was now an old man. He limped back to his town and found—hallelujah!—his termagant wife dead, his daughter married, and a hanging portrait of King George the Third replaced by a portrait of George Washington. Rip Van Winkle learned that though there had been several moves to make him emperor (one suggestion was 'His Magnificence'), he became of course, plain President Washington. But everything around Rip's house and his town, and all the news and talk, all new, and Greek to poor Rip.

Well, that is the way some of us felt when we read the thundering news last Tuesday: 'The Death Of The Old Media'. It says here, we are seeing the beginning of the end of the bookstore, the auction house, the yard sale, the real-estate agent, the insurance man, the post office, the bulletin board, the newspaper, the radio broadcaster (ouch!), the private club, and I should add, the blessed anchor of our daily life: the retail shop or store, what the young folks who spent Christmas week ordering their presents online call, 'the old bricks and mortar'.

What I'm talking about is the staggering news that a company thought to be wobbling (with, however, a booming share price, but likely any minute to be gobbled up by Mr Gates' Microsoft) bought a huge company whose share price has lagged behind the market all through the bull market. A company riddled with debt, it was suddenly bought by this smallish company which paid 70 per cent more for the debt-ridden giant's shares than the stock market thought them worth. This acquisition of Time-Warner by America Online is being hailed as a brilliant formula, not for rescuing staggering companies but for unimaginable success as an institution that will date and replace all those institutions we've been so cosy with for, say, two hundred years. One financial paper calls it the $164-billion enigma. It is certainly an enigma wrapped in a riddle to most of us who don't spend half our days hanging out on the Internet. The *Wall Street Journal* made the best attempt at defining exactly what this enigma is.

246

Here is the enlightening passage. Maybe I ought to say before I recite it that much of the language of this piece will be strange to many of the middle-aged and older still. It may sound like jargon, that is to say the vague, pretentious, tortured English used by ignoramuses, highbrows, pompous businessmen, sociologists, art critics, and most politicians. It's something quite different, professional trade talk—as exact as a doctor's professional talk. Now, having said that, what this merger constitutes is all the things it will replace: newspapers, books, television networks, post offices, retail chains, etc., the piece says.

It is all of the above or, if you prefer, none of them. It is, at its core, an architecture, a set of digital protocols, rules and structures, some of them proprietary, some Internet-based, embedded in software running on servers, and linked up to networks. Amazon.com has done it to the bookstore, and hopes to do it to the rest of retailing. e-Bay is doing it to the auction house and the yard sale. AOL is doing it to a broad swathe of messaging, chatter, publishing and broadcasting. And Time-Warner? The parts—its parts—that really matter to this merger represent a grab-bag of old, analog content: CNN/Time Magazine, Warner Brothers, music groups, a television network, all perfectly good businesses well-managed, and generally profitable. But still, very old wine. They'll hang around for another decade or so, but they're history. AOL is the new bottle and for the next decade, at least, the new digital bottlers will

247

be in complete control.

Is that quite clear? No? Well, the good news came next day with a consoling second thought that it won't all change by next Monday morning. Writers as splendid as Tom Wolfe and as humble as yours truly, who bang out their stuff on old manual typewriters, will still compose prose and have it printed between hard covers and hope you'll read it—better still, buy it. But hurry, before they tear down the old neighbouring bricks and mortar.

Running Mates and Carpetbaggers

11 August 2000

I telephoned my son the other day, way up there in the Rockies, just to hear how things were doing in Wyoming, since Mr Dick Cheney, Governor Bush's choice for Vice President, had rushed from his Texas home back to Casper, Wyoming (his birthplace), to register there as a voter, so that, on 7 November, the people who so chose could legitimately vote for Bush and Cheney. (The Constitution specifically forbids the President and Vice President to be residents of the same state.)

There is a comic aspect to the choosing of Mr Cheney that could have come from a chapter in *Pickwick Papers*. Mr Cheney is a man very little known to the public. We saw him and heard him occasionally during the Gulf War, when he was President Bush's Secretary of Defense. He retired from public life after a couple of heart attacks. He came into the news again, just about a month ago, when Governor Bush chose him to head a small team—first, to suggest a name to be Governor Bush's running mate, then to pick several and do thorough background checks on them, a process that is all the more ruthless these days since, about a dozen years ago, the media started digging out small sins (what the victims called 'mistakes' or 'inappropriate behaviour') on the part of the unlikeliest people, including three Senators, and one man who was made Speaker of the House and lasted one day, twenty-four hours being all it took for the media shovellers to dig the dirt.

So, finally, Mr Cheney, head of the team choosing a Republican Vice President, reduced the list to two or three, when somebody—and they say it was Governor Bush himself—had a brain wave. Governor Bush has confessed he is not a great reader, but he's been to the movies often enough to be suddenly struck with recall of one of the oldest plots in the business. Why this far-flung search for the girl of your dreams when she turns out to live next door? In shorter words, why not pick Mr Cheney himself? So, to Mr Cheney's happy embarrassment (oh, Governor, you really shouldn't have), Mr Cheney—in a Pickwickian sense—chose himself. And now it sounds more than ever like the election at Eatanswill: I gather that the Bush team, not only the search-and-destroy team but the campaign advisers, were sitting around thumping each other on the backs, in a manner of speaking, when somebody, a reader of the Constitution perhaps, suddenly remembered that, while the Founding Fathers said nothing about having a President and a Vice President who are both big oil men, it did say that in picking a Presidential candidate and a Vice President (I paraphrase the Twelfth Amendment), 'one of them shall not be an inhabitant of the same state'. I'd love to know who recalled this provision and how Mr Cheney upped and said something like, 'I have it, I was born in Wyoming, and I can whip up there, transfer my Texas vote to my beloved hometown, Casper, and become a legal inhabitant just in time.' Right on! Bully for you, Dick! And off he went. It was a close call. The public, which does not read the Constitution, had not had time to wake up and cry, 'I say there, hold on, old man, I mean', or 'Take it easy, fella'.

So, it was an historic, and a very necessary, moment when Mr Cheney arrived breathless in Casper to embrace his old town, re-establish himself as an inhabitant, and then fly off to meet Governor Bush and begin the long, punishing trail of a campaign tour.

And within the week, the opposition couple did the same, after Vice President Gore broke the last remaining thread of suspense by naming his Vice Presidential partner—running mate. By the way, that's a phrase I'm afraid I take too much for granted. A listener wondered not only what it meant but how it came about. Quite right. Well, it's a horse-racing term and derived from the practice of one owner, one stable, running two horses in a race, the slower one being put in there to pace the star. The pacesetter was known, is known, as its running mate. The phrase is just one century old. But its use to define a Vice President was coined by, of all the non-practitioners of slang, the most scholarly, the most ecclesiastical, of Presidents,

250

Woodrow Wilson. At the Democratic convention in 1912, the Presidential nomination went to Wilson (he got it after a terrific brawl on the forty-sixth ballot)—Governor Woodrow Wilson of New Jersey—and he announced that his Vice Presidential choice would be another Governor: Thomas Marshall. 'And I feel honoured by having him as my running mate.' It brought the house down, the only squeak of humour they'd ever had out of Woodrow Wilson. If Wilson's mother had been alive, she would undoubtedly have scolded him: 'Is it possible that you have been attending one of those vulgar horse-race meetings?'

Thomas Marshall, incidentally, is, like all Vice Presidents, totally forgotten, except today by students of American politics. He is immortal for two slogans he cranked out wherever he appeared in public, which was seldom, during the election campaign. I doubt that either slogan would do him much good today. He was a droll fellow and sophisticated enough to know well the ringing patriotic phrases, the hackneyed rhetoric that would be expected of him. So he parodied even the most obvious phrase, like 'What this country needs . . .' The Marshall version: 'What this country needs is a good five-cent cigar.' The other one, swiped from Kipling, 'A woman is only a woman, but a good cigar is a smoke.'

Mr Gore's choice of a Connecticut Senator, Senator Joseph Lieberman, gives us at last something substantial, even intriguing to talk about. Senator Lieberman is a moderate liberal Democrat, well liked by Democrats and Republicans alike. He was the first Democrat to stand up in the Senate after President Clinton's famous or infamous lie, and say, 'The President's behaviour was not appropriate. It was immoral.' Lieberman is known to be himself without fault or flaw in matters of personal honesty and marital fidelity.

All these were no doubt considered useful qualities to set off against the constant side-swipes at Mr Clinton by Governor Bush and Mr Cheney as they urge the voters to help restore dignity and decency to the Presidency. But the main point about Senator Lieberman is that he is a Jew—the first ever to be put on a Presidential ticket. The Vice Presidency, for much of the past two hundred years, has been a post in which the party wished to honour a nonentity who had done the party some service. It has sometimes been a useful place of exile to shunt off a man whose ideas were too radical or threatening to the party regulars. Theodore Roosevelt did such a job as Police Commissioner of New York City in reforming a corrupt immigration office and, as Governor of the state, of taxing corporations and going after the sweatshop owners, that he violently rocked the boat of the smooth-sailing Republicans. They had the brilliant idea of tossing him into decorative oblivion by getting him appointed as McKinley's Vice President. Till then, the Vice President had been almost a ceremonial post. Well, McKinley was soon assassinated, and Roosevelt became President and the reforming terror of the Republic. And, however much demeaned the office has been, the public today is well aware of the alarming fact that eight Vice Presidents have become 'accidental Presidents'—as we call them—because of the sudden death of the President, five of them after the President's assassination. These are facts which remind every voter that the Vice President is, as they say, one heartbeat away from the Presidency.

It might be possible to have a secular Jew whose race or religion played little part in his public life. But Senator Lieberman is a deeply religious man, a practising Orthodox Jew. He will do nothing forbidden on Saturdays. He has said that, for serious matters affecting the people's welfare, he would go to preside over the Senate (his only official job) but he would walk, not ride, there.

Somebody has said that Jews may not be welcome in many country clubs but they have been received and respected, even venerated, as justices of the Supreme Court. It's been almost a century since the appointment of Brandeis and Cardozo. Today there are two Jews among the nine justices. But the prospect is there of a Vice President— like eight others—suddenly translated to the Presidency.

There is at the moment very lively and knotty discussion about the wisdom or folly of Mr Gore's decision. The leaders of both parties applaud it as an act of courage. Here in the City of New York there is great elation and among some prominent Jews, apprehension. But New Yorkers are probably the worst judges in America of how the rest of the United States thinks and feels about the nomination of Senator Lieberman. For years, I have played a parlour game with visiting Europeans, British men and women who come to this city on business, by saying to them: 'There are 265 million Americans in the United States. How many of them are Jews?' 'Oh, I don't know, they'd say, twenty, thirty, even forty million?' The answer is, six million. Of them, two million live in this city. In other words, one American Jew in three lives here in the City of New York.

A national poll taken two years ago found that about 90 per cent of Americans wouldn't mind having a Jewish President. If true, it is an astonishing figure and shows a heartening decline in what you might call polite, unspoken anti-Semitism that, in my time, has tiptoed throughout the land. Jews settled mostly in New York, Chicago and Los Angeles. How they feel in Omaha, Nebraska, in Salt Lake City, in Cleveland, Ohio, in Michigan, in the other forty-nine states, we shall simply have to wait and see.

The Day of Judgement

3 November 2000

Finally, the day of judgement: Tuesday, 7 November. I have been following American Presidential elections since 1936—the first time accepting an invitation to join the resident members of the Harvard Club in London, and, thanks to the marvels of modern technology, to listen to a short-wave radio set and hope the signal was steady enough to enable us to follow the results. Most of the time it was. Other times it crackled or whined. Of course, we had to sit up throughout the night because of the five-hour difference in time (an anomaly modern technology could do nothing about), but the officers of the Harvard Club greatly softened this ordeal with copious draughts of the, er, wine of Scotland. It was just as well, for most of the young Harvard men present had learned from their fathers to loathe and fear Franklin D. Roosevelt and his New Deal ('nothing short of galloping socialism', one dutiful son protested), and when the radio gave forth the unmistakable roar of a Roosevelt landslide, they were in urgent need of solace.

They were outraged by the victory (he took forty-six states against the Governor of Kansas' two) because the only poll then extant—a pioneer of polling—was one put out by a magazine called the *Literary Digest*. It had predicted an overwhelming victory for Governor Landon. Soon after the election, a new breed of statisticians examined the *Digest*'s polling method, and found that it had collected its opinions, the numbers, by looking through telephone books and local automobile registration lists. In other words, the *Digest*, and the rest of the country, realized a little late in the day that Governor Landon was going to get the overwhelming vote of the people who had a motor car and a telephone. Sixty-four years ago (in the pit of the Depression), that left out of consideration an awful lot of millions of Americans who didn't own these luxurious conveniences. That infamous poll killed the magazine and opened the way for the beginning of the statistical sample.

Well, today there are at least eight national pollsters, all professing to be objective and for the first time I can remember, they are not only in the dark about what's going to happen—they are not in conflict—they are baffled, bewitched, bothered and bewildered. And even the boldest of them gives either Governor Bush or Vice President Gore no more than a 3 per cent edge, and quickly adds the warning that the prediction is subject to '3 or 4 per cent error.' In other words, for once, everybody has checked out of the prophecy business.

To visitors from abroad, and to foreigners here who follow American politics, a first, even a long second glance reveals no mystery in the relative appeal of the two candidates. This is what they see. On the one hand the Vice President, the Democrats' Mr Gore: twenty-four years in Washington, eight years in the House, seven in the Senate, on the Energy Committee, Science/Conservation, served two years in Vietnam (as a reporter, admittedly, but often close to danger). He's an admitted though self-proclaimed expert on the environment, almost an alarmist on global warming, and deeply concerned about the need to discipline the world's industries. At least half of President Clinton's initiatives in foreign policy were inspired by the Vice President. He broke with his party to vote in favour of the Gulf War, which, you'll recall, was, at the time and ever since, considered President Bush's finest hour. So, for the past eight years as Vice President, Mr Gore has been privy to every public and secret policy of this administration. It has been said of him by many influential politicians, including some Republicans (who dare not of course speak their name), that he is the best trained and qualified man to be President in modern history.

On the other, the Republican hand, Governor Bush, an arrow-straight, handsome chip off the old block—in fact, chipper and handsomer than the old block—Governor of Texas for the past six years, before that an oil man, not doing very well, but well enough to grow affluent during the unprecedented nine-year prosperity to buy and successfully run a major league baseball team. Such a bald summary is cruel, even though it's a favourite Democratic biography of the Governor. It should not be forgotten (remember the Democrats' scorn of Ronald Reagan) that a Governor has to be conversant with every aspect of the political, economic and social life of his state, and for many decades (before Senator Kennedy broke into the White House) a Governorship was thought to be, and in practice *was*, the most favoured stepping stone to the Presidency.

Now, our foreigner, knowing so much and little more of each man's background, has presumably spent the last few weeks listening to the three television debates and to the speeches of the candidates stumping around the country. And the foreign observers agree with the domestic ones, of whatever political prejudice, that if you tap Mr Gore on any issue, he will reel off impressive statistics without taking a breath. I almost said he will give you a detailed answer ad nauseam. And bear that Freudian slip in mind. Governor Bush is not interested in explaining policy and what he calls 'details'. When the Vice President reminds him that an impartial commission found children's health care in Texas to be fiftieth in the roster of the states, the worst in the nation, Governor Bush looks patient and affable and responds quietly: 'We take care of our own.'

But on so many great issues—the long-term protection of pensions (Social Security), the extension of Medicare (the free health system for the old, rich or poor), how much of a tax cut and

257

who should get it—both candidates *have* to go into figures. And they have such different systems of arithmetic, and they're talking about billions and trillions of dollars, that the differences between their policies drown in a boiling ocean of numbers. It's too much for most voters, so the polls report.

But there's one huge assumption that lies behind all this arithmetic which doesn't seem to come up in the campaign rallies. Both the Vice President and Governor Bush assume that the huge moneys for these great reform expenditures will come from the enormous surplus the nation will boast of in 2004, not to mention 2008. Both parties therefore assume that the present economic boom, which is already in its ninth year (a record in the 130-year history of booms and recessions), is going on for ever. This is surely a delusion. It comes up between friends and in families, but it's never brought up to the candidates on the stump for, I believe, the simple, drastic difference between party rallies in Europe and here. In this country, a candidate's rally is a rally of the faithful. You never hear from a heckler. I remember once, in Madison Square Garden, John Kennedy addressing twenty thousand people, Democrats! In between his soaring rhetoric and the punctuating cheers, one time when he paused to take breath, a lone voice cried out 'How about . . .'—the name of a man who'd been falsely arrested in Massachusetts. There was a wave of shocked, responsive, boos. Who was this barbarian? And the cops bore down on the man and carried him out.

However, we have got ahead of ourselves. From the background sketch of both candidates, and the glimpse of the two men's opposing tactics in

258

debate, those foreign observers of mine, say, well, there's no contest, surely. Gore is plainly the man.

But, as we noted at the beginning, to the voters it's not plain at all. And it's agreed, even by the most double-dome commentators, that, probably as never before, appearance, likeability, the manner and the character of the two men seen in public (which today and for evermore means seen in close-up all the time on television), could be the decisive factor. As I talk to you, only days away from the election, more than 10 per cent of the voters, one poll says 15 per cent, are undecided. And the puzzle, the choice, seems to come down not so much to a choice between the looks and manner of the Vice President, and the looks and manner of Governor Bush but between the affability, the likeability of the comparatively ignorant Governor Bush and the knowledge and experience of the unpleasant Mr Gore. For it's also generally admitted—I was going to say universally admitted (except by my passionate Democrats)—that Mr Gore is an unhappy-looking campaigner, like a bad actor running for President, a smart alec, top boy in class, always with his hand up and waving, teacher's pet. And Governor Bush always sounds gentle, composed, authoritative, even when he says we must get our troops out of Haiti (and nobody says, 'wait a minute, all twenty-nine of them?').

So, unable to predict the result, and afraid of falling on their faces, even learned pundits fall back on one of several famous clichés: since no incumbent has ever been thrown out of the White House during an economic boom, they cry, 'You can't beat prosperity.' Then there's 'a new face is always welcome' or 'a new broom sweeps clean', or, as one famous commentator said last night with great gravity: 'I honestly think it'll be either—Bush, or—er, Gore.'

The Origin of the Continental Blow-out

24 November 2000

Last Thursday was Thanksgiving, the first truly American festival and the one that sets more millions of Americans in a turmoil of transit, criss-crossing thousands of miles to join long-separated families at a feast of turkey, cranberry sauce, sweet potatoes and pumpkin, the strange, unknown foods the native Indians introduced to those starving English men, women and children who had landed—three hundred and eighty years ago—on the bleak and unfruitful soil of a Massachusetts cape.

This festival was inspired by a letter from America written by a Yorkshire man, son of a farmer, written as a report on his first transatlantic voyage along with other, mostly humble folk who sought a new land across the ocean in order to practise a religion freed from the corruption—in 1620—of the Church of England. They had none of our advantages, so William Bradford's writing is bereft also of parliamentary English, Congressional English, business English, advertising English, or the lawyers' English we've been exposed to for the past fortnight in the service of Vice President Gore and Governor Bush.

This company of very mixed types, just over a hundred of them, had been sixty-four days out of England and meaning to settle at the mouth of the Hudson River and start a trading post. However, this is William Bradford's account of what happened. I thought it might be a refreshment.

But after they had sailed that course about half a day, they fell among dangerous shoals and roaring breakers . . . and therewith conceived themselves in great danger. [But] the wind shrinking upon them withal, they resolved to bear up again for the Cape to the north [later to be known as Cape Cod] and thought themselves happy to get out of those dangers before night overtook them, as by God's providence, they did. And the next day, they got into the Cape Harbor, where they rode in safety. Being thus arrived in a good harbor and brought safe to land, they fell upon their knees and blessed the God of Heaven, who had brought them over the vast and furious ocean, and delivered them from all the perils and the series thereof, again to set their feet on the firm and stable earth, their proper element.

But that's not what Thanksgiving is about. Within twenty-four hours, they had good cause to bemoan the place they'd landed on. They had intended, when they left Plymouth two months before, to land in Virginia, 'earth's only paradise', wrote an English poet who'd never been there, 'where nature hath in store fowl, venison, and fish and the fruitfullest soil'. But they missed the southern coast of Virginia; storms sent them up five hundred miles north, kept them from the Hudson channel, blew them another couple of hundred miles and on Cape Cod found—what? 'No friends, no houses, no inns, but [I quote from brave Bradford] a hideous and desolate wilderness full of wild beasts and wild men.'

Well, it was, as I hinted, those wild men who saved most of the Puritans—with their introduction of the (unknown to Europeans) turkey, potatoes, and the red berry they'd never seen either but which was the only fruitful growth of the Cape. The cranberry bogs produced this red berry which, as an accompanying sauce, is considered mandatory at the family Thanksgiving dinner. I had better say at once that cranberry sauce is, to me, one of those things you must be born to, like peanut butter and drum majorettes. Today, cranberry juice has become a mad fashion in this country as a health drink of choice, recommended strongly even by cardiologists since the recent large, and I believe first, long-term clinical trial of vitamin C pills, reported that whatever else vitamin C supplements may do, they are first-rate producers of arteriosclerosis (hardening of the arteries). Consequently, an eminent cardiologist predicts the retreat from orange juice will be as fast as the advance to cranberry juice.

I deduced (I think you'll agree correctly) that, of those four dishes that saved the Puritans' life, the cranberry is the one that would most interest most listeners, since most of them today have known about turkey and potatoes for centuries. Not long

262

ago I ran into an old English lady who said, 'Turkeys came from America? What nonsense! Why, my grandmother had a turkey every Christmas, and that was in the middle of the nineteenth century!' I hope I made it clear at the start that William Bradford ate his first turkey in 1621, when he was 43. Many of the Puritans died during the first winter, and it was in the early fall of 1621 that they had their first harvest. They had learned, too, about the crop known from the Canadian border to the tip of Chile as corn, but in England (just to be different) as maize. (I often wondered how that early maker of breakfast cereals would have done if he'd tried to popularize maize flakes, which is what they are.) It was some day after the first harvest was in and the Bradford crew knew they were in Massachusetts for keeps that—legend has it—they held a feast. Somebody made up a hymn (the one we sing now is a nineteenth-century invention) and gave up a public prayer of Thanksgiving. That's what we like to say is the origin of the continental blow-out that took place last Thursday.

In dry fact, it wasn't until the middle of the nineteenth century that somebody thought it would be a charming thing to have a national day of Thanksgiving, really to congratulate each other on having settled in America or having been born American. This year, you'll gather, there are in some places some misgivings. Anyway, it wasn't until 243 years after the supposed event that Abraham Lincoln proclaimed a national day of Thanksgiving. Many states paid no attention. But gradually, over about eight years, it dawned on people that it was yet another excuse for another day's holiday. Finally, Franklin Roosevelt not only proclaimed it, but read it over the radio and put in a little sermon of his own about William Bradford and company. And by 1940 it had become an immovable feast, celebrated by Act of Congress on the third Thursday in November.

Forty years ago this weekend, a terrific national panic blew up when, a month or so before Thanksgiving, the Pure Food and Drug Administration, which passes on the safety of all crops and new drugs, put out a general warning. The cranberry crop set aside for Thanksgiving had been found (two shipments anyway) to contain a weedkiller poison, aminotriazole. The Secretary of Health, Education and Welfare was instructed to go through the entire Thanksgiving reserve to see how much threatened the national survival. Two little bags of cranberries were found to be suspect. The rest of the seven million pounds he searched were safe, home free. On the Wednesday evening before Thanksgiving, an enterprising reporter asked if President and Mrs Eisenhower were going to serve cranberry sauce as usual. None of your business, the White House replied. Quite right. A little later, your own enterprising reporter made enquiries. President Eisenhower, the American hero of the Second World War, served apple sauce.

America's Day of Terror

14 September 2001

Last Monday I woke up and, as usual on Monday mornings, I began to ponder what I might talk about this time. I was out of touch, you might say, with what they now call the real world after two weeks' absorption in the fantasy world of the United States Open Tennis championships. But first, as the anchormen say, the weather. (I like to know if it's cool enough for me to venture around the block.) So, first, I turned on the weather channel, and within ten seconds knew all too well what this talk would be about. The man was pointing to a blurry circle just north of Bermuda. The circle had a bull's eye, and it had a name. Its name was Erin, the fifth tropical storm up from the Caribbean this season, and it was said, by the National Hurricane Center in Miami, to be the most lethal in a quarter-century, its winds swirling at a hundred and twenty miles an hour. And, the point that hit me literally where I live, it was headed due northwest and expected to make landfall on Wednesday at Suffolk County, the eastern end of Long Island. Not since 1986 have we had to retire from a hurricane to the underground bunker my wife designed twenty-five years ago.

I had breakfast and thought about when I might take off for the Island to join my wife, and my daughter over from London. Then I went back to the weatherman, who was mysteriously in a very cheery mood. He pointed to the whirling circle and then across the Atlantic water inland to Pennsylvania to show a vertical line of arrows pointing east. They marked a cold front that the experts positively declared would move swiftly east and not merely block the oncoming hurricane but push it rudely due east to expire in mid-Atlantic. For once, the experts were dead right. No more was heard about Erin, and, waking on Tuesday morning, I was free to ponder again.

But not, you'll understand, for long. I turned on a twenty-four-hour news station and saw a kind of movie I detest, of the towering inferno type: a roaring image, of a monolith collapsing like a concertina in a vast plume of smoke. Just as I pressed my thumb to switch to 'the real world' I caught the familiar voice of a newsman and was in the appalling real world of Tuesday, 11 September 2001, a date which to Americans will live in infamy along with the memories of Pearl Harbor, 7 December 1941, and 22 November 1963, the grievous day of President Kennedy's assassination.

Before nightfall, an old United States Senator was to call it 'the most tragic day in American history'. And by that time, numb from the apocalyptic images, not even a historian was going to question the Senator's definition by bringing up, say, the Civil War and a million dead. But in our time, in my time certainly, it was the most awful, startling, morning I can remember, not because this was the most awful domestic disaster ever, but because, for the first time in the American experience, an act of war aroused, and television pulverized, our senses in a way we'd never known. Before 11 September, most of the Americans who had seen and felt war on their own shores were

266

nearly a century in the grave. The first word I had from my wife, who was a hundred miles away in that so nearly-fateful Suffolk County, was, 'To think, all these years, I've been saying we were the luckiest people alive, never to have known war in our own country.'

For myself, after the first mere announcement, I thought back to another September, by a fluke of memory of another 11 September. The date is confirmed by the books, but my boyhood memory of the newspapers is sharper. You must bear with me in this. The point will emerge. The first great battle of the First World War was over, the Battle of the Marne, on the 11th, and, in the following days, the newspapers hailed the German retreat as a triumph. The sub-headings printed: 'Heavy Casualties On Both Sides.' I didn't at first know what that meant but soon learned as, during the next four years, it became a standard phrase. We often suggested the German casualties—60,000 in one day. We didn't print numbers of our own. Later, when the Battle of the Somme was over, Britain had lost a quarter of a million men in that battle alone. We never knew, nor read, that. Many years later, I wrote: 'Is it conceivable that if the British could have been a population of *viewers*—of television viewers instead of newspaper readers—is it conceivable they would have just shaken their heads and gone to the railway stations, as they did, to wave their boys off on the troop trains?'

So, the first thing I felt was, 'This is a war. It's here, it's happening to us.' It is the first thing, I think, for people outside the United States to realize. It is the same feeling of bewilderment and secret fear (what next?) that Londoners felt after the first night of the Blitz, in September 1940.

What next, now? I have reams and reams of notes, made over four days and three nights. But most of them recount heartbreaking scenes and awful facts you yourself will have seen and heard much of. If there is one note, one small note in this whole monstrous story that can be called heartening, it is the act on Wednesday of the NATO ambassadors in Brussels. For the first time in the history of the alliance, the council voted to invoke Article 5 of the original treaty, which says plainly (something that has been quietly and blandly evaded): 'An armed attack against any of the allies in Europe or North America shall be considered an attack against them all.' This was far and away the best news for the White House and the Pentagon in many a year, for it gave strength and credibility to the President's promise of punishment for the perpetrators.

The word 'perpetrators' points at once to the mystery that has maddened everybody, the military especially, since last Tuesday morning. Since the first microphone was pushed in front of an official of any kind, the line I remember best was that of General Schwarzkopf, the commander of the alliance in the Gulf War: 'That's our main problem: how and where to respond to an enemy we can't identify.'

While he was talking, the FBI had organized around its counter-terrorist squad four thousand agents and two thousand others: scientists, forensic lawyers, weathermen, aviation experts, architects, engineers. They have been very busy all around the country, and already from an avalanche of data have learned enough to alert the entire continental

268

American air defence system, and to discover with careful speed the prime suspect to be bin Laden. From now on it would be wise not to believe the welter of rumours that are bound to flood us, and credit only what is confirmed by the American and European intelligence services. Attorney General Ashcroft and his FBI chiefs have been remarkably patient with the media, most conspicuously with the younger television reporters—as with the dense, super-stupid question of the year from a young girl reporter: 'Sir, do you think this attack had been planned?' It gave an FBI terrorist expert the chance to respond dryly. 'I should say it would be brilliant if it had been planned in less than one year.'

Talking of patience before the interminably inquisitive, and often stupid, press, the Mayor of New York City has stood out as a hero, a hero who apparently has to get along without sleep. And as for the unseen heroes, I recall most vividly a doctor who had been in combat in Vietnam. He emerged from this Hieronymus Bosch inferno in a blizzard of ash and rubble and said, 'Never saw anything like this—this is hell.' And there was a young television cameraman, a simple (late twenties I should guess), all-American boy with ropey hair and good looks, wiping the ghostly ash from his face and talking of the nurses, among the hundred-odd doctors there: helping survivors, staunching wounds, day and night on the move, calmly saying, 'Please make way.' The boy said, 'People—are unbelievable.'

What is more unbelievable than the enormous wasteland of downtown New York is the stamina and courage of the firemen rescue workers (over

269

three hundred lost by now), the thousand or more, on their sixteen-hour shifts before they nap for a couple of hours and begin again, slogging through, so far, 100,000 tons of ash and rubble and tangled steel, pointing dogs into dark tunnels of wreckage, on and on, looking for the shape of a life or a corpse.

There is an old song, what we knew as a spiritual, which goes: 'Sometimes, I'm up, sometimes I'm down—sometimes I'm almost to the ground.' Well, today, tonight, America is down. But between the deeds of the rescue men and the words of NATO—if they mean what they say—America is not 'almost to the ground'.

America on Standby

21 September 2001

I make no apology for beginning, yet again, with a memory which has never faded, of the First World War. The late Dr Sigmund Freud said, 'The unconscious has a long memory and a logic all its own', and the senses of a small child between the ages of 6 and 10 are here to prove it. When last week I first saw what so many firemen, doctors and nurses were moving about in, the huge, raw landscape of fog and rubble and twisted steel and what we now call, without a wince, body parts, my memory immediately matched the scene with the newsreel pictures we saw eighty-odd years ago every week in what to me was known as the local picture drome: skeletons of village churches sticking up in a now rotted landscape, no foliage, no leaves, trees shot down to broken matchsticks in a miles-wide tangle of barbed wire decorated with body parts.

In the middle of one thundering battle there appeared in the night sky a glowing figure in a frame of blinding light. All the thousands of soldiers saw was the figure of an angel. It became known as the Angel of Mons. And in time, the sensible wisdom was that it had been seen by either the very religious or the very naive. But hundreds of soldiers who were neither swore they had seen in it an angel of deliverance. Mons was where the British, in the earliest days of the war, first engaged the Germans. And Mons was recaptured on the *last* day of the war, in the eleventh hour of the eleventh day of the eleventh month, 1918. Ever since, there has been an annual memorial service in Mons dedicated to St George, who, you recall, slew the dragon.

While on that dreadful Tuesday morning a week and more ago, we lay, stood or pattered in the first terrified daze of seeing the hellish scene, there arose (to be less poetic but more correct, I think I should say there popped up) a figure, everywhere pointing, taking charge, in a suit, in a sweater, in a helmet, a human figure in the downtown hell, in an uptown church, a well-known figure, not hitherto thought of as an angel—a fallen angel, perhaps, with a rather messy private life—known to most Americans as a very quick-witted public prosecutor and active public servant who had greatly reduced crime and performed other virtuous services in his job as the second most powerful executive in the United States, namely the Mayor of New

271

York City.

More than any Mayor in my lifetime, except Fiorello La Guardia, Rudolph Giuliani has been loved and loathed. All the truly effective Mayors alienate one group or another: whites, blacks, Hispanics, Jews, the Irish, the Italians, whoever, whatever. The inimitable Ed ('how'm I doin'?') Koch said, with his foxy smile: 'Being well hated in one quarter or another goes with the job.' But before 11 September, if we'd been asked to sum up the mayoralty of Mr Giuliani (his term ends in December), most of us, I think, would have said: a small man, a battery of energy, brainy, ruthless with opponents, and whether likeable or not, immensely competent.

Tuesday morning, within an hour of the shattering of the towers, we saw, deep in the grey-black fog and the writhing steel and the rubble, a man barely recognizable as Rudolph Giuliani, and from then till now, twenty hours a day, everywhere there was trouble, or mourning, or work to be done and ordered, here he was, gentle with widows and old people, enormously instructive at all times, exercising almost saintly patience with the press, never striking a wrong emotional note, never sentimental or platitudinous, never showing a spark of temper. He was what the Greeks called an epiphany, 'a manifestation of a super human being'. And thanks to worldwide television, he was seen for many days as the leader of the nation, an impression that, of course, flashed to us an almost guilty reflection. Where, in a word, was the President?

It took our leading newspaper only two days to write a scolding editorial—I think it is not too harsh a word—complaining that it was not Mr Bush who had so gallantly and quickly stood among the firefighters and the grieving, comforting at a hospital bedside, or praying in a humble church. By a weird coincidence, directly opposite the scolding editorial was a piece written by one of the paper's political columnists. But this was not a matter of opinion, it was hard reporting, and when Mr William Safire turns reporter, he seems to have a direct line to the horse's mouth. It was an account of how Vice President Cheney took command of the whole security emergency, realized in an instant the personal peril the President was in, guessed correctly that the Pentagon bomber was at first intended for the White House, and directed the President to be flown off to secret locations in three other places, one of them, the nuclear control centre deep in the bowels of the prairie in Nebraska. This astonishing story, in effect scolding the scolding editorial, was confirmed in every detail the following Sunday by the Vice President himself in a network television interview.

This journalistic jumping of the gun of judgement should alert us, I think, to the role of the press, the media. Surely a naive question to ask at this time of day. Isn't the media's function what it's always been: to comfort the afflicted and afflict the comfortable? After this catastrophe, the second half of that injunction carries a quite new peril. To afflict the comfortable has always meant in practice to keep an eye on government on behalf of the governed.

But in the past quarter-century there has been a tendency, in this country certainly, to assume that a reporter's job is primarily to smell out corruption and, on bad days, invent it. This drift is due to the remarkable success, in the early 1970s, of the two Washington reporters, Woodward and Bernstein, in unearthing the dirt of the Watergate scandal and pushing Richard Nixon out of the Presidency. Not too long ago I asked a young college graduate what he wanted to be. He said, 'An investigative reporter'. Why not, I suggested, just a reporter?

This ambition flourishes today in reporters who honestly believe that their first job is to find out who's to blame. And already, in the interminable procession of television talk shows and round-table discussions, we discover that the country is absolutely teeming with professors and international affairs gurus, ex-Cabinet officers and journalists who are absolute experts on terrorism.

We're going, I think, to have trouble with this side of the media. I suggest that just now is not the time to stomp around looking for someone to blame. Of course the government must always be open to criticism, but since most living American journalists have never covered a war, there may be lots of ill-feeling ahead if, as happens in all wars, there has to be a form of censorship. Most journalists I've listened to have, I'm sure, no idea that twelve years ago Vice President Cheney, who was then Secretary of Defense, was busy drawing up a study of the care and destruction of counter-terrorism, especially in the Arab world, or *out of* the Arab world *into* America. An old friend, long in government but now on the sidelines of the aged, mentioned how grateful we, President Bush more than any of us, should be that he has on his team Mr Cheney, General (now Secretary of State) Colin Powell, and Donald Rumsfeld, once and present Secretary of Defense, ambassador to NATO, special envoy to the Middle East. These three, and a whole squad of CIA and FBI unknowns, were in the thick of the conduct of the Gulf War and explain, I think, the uncanny job done so far by the FBI in tracking down, without panic or illegal tactics, hot suspects in the most unlikely public places and in obscure suburbs from Maine to California.

For the first week or so, we got mixed signals about the proper military response. The President promised, with thumbs up, that 'we shall smoke them out of their holes and catch them fleeing for the hills'. Next thing, or rather a day earlier, General Schwarzkopf, who spent years in Saudi Arabia, warned us: 'Afghanistan is the size of Texas, desert and rocky mountains, no roads, automobiles, transport by camel and mule, no place to dump missiles and smart bombs. There are a million places and holes and caves in the mountains where people don't hide—they live.' For the great mass of us (the people, I suppose, is a better word), the job ahead is, in the long run, of understanding, along with the government, the nature of this new war.

In the short run, the more difficult task for all of us is the emotional, the psychological one, of knowing this as a new age and knowing how we should act in it. On the first day of the apocalypse, in the midst of the fire and the fog, Mayor Giuliani was asked by a news reporter what we, ordinary people, ought to do. He said, 'Take your kids on a picnic, go out and buy something, pray to God, do your usual job, whatever it is, however humble.' Almost four centuries ago, an Englishman, George

275

Herbert, a poet and later a priest, in a very turbulent time in English history, urged the same advice: 'A servant . . . /Makes drudgery divine, /who sweeps a room, as for thy laws, /makes that and the action fine.'

The Stars and Stripes

9 November 2001

Something that every first visitor to America notices, and I mean during my lifetime here, is the constant display of the American flag, in places both public and private. I couldn't count the hundreds of times that a visiting European friend, off, say, the morning after arrival on a little tour of the town or the village, has seen the flag draping from a pole outside the firehouse or hanging from a humble bedroom window. And the visitor says: 'Hello! What's the occasion, some famous American date? Independence Day, whatever?' No, you say, nothing special. Somebody got up in the morning and felt good, and instead of taking the dog for a trot or cooking up a special batch of pancakes, decided to hang out the flag. In country places, there are always families who make a point of hanging out the flag every Sunday morning in summer.

The first flaming public response to 11 September was an outburst of flags. Overnight, two suddenly famous flag factories were reported to have gone on a twenty-four-hour working day. And orders came roaring in for flags to be woven or impressed or embedded into every sort of item of clothing or decoration. The two teams playing off the baseball championship appeared, the second night, with a neat Stars and Stripes planted above or alongside their team's logo. A hundred flags flew outside Rockefeller Plaza. Flags flapped into the late afternoon fog atop San Francisco's Golden Gate Bridge. Flags were on hats, sweaters, blouses, trousers, motor cars, bikes, shopping bags, from windows, roofs, awnings—a continent blanketed by the Stars and Stripes. I didn't hear or read a squeak of a complaint from anybody about the wholesale violation (punishable by a fine and a prison sentence) that this coast-to-coast flourish represented, which shows just how old I must be. Some days after the original horror which stirred this vast wave of patriotism, I had a most lively recall of a time when I was begged by the newly arrived British ambassador, no less, to do a broadcast to Britain as soon as possible, and acquaint the people of Britain of the hideous crime that an English manufacturer was perpetrating against the law of the United States.

The time was fifty-nine years ago. The United States had come into the Second World War, and the first shipment of American troops was about to arrive in England. A British clothing manufacturer, in the Midlands I believe, had an idea of heart-warming hospitality, to make and deliver an item of clothing for each and every arriving American soldier which should have knitted into it the American flag. Now whether or not the Foreign Office or the Prime Minister was consulted about this idea, all the evidence suggests that they thought it a splendid, a touching, tribute to the

277

arriving allies. Nobody, it seems, had ever heard of the Code of Etiquette issued by the United States War Department in the early 1920s to dictate once and for all how the flag was to be flown, where and when, and especially certain abuses of the flag which must be for ever prohibited. The code is a pretty elaborate one but the gist of it says that the flag is to be flown only between sunrise and sunset, is to be hoisted *briskly* but lowered ceremoniously, and that it must never touch the ground. It may be displayed at night only on special prescribed occasions, and then it must be lit. Another thousand words prescribe the flag's role, position and function in the United States and its dependencies and at sea, whenever a President or former President dies. The really tough part of the code is the list of prohibitions. The flag must not be dipped to any person or thing; it must not be displayed on a float, motor car or boat except from a staff. It is by no means ever to be used—here's the nub, or the rub—as a receptacle for anything, or for any advertising purpose, not to be embroidered on such articles as cushions, or handkerchiefs, or boxes of any kind. The code did not even reach to what a United States Senator once called 'the obscenity' of the flag's being printed on the cover of a box of chocolates, a very frequent and welcome sight to me as a boy at Christmas time, except, of course, the flag was the Union Jack.

You'll gather at once that no such code had ever been thought of in England, where the royal standard and the Union Jack were, indeed, the most popular emblems for advertisers of everything from biscuits to a mysterious potion, I well

278

remember, called 'a lung tonic'. The implied suggestion, I suppose, was that if it could liven up the royal lungs it certainly could ginger up yours.

So, imagine the moment in Washington, when the British ambassador was told, by some American friend, that a British manufacturer had delivered to this American camp in England a whole year's supply of an object of clothing which violated the official American code in a particularly tasteless way. 'What', asked the embattled ambassador, 'is the code, and what is the offending object?' He was told about the code and, according to his own later testimony, blushed with embarrassment. But the blush was nothing to the groan that followed on his hearing about the item of clothing which the innocent manufacturer, bless his warm intentions, had thought would be especially cute. A pair—a thousand pairs—of, how shall I put this? ladies' short undergarments, the seat being composed of the Stars and Stripes. I was asked to broadcast a report on the War Department's code, and the next we heard was (you can well believe) that the panties were immediately . . . withdrawn, I suppose, is the inevitable word.

The result of this famous clanger or boo-boo was that within months, in June 1942, Congress passed a resolution 'amending into public law all existing rules and customs pertaining to display and use of the flag'. The assumption was that from then on, nobody, not even the British, would dare desecrate the American flag in any of the stated or unstated ways. We had a quarter-century to observe the code and, by now, the law.

We reckoned without Vietnam and the uproar of

279

students on the streets in an outbreak of deliberate burning of the flag, an act so outrageous to many Americans in many states that in 1968 Congress passed a law making it a federal crime to burn or otherwise desecrate the flag, on pain of one year's imprisonment or $1,000 fine. For twenty years that law was on the books but only randomly observed, for in several states the students went on burning the flag. Eventually an appeal against the new law—citing the protection of the First Amendment—was taken to the Supreme Court and the Court ruled, only twelve years ago, that burning the flag was a permissible expression of free speech. The effect of this was to have the flag-desecration laws of all the states declared invalid, unconstitutional. And from now on, plainly, you can do anything you like with the flag: wear it on top or underneath, hang it, burn it, flaunt it or, if the war goes on too long for the already chanting students at Berkeley, you can freely flout it. So, yet another old value bites the dust.

Already, though, the wholesale displaying of the flag, on humans in particular, is fading along the gently falling graph of the President's popularity. Only two weeks ago, eighty-seven Americans in a hundred approved of President Bush and the war in Afghanistan. Today it is down to 69 per cent, and these two parallel falling lines are a graphic reminder of something about the American character, if there is such a thing, which is its impatience with difficult, slow solutions.

This is essentially the nation of the quick fix, the miracle drug. And though so many such promises turn out hasty and false, it's surprising in even the last hundred-year stretch of American history how

280

often the sudden flash of intelligence, rather than interminable research, has produced a blessing to mankind. Think of cheap steel, the dollar watch, the refrigerator, traffic lights, the assembly line, the oil freighter, the electric bulb. The President said a month ago that the new war would be strange and long. He never defined long, but day after day at the White House press briefings, the President—or his press secretary, or Secretary Powell—is unceasingly pressed by the media to say how long. There are people, raving enthusiasts in the week after 11 September, who already suggest the war is not showing results. They can't have thought much about the history of Afghanistan and its guerrilla warriors. They've lived on a battleground for eight centuries. In the nineteenth century, Great Britain fought for eight years to conquer them and failed. In 1979 the Soviet Union moved in and occupied the whole country. After fighting for nearly ten years, with 300,000 men, the Soviets gave up and withdrew.

Our trouble is, I think, that to the older generation of Americans, war recalls the long quagmire and defeat of Vietnam. And to the middle and younger generations, the only war they remember is the Gulf War, a spectacular display of night missiles flying, minimum casualties, of the enemy surrendering, and all over in a hundred hours. So how long is long?

If Americans are looking for a role model, a man who didn't flaunt his patriotism but acted on it, they couldn't do better than Thomas Edison. He had one brilliant, bright idea: the electric light bulb. Not before he'd failed with six thousand different vegetable fibres did he find, in a Japanese

281

bamboo, a high-resistance filament that would burn permanently in a vacuum. He had inspiration which was god-sent. But he had something better: stamina. And you can sense, I think, that behind President Bush's gung-ho assurances there is a slightly nervous, earnest, appeal that stamina is what more than anything he wants the people to begin to show.

Messiah at Christmas

21 December 2001

I am not myself a great collector of old letters, but from time to time, riffling through the chaos of what I dare to call my files, I come on a note from someone I'd long forgotten. And the other morning I fell on a funny, shrewd letter from a shrewd and funny man who has been lost to us for far too long, a loss I feel now because at a time of pretentious theories in literature, politics and—help!—architecture, this man was the sanest of critics and a splendid slaughterer of sacred cows in England whether of the left or right, the lowbrow or the highbrow, as Tom Wolfe has been in America: Philip Larkin.

I had the privilege of keeping up a correspondence with him in what, alas, turned out to be the last year or two of his life. We exchanged ideas, mostly about poetry, and always about jazz—the word jazz being understood as only and always what *we* agreed to like—namely, jazz from the earliest New Orleans days up to the 1940s—and there an end. The arrival of bebop we both heard as the death knell. Larkin called Thelonius Monk 'the elephant on the keyboard'.

In this—as it turned out—his last letter there was a PS: 'Another thing I note we have in common: you say you play the *Messiah* right through every Christmas. So do I.'

I must not assume, as people of my and indeed the previous generation always do assume, that a permanent item of our culture passes on to the next and the next generation. Nearly fifty years ago, I had the rare, weird pleasure of introducing *Messiah* to—Leonard Bernstein.

Leonard Bernstein came to fame, with a national audience as distinct from the concert audience, everywhere when he appeared first on television. The show was the first ninety-minute show of any kind. It was a collection, collage or mishmash of music, science, drama, politics, history, anything and everything; and Bernstein was one of our earliest stars, when he was already blazing his way from Boston to Vienna in the works of the nineteenth-century romantics, the Russians especially. One day the small core of the staff of our show, a half-dozen of us, were sitting around tossing ideas and we came to sketching out the Christmas show. It was then I threw in what I thought was the very hackneyed but beautiful idea of having Bernstein conduct a short version of *Messiah*. Bernstein, I remember, looked up— 'Handel?' he said with a rising inflection, as if it might just as well have been Gershwin. That's the man. 'You know something,' said Bernstein, 'I don't know it.' Well, need I say he came to know it, and I—as one brought up in the Nonconformist north of England and therefore having known every note of *Messiah* since the age of 5—had the pride of standing before a television audience of two hundred and ninety stations and introducing George Frederic, a pretty old man (56 was beyond the usual span in 1742), not doing well with his concert music or operas, in bad financial trouble, being invited to go to Dublin for a few weeks and for a price compose an oratorio. He lived alone in two rooms in a small house but, once he had this conception of writing the life of Christ, not as a chronicle but as a series of spiritual musical themes, he scarcely paused from dawn to midnight. He had his meals pushed under the door. At the end of fifteen days only, during the last twilight, he finished the 'Hallelujah Chorus', and wrote in his journal: 'I felt that the Lord God Almighty had come down and did stand before me.' At the end, Bernstein embraced us all. 'What a sublime work,' he said.

One of the oldest musical traditions of New York City is a performance of *Messiah* given with the instruments of the original scoring, first done here in 1770 in a church which stands, miraculously, today only three blocks from the mountainous rubble and ashes of the twin towers. On that 12 September, the minister and the choirmaster padded in gas masks through the horrors underfoot and knew that this 230-year-old tradition was bound to be broken. However, three months have passed, and the ninety pipes of the old organ are still choked, and the burning smell is everywhere, and, though the church has stained glass but no open windows, the ash and the grime and smoke came in through the leading. But last

Sunday once more, into an acrid atmosphere, the old tradition stayed unbroken.

It may strike some listeners as odd that of all cities, New York, which houses two million of America's six million Jews, should hold to this by now ancient Christian tradition. But if you knew New York City, as this administration is desperately trying to have it known to the Arab world, you would know this to be most characteristic of the city. Long ago, the most elegant essayist of the twentieth century, E. B. White, wrote: 'the most admirable thing about New York is not the conflict of the races and religions but the truce they keep.'

The word 'Messiah' exists in many languages, though it wasn't until the sixteenth century that translators of the Bible chose to fix its spelling with an aitch—Messiah—as sounding more Hebrew. And that's the way it stayed. It meant, as everyone knows, the one who would come and set free the oppressed children of Israel. And ever since, it has been used in general in other languages, to signify the liberator of the oppressed.

When I was watching that appalling tape of bin Laden it struck me that one of the tragedies of this war is the fact of his striking good looks: a sombre and handsome presence, the fine eyes, an expression almost of tenderness. It was hard from the beginning to appreciate that this man is the latest of a dreaded breed we have known to our rage and sorrow in the twentieth century: Stalin, Hitler, Pol Pot, Saddam Hussein, all of them either ordinary or ugly. And here is a totalitarian fanatic whose majestic presence lends itself at least to the role of Robin Hood, which is how he sees himself and—at most—as a Messianic figure who will deliver the impoverished peoples of Arabia from what some see as the superpower bully of the Western world.

Enough of these morbid musings—though I believe they are, unhappily, very relevant to the main American propaganda problem: which is how to define this new, strange war and how to make people recognize the chief personal enemy as an old tyrant in a new guise, let alone to see this war as a bizarre revival of the medieval religious wars: the Middle Ages returned with a bomb and a germ.

*   *   *

But, as I settle for Christmas Eve sipping the twilight wine of Scotland, I shall think of another tape, another television interview, which, in this season of good will it's a pleasure to remark on.

Everyone who has followed a sport for long is frequently caught, I believe, between two emotions in watching the stars of the game: horrified awe at the huge money they earn, and yet relief that they are not paid, as they used to be, at the going rate of plumbers' assistants. We're bound to wonder from time to time what they do with all this loot. And too often the answer is—as one famous golfer put it—'Well, what d'you think? I used to ride the subway. Now I have six cars, a yacht and a private jet. How *about* that?' The tale I have to tell is quite another story and shines like a good deed in a naughty world. The interview came at the end of the final tournament of the season. It was won by the young man who is without question the best golfer in the world. He had just picked up $2

286

million from winning this one tournament and was asked if it was true that the money would go to the Tiger Woods Foundation. Yes, it would, he said. His foundation he described simply as a fund with the simple aim of helping poor children of colour make something of themselves. What, asked the breezy interviewer, is your main goal in life? Tiger blinked, as if we'd just had another glimpse of the obvious. 'I said—the Foundation—my aim is to make it global, based in the United States but taking in many, many countries. That's far more important than winning tournaments.'

Here is a young man, just 26, who was urged only four years ago by an old and well-wishing friend, an old man and a ravenous golfer, to stay one more year in college and 'enrich' his life. Tiger decided, on the contrary, to turn pro and sign a first sponsor's contract for $52 million. Since then, new contracts and renewals have poured in like Niagara. And he has grown in maturity as a human being ever since, stayed remarkably modest, and, with his enormous fame, level-headed. From the start, he decided to hand over his fortune to enriching the lives of impoverished coloured children across the globe. At Christmas time, I can't think of a finer role model, young or old.

Ringing the Changes

4 January 2002

We had the warmest fall in recorded—meteorologically recorded—history, a mainly frostless system across the whole state from New York City in the south to the Canadian border (remember, New York State is exactly the area of England).

On Christmas Day there was a now famous photograph of two young women, sunbathing on a bench in the most western city (Buffalo) heretofore famous for having been settled three generations ago mostly by Russians and for having more and earlier big snowfalls than any place in the state. Last week Buffalo paid the price for that very late and continuing warm spell. The usual icy Canadian wind came hurling in from the west, collided with this strange layer of warm air we were basking in, and in four days deposited 7 feet—83.5 inches to be precise—on good old Buffalo, provoking loud choruses in every pub that had candles to see people with, ribald variations of the famous song urging Buffalo gals: 'Won't you come out tonight?'

So, the winter bore down like a wolf on the fold. Down in the city here, it's been so far too cold for snow, but the days have been as bright as diamonds and I look down to a meadow in Central Park and see tiny muffled moppets frisking around like children in a Dutch painting. It is a very peaceful scene, and only the occasional ripping of the sky by a fighter jet reminds us who keeps it so.

Well, I couldn't keep up this reverie all the short day long. Back to the television, and a review of some of the stories from the past year we'd forgotten, some we're only too happy to have forgotten. Three million animals destroyed in England. That plane mysteriously lost off Long Island. Better forgotten as soon as possible were three topics so shocking at the time that we may never forget them. Mr Clinton's pardoning of the convicted felon and campaign contributor, Marc Rich, and the Clintons' subsequent departure from the White House with a load of furniture—an exit the mildest critic called tacky, and which former President Carter called 'simply disgraceful'. There was, I'm afraid, the indelible memory of those awful weeks during which there was no President-elect. Most memorable of all was the still debatable intrusion of the Supreme Court in a matter the Constitution leaves to the state courts of any state whose tally is disputed. And after that, the twenty-four-hour panic of the United States Supreme Court—so uncertain how to act that they reached the most unsatisfying verdict they ever can: a split 5 to 4 decision, which meant, in a Presidential election, that a President was elected not by the recorded seventy million or so voters, not even by the nine justices of the Supreme Court, but by the one vote that broke a tie of 4 to 4, the swing vote of one person. In a phrase, Justice Sandra Day O'Connor appointed the President of the United States.

There is one man who is not forgotten yet and perhaps never will be forgotten by anyone alive and sentient on 11 September. Time was when *Time* magazine published on its New Year cover its main story with a photograph, the title: Man of the Year. It's now, need I say, Person of the Year. And that person, who is also a man, seems to have met the general national choice of a human being most deserving the title. He is Rudolph Giuliani, who for seven years was known to New Yorkers as the most active, crime-busting, ruthless and best-hated Mayor since the late, great Fiorello La Guardia. I never met any New Yorker who was in two minds about Giuliani, just as I never met an adult American during the 1930s and 1940s who was in two minds about President Franklin Roosevelt. You either worshipped or loathed him. And that was true till the day he died. The eerie thing about Mr Giuliani is that during his seven and a half year reign as Mayor, even the New Yorkers who decided he had become a good Mayor did so grudgingly. Yes, New York City was orderly again, race relations were at least subdued, and the drop in crime was really dramatic. A final figure appeared on the last day of the year, the last day Mayor Giuliani was in office. The year he came to City Hall, the homicide rate for the year was 2,400. Last year, it was just over 600. All this made Mr Giuliani admirable. His transformation into a man greatly admired but also lovable is the mystery story of 2001.

It induced in a few serious people serious discussion about whether redemption is possible all at once, during a lifetime. Once a year at least, we all enjoy Dickens' happy absurdity of taking a tough, malicious, shrewd businessman and making him over, overnight, into a genial, gregarious, almost saintly old man. No matter how much *A Christmas Carol* may be dismissed as a rollicking good story but a deeply sentimental one, I believe it has stayed alive for a hundred and sixty years because in even the most cynical, rational, irreligious human, there is from time to time a twinge, even an unacknowledged wish, to be a better person.

From 11 September and on till the moment he said farewell to the city, Rudolph Giuliani was no longer merely the impersonation of a successful Mayor. He was acknowledged throughout America to have been a good man who behaved finely through an appalling ordeal. Inhumanly patient and attentive, totally unaffected, open, for twenty-four hours, to any help he could give to every victim in sight. At the very end he was asked if he was not sad to be leaving the Mayoralty. 'Of course,' he said, 'but when, like me, you've seen real sadness all around you day in and day out, you're just grateful to have had the privilege of serving.'

I no sooner had these solemn thoughts than an appropriate sound put an end to them. It was the sound of a tolling bell, very familiar to me. If you were here with me and wondered why it is so loud and clear, you could climb a staircase and go up on our roof and look straight to the north and east— no farther than forty yards away you'd see towering above the adjoining apartment building five onion domes and below them two huge shining gold crosses. You would be looking at the Cathedral of St Nicholas, and might well believe you were in Moscow. But no, you are just off Fifth Avenue. Such are the mind-your-own-business habits of many New Yorkers, there are people who live in the same block as the cathedral and don't know it is the largest, the most prestigious Russian Orthodox church in the United States. It has been there for all and more of the fifty-one years we have lived in this apartment. And in all that time, I never heard its bell or bells ring out merrily. Always at twilight, two melancholy tollings at intervals, bemoaning, it always seemed to me, the enslavement of the Church, of all Churches and church-goers, for seventy years and more, under the tyranny of the Soviet regime, which, you remember, in the very beginning called religion 'the opiate of the masses'.

Well, only a few weeks ago, something most remarkable happened at the cathedral round the corner. The bell tolled continuously. Evidently, something was going on. Across the street from our entrance were two police cars and a cordon closing off 97th Street and the approaches to it. This little ceremony lasted the shortest time. Whoever the big shot was, he prayed briskly and was gone. I was very sad. If I'd known, I would have pattered round the corner and raised my hat to the slim little man who emerged and stepped swiftly from his devotions to a car guarded by two men in dark suits. I can tell you who it was in a short sentence no listener would have believed for sixty years at least. The President of all the Russias had just been to church. Yes, Mr Putin had been to church.

So, on New Year's Eve, though St Nicholas' bell tolled in its usual way, it sounded a new note to me, as I watched one of our television networks tour the festivities in all the capital cities that are well ahead of us in time. We saw a positive blizzard of fireworks from New Zealand to Paris. From Moscow, though, was a note more dazzling than any fireworks display: a national poll in which 78 per cent of all the Russians declared their best friend to be the United States. Bearing in mind our ignorance of Mr Putin's deepest motives, but allowing for his saying in a private interview that he had developed a close and trusting relationship with President Bush, and that not too much should be made of the abrogation of the Anti-Ballistic Missile Treaty—the prospect of, at last, a genuine alliance between Russia and the United States could be the brightest light to shine from the ashes of 11 September.

Arise, Sir Rudolph

22 February 2002

Long ago, New York City had a monthly magazine of great elegance. It was published by a man who hired the most famous writers, the best photographers, reproduced the Impressionists (then coming into fashion) in the finest colour reproductions, printed everything on touchably beautiful papers. The whole magazine was maintained with style, and damn the expense: an attitude that, alas, could not be sustained for long after the Great Depression really set in. The magazine folded in the mid-1930s.

One of its renowned features was a monthly full-page colour cartoon by a fine caricaturist, a Mexican named Covarrubias, whose cartoons brought two people together for a social meeting, an interview, two famous people whose appearance in life together anywhere at any time would have been inconceivable, preposterously unlikely. The series was called 'Impossible Interviews'. I won't give you any actual examples because I'm sure the stars of this series are long gone and you would never have heard of them anyway. But if Covarrubias were alive and practising his cunning art today, you might have Tony Blair taking tea with Saddam Hussein, or wilder still—Madonna sharing a cocktail with the Pope.

I thought with affection back to Covarrubias, and not a little yearning, because he drew at a time when there was an abundance of fine cartoonists on both sides of the Atlantic—the *New Yorker* and *Punch*. Each had at least a dozen brilliant cartoonists with a finished individual style recognizable at a hundred feet. Alas, this yearning is sharpened by the recognition that we—both countries—today live in the Dark Age of comic draughtsmanship.

What made me think of Covarrubias and his *Vanity Fair* series was a scene, a shot on television and next day in the papers, which was, indeed, an Impossible Interview. A photograph of one Rudolph Giuliani bowing before the Queen of England. The caption read, 'Sir Rudolph?' And the underlying piece went on to tell us why he might not properly or legally be addressed as Sir Rudolph. Because, the papers said, the Constitution forbids: a delusion which, I am sorry to say, even the good, grey, authoritative *New York Times* appears to share. I have had it explained countless times—once even by the British ambassador to Washington in the act of hanging the cherished silver star around my neck: 'Because, you see, you became an American citizen—the

Constitution forbids.' Ah, so! Also, not so!

The Constitution is quite emphatic but also quite precise about who may not accept a foreign title and who, by inference, *may*. During the seventeen-week convention in Philadelphia which eventually produced the written Constitution, the chief authors had, over several days, recited the great range of powers enjoyed by monarchs that would not be allowed to a President. One deprivation was most pungently expressed by the brilliant young Alexander Hamilton: 'this plan [the pending Constitution] gives the express guarantee of a republican form of government . . . and the absolute and universal exclusion of titles of nobility.' The Constitution laid down this guarantee without quite such a burst of emotion. It forbade the granting of titles *by* the United States and forbade federal government officials accepting titles from a foreign state. Here is the crucial clause, in its original eighteenth-century language: 'No title of nobility shall be granted by the United States and no person holding any office of profit or trust under them [these United States] shall accept of any present, emolument, office or titles of any kind whatever from any king, prince or foreign state—without the consent of Congress.'

I don't know of any case in which an American about to be entitled went to Congress and asked, 'please may I use it?' But the point I'm making can be simply stated: no foreign title may be accepted by anyone 'holding any office of trust' in the federal government. So, Secretary of Defense Donald Rumsfeld could not accept a knighthood. But Rudolph Giuliani is not an employee of the federal government. And there is no legal or constitutional

295

reason why he shouldn't be called Sir Rudolph, as P. G. Wodehouse, an American citizen, was dubbed and called Sir Pelham Greville Wodehouse until he died. But there is one very powerful reason that down two centuries has overwhelmed any legal right. It came from Thomas Jefferson, who was in Paris during the early debates on the Constitution. He kept an eagle eye on everything in dispute. He was full of suggestions and recommendations of what should and should not be done. If they'd had e-mail in their day, the delegates wouldn't have been able to keep up a continuous discussion without a blizzard of notes and urgings from Jefferson. First, he was shocked to learn that there was no attached Bill of Rights, and was mainly responsible for its creation. He added all sorts of private fusses. One day after a walk through the centre of Paris, he scribbled down 'No public statues', and rushed the idea off to the next packet. He lost out on that one. But he did have his say about titles of nobility, and it was so sharp and memorable that the delegates quoted it long afterwards. All Jefferson said was: 'Titles of nobility—*a very great vanity*', which, he went on to imply, no proud Republican with any sense of self-esteem would dream of accepting. This sentiment became so firmly planted in the American consciousness that to this day, even distinguished Americans cannot believe in the acceptance of a title by democratic, especially socialist, Englishmen. I remember an American Secretary of State, a powerful intellect and a very sophisticated diplomat. Yet he marvelled when the most famous Labour leader of his day moved to the House of Lords. 'Lord Attlee—sounds absurd does it not?

296

Why would he take it?' The soft answer came from a waspish friend of the Secretary. He said, 'Well, I suppose even an occasional socialist has his quota of human vanity.' Since everyone present had great admiration for Clement Attlee, we moved on to other topics.

However, if Mr Giuliani found himself in London again and wanted to get the feel of what it's like to enjoy his permissible title, I recommend that he drop in for lunch or dinner at any one of London's top hotels. He will be greeted by a tribe of men who scorn the niceties of the uninformed. They are the maîtres d', the head waiters, the commis waiters, doormen, men in the profession of greeting and serving the citizenry. They know what is what and who is who. 'Good evening, Sir Rudolph.' 'Would you care for an aperitif, Sir Rudolph?' 'And after the flutes of sole, Sir Rudolph?' 'Thank you, Sir Rudolph.' 'Goodbye, Sir Rudolph.'

On the other hand, he has cause to be glad, when he gets back home, that he is not a British citizen. I recall the wearisome experience of the actor, the late Cedric Hardwicke; in his day, a very distinguished stage actor indeed, George Bernard Shaw's favourite actor, and the one for whom he wrote a special play, casting him as King Magnus in *The Apple Cart*. Long before Olivier or Richardson, he was knighted—way back, I'm shocked to realize—in 1934. Very soon he took his career and his title to Hollywood. And in the beginning there's no doubt that his title was not an obstacle to Sir Cedric's acquisition of agreeable roles. Years later when, towards the end, he was having a rough time, having to do with the high cost of a second divorce, he told me that his title had become 'a very expensive albatross around my neck'. 'Every American', he said, 'who does any kind of service—a bootblack, a waiter, a delivery boy, assumes that a knight is a very wealthy lord with twenty thousand acres—something they hadn't known before. So where I normally gave a quarter tip I had to give a dollar, and at expensive restaurants, where the car parking attendant used to get a dollar, now, unless I give him five, he positively sneers and mutters "cheap skate" to his cronies.'

Which reminds me of a friend who, I discovered fairly recently, shared the universal delusion about knighthoods and American citizens but thought, that 'holding any office of trust under these United States' was a comic invention by a journalist we both admired. No sir, right there, Section 1, Clause 9 of the Constitution. He was thinking of a memorable column by the most famous American journalist of the last century: H. L. Mencken of Baltimore. In the Roaring Twenties, the wonder-boy amateur golfer, Bobby Jones, inspired a new national fad: young and old, the famous, infamous and obscure, took up golf. One day a young reporter walked into the Baltimore *Sun* office wearing plus fours and carrying a golf bag. Mencken was appalled at the costume—'it makes its wearer look like a stud horse with his hair done up in frizzes'. He sat down and wrote an indignant column which ended: 'If I had my way, any man guilty of golf would be ineligible for any office of trust under these United States.'

The Day the Money Stopped

8 March 2002

The 4th of March is a frightening date in American history, and every time it comes around I am drawn, as by a magnet, back to 4 March 1933. Anyone who was alive and sentient in this country then, most especially in Washington or New York City, will never forget it. I think I ought to try and give you something of the feel of it, so that we may better glimpse what may be ahead of us after the omen, I'll call it, of 4 March 2002, last Monday.

Saturday, 4 March sixty-nine years ago was an almost balmy winter's day, after several roaring blizzards. I was in New Haven, Connecticut, because that is the seat of Yale University, and I was in my second term there, taking no lectures because I was 24, on a fellowship, in the graduate school, and doing my own thing. I was about to take to the train, a ninety-minute stint, to New York City, there to meet on an incoming Cunarder, a young and jolly woman who was the daughter of an old family friend. She was on her first visit to America and I had pledged to spend the weekend showing her, as we used to say, a good time. If this tale is already eliciting a giggle in the expectation of some hanky-panky, I had better disabuse you at once. I was very much in love with an English girl who was, alas, not coming in on any Cunarder. Never was a more high-minded weekend to be spent by a young couple in their early twenties.

In those days, I was blankly non-political, never

read a newspaper, except for the theatre page. In America, more than in England, I was a 100-per-cent ignoramus about government and politics. I was aware of the grimness of the Depression from the evidence of my senses, every day seeing the long breadlines of very mixed company: shabby men and elegant men and poor women, people of all classes and ages, and every evening, out with a friend, being solicited half a dozen times by smart middle-aged men who told their wives they were looking for night work. So they were. They were begging for dimes and quarters.

I had enough ready cash to see us through the rest of the day. I checked my theatre tickets, and was on my way. As the Cunarder blew its baritone horn, it little knew it was sounding the trump of doom. But the young lady was in good spirits and in no time I was checking into my usual hotel. I walked over first to the cashier and wrote out a cheque for some, in those days, very lavish amount: could have been $20. He looked at it as at an obvious forgery. 'What is this?' He couldn't possibly cash it. I responded with a line from the then fashionable Noël Coward: 'Do you imagine there's a bank anywhere in the United States that might have the kindness to cash this cheque?' He looked at me with all the zeal of a codfish. 'I don't think so,' he drawled. 'Better go and read the papers, sonny.' (He was, you'll gather, a very old man, couldn't have been a day under 50.) Well, I did. I walked over to the news-stand and saw, across the whole front page of the *New York Times* no less, the blanketing headline: 'Roosevelt To Be Inaugurated At Noon. Declares Moratorium On All Banks.'

All banks. That made no more sense to me than

an announcement that the sky would turn to midnight-black for the rest of the day. Still, I was young and sassy and not to be intimidated by a cashier and a word I hadn't a clue to: moratorium. I stopped a passing lift man and enquired. It meant the banks were shut. All the banks, said the lift man, 'of the *You*-nited States'. In other words, he said, 'This is the day the money stopped.' It was a piercing phrase and passed into the language. A later friend of mine wrote a book with that title. But what did it mean, by way of living? And how about a receptive hotel? Mine would have no truck with us, not with a young con man who heard the news and thought to cheat the crisis by cashing a worthless cheque for a king's ransom.

These doubts and questions only came later. At the moment, the young lady and I were looking forward to a lark. How to spend a holiday weekend in New York without money, without even a bed? I had a triumphant idea. I sat the girl down in the lobby of the hotel, told her to eat, read, walk, do anything she chose for two, possibly three hours and I'd be back loaded with lots of lovely money. My ace up the sleeve was a New York to New Haven railway season ticket, or what is called a 'commutation ticket'. It had been provided to me— an advanced student of drama—to help me go to New York whenever I wanted to catch up with the latest plays. (The Commonwealth Fund was nothing if not a thoughtful provider.) So I caught the train and, back at Yale, went the rounds of my friends to borrow what would be my reserve of walking-around money. To my horror, most of them were out, and three of them could cough up only a dollar or two. The last man I called on was my oldest—six-month-old—American friend, a merry-eyed athletic type who had knocked on my door the first night at Yale wondering if I needed help of any sort. He gave me a happy but quizzical look and said a sentence that changed my life.

'Do you know', he said, 'what a due bill is?' I hadn't a clue. But I learned within thirty seconds. Yale's student publication, a very serious, double-dome quarterly was called the *Harkness Hoot*, and its editor was the very man before me. He said that the Hotel St Regis in New York, a positively upper-crust hotel on Fifth Avenue, had an outstanding bill with the *Hoot* for an advertisement at an unpaid cost of $100 (about $1,000 today). 'I think', he said, 'they'll put you up.' No wonder this merry-eyed, quick-thinking lad became Dean of the Yale Law School at the age of 26 and subsequently the President's adviser on atomic energy.

I took the bill and took the train, whipped in and out of my old hotel with a sneer and whisked my girl off to the St Regis. We ran into a small tide of outgoing guests. I guessed, correctly, we were the only new guests. The reservations clerk was suspicious of this young, carefree and probably illegal couple. He summoned the manager, whom I can see now: a dapper, grey-haired man in a cutaway. 'Can I help you?' he asked with the bored tone of a cop turning his flashlight on a burglar. Yes, I said, two separate nice rooms on the top floor. He coughed a high sarcastic cough. I showed him the due bill. He was transformed in a flash. He started clapping his hands like a flamenco dancer, and minions came running. We were swiftly ensconced in a suite with two bedrooms at the outrageous price of, say, $7. We laughed, we lolled, we prepared to see the town. I think there was one other couple in the dining room. We went to the theatre, the stalls were littered with depressed men in crumpled tails and white tie roused by the chorus, which suddenly broke loose from its opening song and changed, to a rhythmic beat: 'We depend on Roosevelt, we depend on him.' Tumult and universal cheers.

We danced some of the night and spent the rest at various Harlem nightclubs, dispensing carefree tips until the ready cash had gone, when I took out my chequebook and faced the taxi driver. He was shocked, insulted, but not for long. He took it, and he was the last cab driver, shopkeeper, waiter, café bartender to demur. A month later, I looked over my bank statement covering that weekend, and saw that my account was sadly depleted: to Helmut Schmidt 45 cents. Antonio Collucci, 65 cents. Connie's Inn, $1.65. And on and on. Next morning, the Governor of Connecticut issued scrip money, and we exchanged that on the promise of repayment in better times.

This experience germinated a lively interest, first in the banking system (what Roosevelt left of it), then in economics, and then in the origins of the Depression.

I learned about Black Thursday, 24 October 1929, the day when blocks of shares went down the river of the New York Stock Exchange, in 20,000 lots. J. P. Morgan and his banker-rescue team plugged the flood with $25 million, and for a month or two things steadied, till the bigwigs said that was nasty but the recession was over. But this was to Congress a band-aid solution. Two Western Senators, one Mr Smoot and one Mr Hawley, proposed a major, curative operation: a radical new tariff bill on imports. A hundred top economists petitioned President Hoover not to abandon his free-trade prejudice. But he signed the bill. The market started to go down, unemployment rose alarmingly, the angry Europeans were less able than ever to pay their huge First World War debt. They retorted in kind. It was depressingly plain, in the spring of 1932, that the Smoot–Hawley tariff had guaranteed the descent into the pit of thirteen million unemployed, and what would be known as the Great Depression.

This past Monday, 4 March, President Bush, over the warning words of the American and European conservative financial papers, and a plea—this time from several hundred American economists—signed a tariff bill, of 20 per cent on imported steel. There was an instant outcry from Japan, Europe, harshest of all from Russia, which sells one-third of its slab steel to the United States and threatened a ban on American poultry. Retaliation has always been the name of the game and the harbinger of recession at best.

An old, wily economist who was there in 1933 said, 'After this, the deluge, remember?' Let us hope, pray, that for once, he's wrong.

Memory of a True Great

15 March 2002

On Sunday, 17 March, St Patrick's Day, in the evening there will take place a continental span of celebration dinners—from New Zealand and Australia, to South Africa to several cities in the United States, and across the ocean, most notably to Scotland—to celebrate the one hundredth birthday of the only American, two hundred years after Benjamin Franklin, to be given the freedom of the city or burgh of St Andrews.

What we might call the shrine dinner was set for Atlanta, Georgia, the birthplace of the man I am talking about: Robert Tyre Jones, lawyer, scholar, engineer and amateur golfer who, in the summer of 1930, performed a feat never accomplished before or since: to win in succession all four of the major golf championships in one year, which, in those days, meant the British Amateur championship, the British Open, the United States Open and the United States Amateur. Like Alexander, having conquered all known worlds, he retired.

But this talk is not to be about the greatest golfer of his day. It is a memoir and personal recollection of, I do believe, the most singular human character I have ever known. The standard reservation to make now is to say of course he was no saint. We always toss in this reminder, forgetting along the way that the early behaviour of some of the saints was not so saintly either.

So, on St Patrick's Day, 1902, in Atlanta,

Georgia, was born to a young-middle-aged Southern lawyer and his wife a son. Almost from babyhood, he was enfeebled by a puzzling disease which later he called 'a digestive system that did everything but digest'. In those days, the automatic remedy for any affliction, from flat feet to a brain tumour, was to take a vacation in a balmy climate. But the Joneses were already *in* a balmy climate. And Mr and Mrs Jones took up golf and lugged the 4-year-old along with a sawn-off club. What for? To do him good. His disease vanished as mysteriously as it had arrived. He took to hitting a ball the way other boys take to kicking or throwing a ball. He watched the new Scottish pro. He was a marvellous mimic, and the gift passed over to driving a ball, and pitching and chipping, and by the time of his teens he had invented shots nobody else had thought of.

His early prowess was such that he was, at 14, Georgia amateur champion, at 15—with the United States in the First World War—touring the country with the reigning professional golfer, giving exhibitions for the Red Cross. At 15, too, he had done with school and went to Georgia's famous Institute of Technology to take the four-year engineering degree. He won it in three years, so on to Harvard for an honours degree in English literature, while there picking up the United States Open championship during his summer vacation.

At 24, he decided to become a lawyer and went back to Atlanta, to Emory University, to take the four-year course. But towards the end of his second year, he thought he'd like to see how tough was the bar exam. He took it, passed easily, so left colleges for ever, became a lawyer and so remained for life.

Quite simply and incredibly, his summer holidays were spent entering twenty major championships, winning thirteen, coming second in five, and, at the veteran's age of 28, retiring for ever from competitive golf.

He had, of course, not earned a nickel from the game, so he started to make some money to keep his wife and three children. He made for Hollywood (with a string of stars) sixteen fifteen-minute movies about playing golf, which, amazingly, were a hit in the movie theatres on three continents. He did a radio talk show, he wrote a weekly column—the most exact, finest instructional writing we have. During the Second World War, he was exempted with bad varicose veins from military service but managed a commission and served in France under Eisenhower. You'd expect he'd retire and spend the days happily with his family, playing golf several times a week. But his fame was enormous and during the Depression he had myriad calls for help. He devoted all his spare time to innumerable charities, playing only occasional golf.

After one round, in his mid-forties, he told his partners, 'I don't think I'll be playing with you boys for some time.' He had been struck with an agonizing back pain and had an operation. It didn't help. He began to feel tingling in his fingertips, a leg grew numb. He had a second operation in which bony vertebral spurs were removed to relieve the compression on his spinal nerves. The numbness and muscle atrophy spread to both legs. Finally he was diagnosed with a very rare progressive degenerative disease of the spinal cord, for which there was no cure, and still isn't. Although he was beginning to be paralysed, he

307

determined to appear as a cheerful invalid, kind and genial, without affectation, to friends and strangers and, always, looking out for the shy one in a corner.

The diabolical disease progressed, in the harsh professional language. Soon, all feeling had gone below the waist, his fine hands were reduced to stiff, curled little claws, with which he clutched a cigarette, a tumbler, and always signed his letters with a sprawling three-letter word—B-o-b, done with a pen taped to a tennis ball. He never complained, for twenty-two years retained his matchless courtesy, his ironical amused gaze at life. His last public visit to Scotland was in his mid-fifties, when the provost of St Andrews gave him the freedom of a city Jones said 'has a sensitivity and ability to extend cordiality in ingenious ways'. He hobbled off to his electric cart and began to propel himself slowly down the aisle, as the audience stirred to a single voice and rose to sing 'Will ye no come back again?' The start of the hobble and the fact of the cart were enough to remind us that he never would.

The last two years we were, rightly, not allowed to see him, a tortured wraith of sixty-five pounds. I pray he was well sedated. On the last day, he turned to his wife (to whom he had, as a friend put it, 'in his old-fashioned way kept the faith') and said, 'Is this all there is to it?' and died in his sleep just before his seventieth birthday.

As a boy on his first round at St Andrews, he played badly and withdrew from the championship and threw a little temper tantrum. It was his first and last. He made 'a general apology'. Later he wrote, 'In golf, and maybe in life too, it is not enough to play by the rules, if you don't play by the etiquette, it's not worth a damn.' I suppose what we saw, what we had in him, was something rarer than a great athlete, writer, artist, actor, composer, statesman—a masterpiece of a human life. So, at a time when, across the globe, many nations and two civilizations are busy deploring each other's national character, I thought it might be useful for a change to talk about one human being who, everybody of every nation who met him agreed, was a credit to his race, the human race, that is.

I have written and spoken a good deal about Bob Jones down many years of watching him, covering, being with him—from his last appearance at Augusta way back to his first appearance at Lytham St Annes in 1926. (I was 17 and within hearing distance of the roar that went up for that magical shot to the seventeenth green that sealed the match and his first British championship.) The best I can do to sum up my long view of him is to say again what I wrote in my history of America twenty-eight years ago:

The 1920s were a prosperous, garish, pleasure-bent, often vulgar decade during which New York City started the colorful custom of paying tribute to national gods with what were called ticker-tape parades up Broadway: mainly for generals, admirals, aviators. There was one peculiar choice, but, in him, the 1920s were saluting not so much an athlete but unknowingly an old ideal in the moment of its passing. He was Robert Tyre Jones, Jr., a weekend golfer but the best of his time, amateur or professional. He had a grace and charm on and

309

off the course that, combined with great good looks, made him the idol of two continents, and *that* to people who did not know a putter from a shovel and had only the weekly newsreels in the movie houses to go on. His universal appeal was obviously not as a golfer.

What then? The word that comes to mind is one that is fast becoming an extinct word with no meaning to present generations except as an obsolete class distinction: the word is a gentleman, meaning in Bob Jones' case a combination of goodness, modesty and social ease, unwavering courtesy, self-deprecation, but first and at all times an alert instinctive, consideration for other people.

As for the last dreadful twenty-odd years of his life, even this long decline was heroic. The American golf historian, Herbert Warren Wind, has said it better than anybody in the fewest words: 'As a young man, he was able to stand up to just about the best that life can offer, and throughout the later years he stood up with equal grace to just about the worst.'

It is in the evening, at around 6 p.m., that I recall Bob Jones best: the moment that E. B. White called 'the time of the most beautiful sound in America: the tinkle of ice at twilight'. I think it is appropriate, on this surely American-Scottish occasion, to tell you that of the whole pharmacopoeia of medications I take every day, far and away the most effective is what I call the twilight wine of Scotland. I had the honour, from time to time, of sharing a teaspoon or two with Bob Jones, and he agreed with me about its power to heal.

310

The Last of the Old-Time Gangsters

14 June 2002

'John Gotti Is Dead.' To many Americans in the seedier section of cities from New York to Miami to Las Vegas to Los Angeles, that simple sentence was as stunning as, to Frenchmen two centuries ago, the sentence 'Napoleon is dead' must have been.

In random street interviews in New York and New Jersey, you could see and hear that the name John Gotti inspired fear in some, relief in most, and in everybody, awe. Unlike most top officers of the Mafia (who moved swiftly and warily in public in the middle of a wedge of bodyguards), John Gotti, five feet ten inches, two hundred pounds, beautifully garbed in the most opulent Italian suits, his handsome and daily barbered face surmounted by a breaking wave of silver hair (which was also tended once a day), John Gotti made his daily excursion from a barber's chair to his office something of an informal royal procession, bowing to fans known and unknown, scattering smiles and autographs and at regular intervals saluting detectives or FBI men posted on a stake-out. The Dapper Don, they called him. The FBI more testily called him the Teflon Don, because for many years he evaded the law, or defeated it in court, more agilely than anyone since Al Capone.

John Gotti was one of thirteen children born to an under-employed day labourer, son of poor Italian immigrants. A quick-witted, restless boy, he

311

was bored by school, did not pay much attention, and dropped out when he was 16. (Interesting to some Europeans, I think, is that even back then the normal school-leaving age was 18.) The family moved from the comparatively alien borough of the Bronx, downtown among fellow Italians in the Lower East Side, which was in the early 1950s a jungle of petty crime and a recruiting ground for the 'crews' of the Mafia families. At that time, there were five Mafia families: the Bonano, Columbo, Genovese, Luchese, and the one young John Gotti would come to join and eventually dominate so that he could boast, and justly so, that he was *the* Godfather of the United States.

Each of the five mob families worked through crews of about a score of young men, who started as errand boys and moved up, if they were good and ambitious, to be thieves, protection bullies, and odd well-paid hit men. The crews in turn recruited their members from boys' street gangs. John Gotti began his life's work by immediately proving with his fists that he could lead a gang. He recommended himself to the capo (captain) of a crew by his quick mind, and the almost delightful ease with which he could suggest to shopkeepers and restaurants that they badly needed protection from some unseen enemy. In no time, he was himself well in with the Gambino family, and for eight years practised much theft, street assaults and stealing of cars, for which he served six months in jail four or five times. These little stretches were not signs of failure. They were exercises in the normal apprenticeship of a first-class mobster.

Just before he turned 30, he pleaded guilty to holding up and stealing cargoes being delivered to

Kennedy Airport. This time, he served three years, and when he got out, at the age of 32, he was ready for the big time. He became the captain of a Gambino crew. A nephew of Gambino himself was murdered, and John Gotti was ordered to perform the necessary act of revenge, which he managed successfully through a three-man ambush which disposed of the murderer. Gotti was indicted and went to trial. But by now, John Gotti had learned a lesson that the Capone school of criminology had taught long ago: find and clutch to your bosom for life a brilliant and conscienceless lawyer. Mr Gotti's man not only got a life sentence reduced to four years, but did a deal with the county district attorney's office to be allowed out from time to time, to see his family, to dine at a fancy New York restaurant, to visit friends and—in a soft voice—conduct the business of the Gambino family. Only after he was free again was it proved (but not beyond doubt) that some prison guards and bodyguards had been bribed.

Out again and settled for life—like all the top gangsters in a quite modest suburban house—John Gotti very soon moved onwards and upwards from being the capo of a Gambino crew. Through the accident of a series of deaths or jailings in the family, he established himself as the head of the Gambino family itself, and was very busy presiding over big robberies, drug deals, corrupting trade unions, and ordering the 'liquidation' (as Stalin used to say) of rival mobsters, sometimes of ordinary citizens who got in his way, like a motorist who accidentally ran over Gotti's 12-year-old son riding a bicycle. The motorist was never seen again.

It would be excessive to say that all this—Gotti's

very active criminal life—went on in the light of day. The only time his innumerable crimes came to light was in the glare of a courthouse. Time and again, Gotti was indicted and tried. And time and again the jury acquitted him. Once, after he'd been acquitted, it was discovered that the foreman of the jury had received a whopping $80,000 bribe. But most of the time the jury lacked the absolutely certain evidence of guilt. Inside a courtroom, Gotti every time defined his profession as that of a plumbing supply dealer with a maximum annual income of $100,000. The investigators, though, had certain evidence that in his life of racketeering he received from his employees something between $10 and $12 million a year.

At long last, the Feds moved in on state and county investigators and examined the extent, the appalling extent, to which the Gambino family and Gotti in particular controlled the pay-cheques and working hours of some of the nation's most vital industries: the labour of the waterfront, the construction industry, the collecting and disposal of everybody's garbage.

Finally, in 1990, with court-approved telephone taps, Gotti was heard by the jury planning hijackings, boasting of murders done. In all, he was successfully charged with thirteen counts of racketeering, five murders, conspiracy, obstruction of justice, and—Al Capone's only punishable sin—tax evasion: fraud.

I go into all this not to indulge a passing bow to the *New York Times*, which had a two-page obituary of him, or because it was time to notice the last of the old-time gangsters, but because from time to time listeners, and friends, say, 'By the way, what ever happened to the gangsters?', such a star feature of American movies in the 1930s and of American crime stories in the 1940s.

The official answer is that in the 1940s, the famous reform Mayor of New York, Fiorello La Guardia, went after the top mobsters in the biggest way by appointing a special prosecutor of rackets, a city lawyer, one Thomas E. Dewey, who sent to jail the New York leader of the Democratic Party, and a federal judge, and broke Lucky Luciano's prostitution racket, and is also credited with crippling the highly lucrative protection racket. Until the Second World War, every resident of the island of Manhattan paid extra high prices for laundry, fruit and vegetables, in fact most foodstuffs that came on to the island by ferry or tunnel from New Jersey and the South. There were alert gangs on the New Jersey shore very anxious to see that we had clean laundry and edible fruit and vegetables—at a price. Prosecutor Dewey was so successful, he became Governor of New York and twice ran for President.

In the 1970s the federal government appointed a supervising team over the chronically corrupt teamsters union—the truckers—the most influential union in the country since it had come to replace the railroads as the nation's main carrier of goods and foods. In the 1980s–1990s, Rudolph Giuliani, as a federal prosecutor, weakened four of the five families, cleaned corruption out of a big downtown trade show centre, and really broke the grip of the mob on the city's chief fish market.

It is difficult to say today how wide the mob's influence spreads, because down two or three generations, the First Families, so to speak, have

315

transformed their image and, optimists say, their character. The children of the old bosses stayed in school, went to the big universities or to business school, sometimes under new names. Looking, talking and acting like the genuine preppy article, they moved quietly into the more respectable fields of investment banking and related enterprises. So, only a first-rate and daring investigative journalist could say how deep and wide is the Mafia's influence. (A former governor of New York with an Italian name maintained, through the most gruesome days of the mobs, that there was no such thing as the Mafia.)

Today it would be utopian to believe that their hands have been permanently crippled and plucked from the fabulously rewarding industries of construction and garbage removal. Certainly, our garbage everywhere costs a bundle, and the unexplained freakish item of the economy is that, while the stock exchange declines steadily every week, and since half the country owns stocks and people worry about their shrinking income, the cost of building new homes and of rented houses and apartments goes higher than ever.

Farewell to San Francisco

18 October 2002

From time to time, an old acquaintance will call me just before I do my talk and say, 'Well, I think we all know what you're going to talk about this week.' I tend to say, 'That's right', or 'You got it', because

316

I know in my bones, from years of such calls, that they haven't got it. It's always about some appalling natural disaster, a fire, an earthquake, perhaps the assassination of a foreign statesman. In any case, I find no occasion for intelligent comment about the lamentable snipings in the Virginia–Maryland country, or about the nightclub bombing on the once island paradise of Bali. The only reaction must be, 'Isn't it awful?' There is nothing useful you or I can do about it, except to add that Bali and, possibly, the snipings miserably confirm our discovery that the explosions of the past few years, from Scotland to the South Pacific, are not the spontaneous outbursts of fanatical loners but the long-prepared world war of a worldwide network called al-Qa'ida.

But now there is a topic which is not to be guessed at, and was dictated quite simply by my looking at the calendar and reflecting: ah, yes, the third week in October, which has meant for so many years, 'San Francisco time'. Certainly, for the past thirty years or so I have been going four times a year to my favourite city to see how America, its life and affairs, looks from the Pacific Coast.

Visually, the first thing that struck me, from the start, was the Oriental connection. It has been there since the first Chinese labourers were brought in by the Central Pacific Company to work their way east and meet the Irish working west, together to create the first transcontinental railroad. In the middle of the Utah desert in May 1869, two locomotives timidly nosed together, and a lad on a high telegraph pole tapped out for the wonder of the world the message: 'The last rail is laid. The last spike is driven. The Pacific railroad is

317

finished.' That moment has been celebrated in many a sentimental calendar painting with railroad company dignitaries in cutaways banging in a gold spike. A more prosaic, not to say brutal, memory has stayed green in the recollections of the railroad crews and their descendants. Several days before the historic moment, the two grades had run side by side for a stretch, and the Irishmen took such an instant aversion to the little slant-eyed Chinese that they blasted them with dynamite. The Chinese swiftly buried their dead and returned the gesture with pickaxes. The massacre was brief and bloody but the racial feud it brewed simmered throughout the nineteenth century.

By the time I first arrived in San Francisco, just on seventy years ago, Chinatown was the most compact and orderly of all the ethnic settlements. It had a thriving tourist business, and the California–Oriental connection was strong and detectable everywhere, from the old Chinese in the early morning on Nob Hill doing their slow-motion graceful exercises, to the furniture, porcelain, murals and other Chinese decorations in friends' houses and in hotels. Just along the block from the first hotel I ever stayed in was a glittering metallic statue of Sun Yat Sen, for many decades a cult figure among Californians. He had been a revolutionary who overthrew the last dynasty and was the first President of a Chinese republic.

By the late 1930s, China, overrun by the Japanese in Manchuria, had become California's favourite victim state. However, at that time the ranking villain to Californians as well as to all other Americans was Adolf Hitler. Only experts at the State Department worried about Japan. Only experts, and one Californian, William Randolph Hearst, a national newspaper tycoon, who sat in his castle looking across the Pacific and rang editorial alarm bells warning about the Yellow Peril, about an actual threat of the Japanese to the security, to the shores, of his beloved California.

To visiting Easterners and Europeans, these foaming outbursts were always thought fanciful to the point of absurdity—until 7 December 1941, when out of the blue the Japanese destroyed half the United States Pacific Fleet (and its air arm) at its base in the Pacific, which most Americans, or for that matter ranking members of the British Embassy (and yours truly) had never heard of. It was called Pearl Harbor.

By now, of course, everything has gone into reverse. Japan is, has been, the great modern trading partner, and China, though vilified and warily watched since it went Communist, is being wooed as the second largest Pacific trader. But in San Francisco, the Oriental, or as we must now say the Asian, presence is as triumphant as anywhere in the country. A medical office building I know which twenty, thirty years ago was inhabited by doctors with American-European names now has a third of its tenants Asian. They are refugees from the Communist takeover of Vietnam, or Hong Kong Chinese whose parents came to this country, say twenty-five years ago, without a word of English. Today, they are young medical specialists.

These things I shall miss, but most of all the daily sights and sounds that are San Francisco and nowhere else. First, of course, the nine tumbling hills, and how remarkably the people troop up and down them like one of the great race migrations of the Middle Ages. The white city is seen from across the bay as a vast pyramid of confetti. The genial sun most of the year, the bafflement verging on outrage of the summer tourists shivering atop a hilly street, not having been told that July and August are the coldest months. But summer is memorable also for the arrival from the Pacific in the late afternoon of great plumes of white fog moving in on the city with the motion of a slow freight train. The double moan of the foghorn at night. The deceptively blue waters under the Golden Gate Bridge in whose icy, thrashing currents no Alcatraz escapee has ever been known to survive, only the corpse of one Aaron Burgett.

Over and over again, I recall a short piece of Mark Twain's which says so much about San Francisco in so little. It reports Mark Twain's arrival in San Francisco after he'd been thrown out of the silver-mining town of Virginia City, Nevada, for having written that 'in this noble city, there are two churches and seventy-six saloons—which is just about the right proportion'. This line aroused such fury in the local church matrons that Mark Twain thought it was time 'to get lost—so I absquatulated.'

> After the sagebrush and alkali desert of Nevada, San Francisco was heaven on the half shell. I lived at the best hotel. I exhibited my clothes in the most conspicuous places. I infested the opera.
>
> I enjoyed my first earthquake. It was just after noon on a bright Sunday in October and I was coming down Third Street . . . As I turned a corner there came a terrific shock . . .

320

the entire front of a four-story brick building sprung outward like a door and fell sprawling across the street. The ground rolled under me in waves. The streetcars stopped. Their horses were rearing and plunging. Every door of every house was vomiting a stream of human beings. . .

The first shock brought down two or three organ pipes in one of the churches, and the next instant, in the atmosphere where the minister had stood, there was a vacancy. In another church, after the first shock, the minister said: 'Bretheren, keep your seats. There is no better place to die than here.' After the third shock, he waved his flock good-bye and added: 'But outside is good enough for me.'

After a time, I had to cease being an onlooker at the peculiar life of San Francisco and get down to earning a livelihood. My first job was with the *Enquirer*, and my first assignment was accidental: a set-to between a Chinaman and some Irish. Now, the Chinese are a harmless race when white men let them alone or treat them no worse than dogs. Their chief employment is to wash clothes, which they do at low prices with their usual patience and industry. One day, I saw a bunch of Irish toughs descend on an old Chinaman, on his way home after laundering the clothes of his Christian clientele. They sat on him and beat him up. I went back to the office in a state of high indignation and wrote my fill of this miserable incident. But the editor refused to print it. Our paper, he said, was printed for the poor, and in San Francisco the Irish were the poor. In time, I cooled off. I was lofty in those days. I have survived.

Most poignantly I recall and miss most a contemporary—long gone—writer, a columnist for the San Francisco morning paper. I often wonder if San Franciscans deserved him, for he never received any special tribute as the best writer ever to come out of that city. His name was Charles McCabe, a funny, beautiful writer of great simplicity, by which I mean he felt deeply and thought clearly. He was never syndicated outside that one paper. 'Why not?' I once asked the editor. 'Well,' he said, 'who's going to buy a man who's more of a meditator than a columnist?' It's true. One day he wrote about the pain of being jilted, next day on Cicero, next a dangerously funny swipe at the women's libbers, next day the life of St Thomas Aquinas.

McCabe looked like a giant, dignified W. C. Fields with a similarly glowing nose. It came at you like a beacon, but before you sighted it your nostrils picked up the unmistakable odour of 'the poteen'. At the end of his life, Charlie McCabe became aware of the one thing that makes any life worth living. 'These days the love I give and the love I get seems spread around rather thin. I am often lonely but seldom bored any more. There's a lot of peace and quiet but I now know it would not be possible without friends. Without friends? I can hardly bear to think about it.' Nor can I.

They are the San Franciscans it will hurt to miss.

Remembering a Dear Friend

13 December 2002

An old journalist colleague was taking his first holiday on a cruise ship. They were sailing along the Mediterranean and the ship stopped at Tangier. It came up on the horizon as what he called 'a featureless strip of sand'. 'Not', he said, 'my notion of Africa.'

I suppose this happens to all of us, though, from not wanting to be thought a bonehead, it's not the sort of thing we mention aloud. My own experience in first sighting America was to the contrary. Sailing into New York, up the bay at twilight on a late September evening; a clear purple sky and thousands of people still at work, which meant that the downtown and midtown skyscrapers were all lit up, a forest of giant firecrackers; nothing could have better fulfilled the imagined scene. New York City, in short, lived up to its billing. 'Not my notion of America' came later. One week later, to be exact, when I took the train fifty miles north to New Haven, Connecticut, where at the Yale School of Drama, I proposed to polish up my directing skills and return to England to revolutionize the English theatre. How that came not to be is another story you'll be relieved to hear some other time, or not at all.

Yale! The only vision I had of an American university had been formed by the musical comedies of the 1920s and the silent movies of Harold Lloyd. The musicals were so rowdy, so

323

facetious, and all turned on the dopey hero winning the football game, and the girl cheerleader on the sidelines, that I knew this couldn't be anything but farce set to music by Hollywood scriptwriters who had never been closer to Yale than the Bronx.

We chuffed into New Haven, and later that day I came on the campus. First thing, I was told to go to the Dean's office and he would tell me where I was going to live. I was made a member of Harkness College (called Hall) and padded off there to find my own cosy room. It turned out to be a suite—a large study, bedroom, pantry, and, best of all (and new to me in a college) a private bathroom with its own radiator.

It was all splendid, but as an American object it was a shock and a letdown. It was a high, Gothic, gloomy room. At my own college in England, I had looked out on a medieval cloister, dank and melancholy and mouldy with distinction. And I travel three thousand miles to the New World, to the land of Douglas Fairbanks, and George Gershwin, and Bobby Jones, and the lovely white colonial eighteenth-century houses I'd read so much about, and here I was under house arrest in a grey, grim, Gothic room with heavily leaded peekaboo owlish windows. I took a quick walk round the campus and found that everything was Gothic, but strangely new. Later on, I discovered that one architect was put in charge and was given a free hand in 1919 to go berserk with his Gothic mania, and in the next sixteen years he built practically a small city, or large campus, of Gothic, as being most suitable for a historic university. On that first evening, I sat alone in my cloistered prison and silently deplored my fate. A knock came at the door. There stood a middle-sized, athletic-looking young man, black hair with a lick of curl, strikingly black-brown merry eyes and an air of geniality he was never to lose. 'My name,' he said, 'is Rostow, Gene Rostow, and I understand you're a new Fellow.'

'Commonwealth,' I said.

'Commonwealth Fellow,' he said. 'I wondered if you'd care to come over to my place and meet my room-mates.'

Of course, my trajectory to his room was that of Bugs Bunny in pursuit of a carrot. And he had a rather grander suite: a living room, and off it four bedrooms. He had three room-mates, two of whom I knew till the end of their lives. Eugene Victor Rostow, however, was plainly to me the key man and stayed my oldest American friend, with nary a cross word, till the day he died, which was on Monday of last week.

He was the son of a Russian immigrant, a dedicated socialist who christened his son after a famous socialist candidate for the Presidency: Eugene Victor Debs. His younger son (who was to become Lyndon Johnson's national security adviser) was named after the poet Walt Whitman.

The lithe, athletic shape I noticed about Gene Rostow at first sight was well taken. First thing I knew about him was that he was the polo captain. A Jew Polo captain at Yale which had, at the time, an unspoken, unacknowledged quota system. However, Gene was captain of *water* polo, and a powerful thrashing performer he was. But very soon I learned that he was an intellectual whizz, graduating after four years at Yale when he was 19, when most students are in their sophomore (second) year. At the age of 40, he became Dean of the Law School, had several famous pupils (including two later Presidents) and in ten years made Yale Law School quite possibly the finest in the country. His passion for international law and his large knowledge of constitutional law made him destined for politics. And not long after he went to Washington, he drew the attention, and the affection, of Truman's later Secretary of State, Dean Acheson, who looked like a tweedy Spanish grandee with a guardsman's moustache. There was a little private talk that, come the right day, Gene Rostow might make a fine Supreme Court Justice. His intellect, his tolerance of opponents' views, but most of all his genuinely judicial temperament: open-minded, objective, disinterested. It is a rare possession, even among justices of the Supreme Court. However, the talk came to nothing. Gene went on to become an Under-Secretary of State, was put in charge of economic warfare in North Africa, and at the end, of arms control and disarmament.

However, it is not politics but his character I wish to end on. At the height of his fame as Yale's Law School Dean, he was offered a visiting professorship in a famous European university. In a postal muddle, the invitation went to the wrong man, who accepted the post and enjoyed it. There was never a hint or a sigh of complaint from Gene Rostow. He was the first public official of any standing who, in the wake of Pearl Harbor, angrily protested the unconstitutionality of herding practically the entire Japanese-American population of California into detention centres— three generations of them—for the rest of the war.

Forty years later, everybody apologized, including the Supreme Court, which made belated restitution to the survivors of the detained.

In a Kennedy year, it was (I'll never forget) 1962, Gene stayed on Long Island with us but at the week's end, he had business in town, and so did I. I drove him back to New York to stay the night. We arrived in the late afternoon, eased off, sat down for a drink. The telephone rang. I took the call. A voice said 'Is Professor Rostow there?' He is. 'This is the White House. The President wishes to speak to him.' After what novelists call a sudden start, I handed over. And this was Gene Rostow's part of the dialogue. 'Yes, sir, Mr President. Well, thank you, and the same. Uh-huh. Uh-huh. Uh-huh. Yes, I know, of course, everybody knew. Uh-huh. Well, I understand, sir. Thank you all the same.' A bright swift chuckle and he hung up. He came back to the sofa, sat down and we went on with our merry conversation. I did not think his business with the President was any business of mine. We sallied off to dinner, came back for a nightcap. At some point, looking both cheerful and mischievous, he said, 'You might wonder what went on with the President, if you can keep it to yourself for a time.' I said something like: 'For a lifetime.'

To understand Kennedy's part in the exchange, I have to draw in a little background. A famous justice, one Felix Frankfurter, had decided to retire from the Court. He was a Jew, and though there is no rule, over the past fifty years or so there is a binding tradition that there must be one Jew, since Thurmond Marshall one black, since Sandra Day O'Connor one woman. Kennedy had offered the coming vacancy to a former Governor of

327

Connecticut, a Jew. Everybody soon knew he'd had the offer. But for personal reasons he told Kennedy he could not take it. Moving swiftly forward in the dark background, Dean Acheson came to Kennedy's aid. Rostow must be the man. Kennedy thought it over. After all, Gene was a Jew, born in New Haven, Connecticut. Kennedy made up his mind and put the call. And this is the brief speech to which Gene Rostow responded with his usual geniality, even with a chuckle: 'Gene, I have a problem. I offered Frankfurter's seat to Abe Ribicoff but the Governor had to turn it down. Yes . . . yes . . . yes, as everybody knew. That's the problem. Well, you were right up there as most qualified. But I'm afraid, I'm sorry, I decided that it's going to Goldberg, of Illinois. Two Jews from Connecticut is one too many. I'm sorry.' 'Well, I understand, sir. Thank you all the same.'

Gene never, to me or anyone I knew, ever breathed a mention of this appalling letdown in his life. But here in the room I speak from, I saw for the first time—and never again, I prayed—a lifetime's ambition shattered in a moment with a chuckle.

Eugene Victor Rostow, a darlin' man, died last Monday week, aged 89.

Meeting the Stars

4 July 2003

One of the comical pains of living on and on is something I hope most listeners will not feel for some time to come. It's the pleasurable moment of remembering an anecdote about some famous person you'd once run into, and then suddenly discovering that the famous person is totally unknown to the friend, possibly even grey-haired friend, you're about to amuse.

One time, staying with some friends who lived on a hacienda up in the hills behind Santa Barbara, California, my host remarked, 'Oh, by the way, we're having drinks with the Colmans.' The Colmans? 'Yeah, Ronnie and his wife.' 'Ronnie and his wife!' To me, it was as if a young beginner with the violin had been told by an uncle, 'Oh, by the way, we're dining with Luddy.' Luddy? Ludwig— Beethoven! Ronald Colman, although then in the twilight of his career, had been for three decades just about the most world-famous English movie actor alive. We went to his house, and who should open the door but the man himself. He offered his hand first to *me* and said in his famous velvety voice, 'My dear fellow, do come in. My mother is your greatest fan!' I was moved to say, 'Never mind your mother, how about you?' but was too overwhelmed to say anything by the mere thought of Ronald Colman's mother listening to my talks. This was sometime in the early 1950s.

A year or two ago, I thought this was the sort of

329

anecdote that would appeal to a friend who had stopped by: a pretty, cultivated, on-the-ball woman in her early fifties, who had a professional interest, as a television producer, in actors and acting. I had long ago learned my lesson of never assuming (especially in anybody under 60) a familiarity with *my* heroes and heroines, writers, politicians, movie stars and so forth. So to my woman friend in her early fifties I said, 'Does the name Ronald Colman mean anything to you?' She paused, and looked thoughtful. 'He was, was he not, a United States Senator?' End of Colman story.

So, I begin guardedly this time and introduce the character I'm going to talk about by having you meet her the way I met her. Last Monday morning, her picture, accompanying a huge obituary, took up a page and a half of the *New York Times*. When I saw the photograph, I realized, from the calendar, that it was exactly seventy years ago that, visiting Hollywood for the first time (as a student/tourist), I had the august sensation of being picked up at my humble hotel by a studio limousine—a limousine sent expressly for me, a totally anonymous graduate student driving round the country, the USA, in a second-hand, $45 Ford. It came about this way.

During the previous winter and spring, I had sent to one of the two distinguished English Sunday papers a few theatre reviews of a new O'Neill play (Nobel Prize playwright), and a play by one Noël Coward (then the chicest of English playwrights). Out of what in New York is called chutzpah, I had had the audacity to write to the editor of this Sunday paper, an awesomely famous man, suggesting that, on my summer trip—since I

330

should be stopping by Hollywood—how about my writing a series of six pieces on the movies, beginning with an interview with Charlie Chaplin, then with the celebrated German director Lubitsch, with an English star (how about the monumental C. Aubrey Smith?), an Oscar-winning cameraman, and so forth? Of course, I knew none of these magnificoes. But when, to my astonishment, the awesome editor wrote back and said it just so happened that their film critic, Miss LeJune, was taking off for just six weeks, I might submit the pieces. This made it automatic for me then, swollen with chutzpah, to write to all the stars and say, 'On behalf of the London *Observer* . . . I have been commissioned, etc. . . .' Not one refused to set a date. On the contrary, before they'd even glimpsed this brash 24-year-old, several of them wrote back to be sure a day could be set apart at *my* convenience. I remember an ingratiating letter from Mr Chaplin, the beginning of a beautiful friendship.

When I got out there, I started my grand tour by deciding to write first about a famous director at work. The man I chose, then in the first flush of great success, was one George Cukor. He had just started shooting the immortal Louisa May Alcott's (an immortal woman writer) *Little Women*. Why not come out and spend the day with the cast, in a stretch of what they had turned into a New England landscape, about twenty miles out from Beverly Hills? And so I was driven off and greeted in the warmest way (after all, I represented the *Observer*, owned by the Astors, no less) by Mr Cukor and the cast. I'll call off their names without further definition—you may take my word for it—it was a very starry cast, palpitating in the wake of the veteran actors Paul Lukas and Henry Stephenson and Edna Mae Oliver, Joan Bennett, Jean Parker, Frances Dee *and* Katharine Hepburn. Of course you know her (thanks to television re-runs).

Katharine Hepburn was, indeed, the subject of the *New York Times* obituary. And it was not a lament. She was 96 and long a martyr to an embarrassing trembling of the head and hands, which she swore to the end was not Parkinson's disease.

Back there (seventy years ago in that California valley), what struck me, in watching the shooting of this famous story of four young sisters growing up in New England before the Civil War, was nothing about the play or the shooting of it, but the—how shall I put it?—the social oddity of this girl Hepburn. She stood out, it seemed to me at the time, as a kind of attractive freak. All because of her accent, which was that of a well-schooled, upper-middle-class New England girl just out (she was four years out) of Bryn Mawr (a college of high academic standing but also notable for breeding well-bred, upper-class young women). It had its own distinct variation of an upper-crust New England accent, which is not, by the way, anything like British English of the same class. Miss Hepburn had it, and, in that place and time, it was quite strange.

I don't believe it will be news to older listeners to hear that the majority, maybe a large majority, of American screen actors and actresses in those days—whatever parts they became trained to play—came from humble immigrant South and Eastern European backgrounds. Since the top

332

producers who founded Hollywood had also that background (most of them pedlars who had fled from Jewish pogroms in Europe), one of the notable signs of their feelings of social inferiority, throughout the 1920s into the 1950s, was the alacrity with which they rushed to change the given names of rising stars to English names, since, way back then, those cunning but simple Russian and Lithuanian and German producers thought, wrongly, that the absolutely top social class in the United States was English. Hence, Emmanuel Goldenberg became Edward G. Robinson, Bernard Schwartz—Tony Curtis, Frances Gumm—Judy Garland, Allen Konigsberg—Woody Allen, Issur Danielovich Demsky—Kirk Douglas, Marion Levy—Paulette Goddard, and so on and so on.

Katharine Hepburn was born and stayed Katharine Hepburn, daughter of a distinguished surgeon in Connecticut and a mother who was, as in England, a fervent socialite suffragette. This rationalization of mine, of course, came to me much later, during a period of Hepburn's life, in her late twenties, early thirties, when she made some indifferent movies and was famously dubbed 'box office poison' because, I now think, the movies she was making then were not good enough to overcome the general popular dislike of what was called her fancy accent. In that summertime, all I noticed is that the rest of the cast treated her with particular respect not usually due a young actress. She had, however, won an Oscar the year before. But the three other sisters somehow gave off the feeling that she was not the normal Hollywood product. But she was totally unaffected, she was who she was: an upper-class Yankee of character.

They took to her simply because of her character. And what a character. She refused to be bought and sold by a studio, no matter how tyrannical and fearsome a Zukor, a Goldwyn, might be. She had a play written for her by a famous Philadelphia playwright, bought the play, acted in it, and then sold it to a Hollywood studio to be made *her* way on *her* terms. They hated her but the actors (slaves to anything the studio picked for them) cheered her. And for the rest of her screen life she ran things her way, and made tyrants say, 'Yes, Miss Hepburn.' 'Well, Kate. Okay.'

Late in life she said flatly that she had been born of a well-to-do family and felt an obligation to live up to its responsibilities. 'I was not', she wrote, 'a poor little thing. I don't know what I'd have done if I'd come to New York and had to get a job as a waiter or something.' She added she was a success, not because of any great individual talent; 'I had advantages,' she said, 'I had *better* be a success.'

The Pledge of Allegiance

17 October 2003

Every Monday morning, in every public-elementary school in America, the children rise and may recite, if they choose to, otherwise listen to, the chanting by the class of the Pledge of Allegiance to the Flag of the United States. It is a single sentence. This is how it goes: 'I pledge allegiance to the flag of the United States of America and to the republic for which it stands, one nation under God, indivisible, with liberty and justice for all.'

Last week it was announced in Washington that next February or March, the nine justices of the Supreme Court will begin to consider the complaint of an atheist parent who says it's against the Constitution that he should have to make his daughter listen to 'a ritual proclaiming that there is a God'. When it does come up, I imagine that the young atheist parent will have a hard time restraining himself from a cry of 'shame' as he watches the nine justices bow their heads in prayer, as is their custom.

Which clause of the Constitution does he believe is being violated? Why, the very First Amendment—the first item in the Bill of Rights. It is written in the most guileless English. 'Congress shall make no law respecting an Establishment of religion or prohibiting the free exercise thereof.' What could be simpler? Also, what could be vaguer, the moment you reflect what the eighteenth century meant by 'establishment', for

335

instance? So many, many words have changed their meaning drastically since the seventeenth and eighteenth centuries that much of the Bible, much more of Shakespeare, is not understandable without explanatory footnotes. To the Founding Fathers who wrote it, 'establishment' meant a religious sect. What a pity they didn't write the sentence the other way round: 'Congress shall make no law prohibiting the free exercise of religion'—oh!—but, by the way, we are not going, as a nation, to have a preferred sect. Too late for that. It would lead to endless dissension between the Congregationalists of Massachusetts and Connecticut, the Catholics of Maryland, the Quakers of Pennsylvania. So, gentlemen, let's make it plain that we shall not have a national religion like the Church of England. That being so, it should be well understood that no law of Congress can prohibit any man or woman practising his/her own religion freely, everywhere, in church, in the street, in Congress, at home or away—freely.

For a hundred and fifty years, this reading was simply taken for granted by most people. As a learned history of the Supreme Court tells us: 'From the founding era at the end of the eighteenth century well into the twentieth century, religion was thought to be a significant and legitimate component of American public life. By the 1940s, however, American public life had become largely secular.'

One short, offhand sentence covers a tremendous fact: the decline of religious belief in the general population of the Western nations. It has been deeper still in Europe. In France in 1960, one family in three were weekly churchgoers.

Today, one in eight. In England today, only six people in a hundred claim to be devoutly religious. In the United States, the comparable devout figure is 65 per cent, but there has been a dramatic increase in the Americans who don't want religion to appear in any shape or form in *public* life. Hence, these continual appeals to the court from keeping religious symbols off any public building, all the way to banning the use of the word God in political speech! To put it more formally, the atheists have gone bananas in the extent to which they misinterpret the First Amendment, as you see from the final appeal of the young father from Oregon who wants 'under God' taken out of the Pledge of Allegiance.

First, let's go back to the pledge and its invention. It was composed by an ex-minister and published in a magazine called the *Youth's Companion*. When? Aye, that's the point. Eighteen ninety-two. The Congress leaped at a happy idea: since 12 October marked the four hundredth anniversary of Columbus' discovery of America, that would be the perfect day to introduce the chanting of the pledge as a daily ritual in the elementary schools. And so it was. But no mention of God. The 'one nation under God' did not appear until 1954. Why 1954, I wondered. I never saw a story explaining why. I thought some digging was necessary. It has turned out that a little digging produced a load of pay dirt.

In early 1954, at a conference of the four allied powers occupying Germany, the United States, Britain and France were all for reunifying Germany under one government. Stalin was absolutely opposed. Stalin had in Europe armies five times the size of the combined other allies. So that was that.

Far away, in French Indochina, the French were collapsing against Vietnamese guerrillas who were fighting to be independent. The French begged President Eisenhower to help with American troops. Eisenhower said 'no troops', but made an impassioned public assertion that the defeat of Communism in Southeast Asia was 'vital'—that if one country went Communist, the neighbours could fall too like a row of dominoes. This was a pressing fear in Washington at that time—fears for Malaysia, for Indochina, for Burma, most of all for India.

Also, 1954 was the heyday of a Midwestern Senator who, after a high State Department official had been convicted of passing papers to the Soviet Union, launched an immensely popular campaign to root Communists out of American government. He gave us alarming numbers but never actually came up with a positive Communist who had not declared himself. Nevertheless, it was the fear of the time that from Moscow to Asia 'godless Communism' might prevail. President Eisenhower and many public men and women used that phrase over and over. And it was by executive order alone that President Eisenhower ordered the pledge now to read: 'I pledge allegiance to the flag of the United States of America, and to the republic for which it stands, one nation *under God*, indivisible, with liberty and justice for all.'

So far as Michael Newdow, the young protesting father, is concerned—the villain of the piece is not, as most people think, the Congress of the United States but the late, great Ike, Supreme Commander

338

of the invading forces in Europe and later President of the United States. If Mr Newdow wins, surely somebody will then mount a crusade to have erased from all dollar bills, of whatever denomination, the sentence printed in brazen capital letters: 'In God We Trust.' And if *he* wins, that will entail destroying every bill and totally reprinting the US currency. It would cost the Treasury (the taxpayer, that is) an estimated $7 or $8 billion. But what's that to the average taxpayer? He's already going to have to find $20 billion for tidying up Iraq.

Towering Glass and Steel

31 October 2003

Forty years ago last Monday morning, a gentle southwest wind carried up through Manhattan what many New Yorkers at first thought was a series of explosions of some kind. Pretty soon there came on television what to most New Yorkers was an incomprehensible sight and sound. The picture showed jackhammers clawing away at the walls of a famous building, and then at slow rhythmic intervals, a huge airborne shining ball swung and crashed against—were they mad?—the long stately Doric colonnade of—were they mad?—the Baths of Caracalla? Well, yes, not of course the original but a superb re-creation of a Roman architectural masterpiece.

Why were they doing this, and who were *they*? What we saw was America's most famous railway station, the Pennsylvania Station. It had been designed at the turn of the twentieth century during the finest hour of the new millionaires, especially the robber barons who had made their fortunes in coke, iron ore and railroads, and when little old Andrew Carnegie was proclaiming the new age of steel. Once such a man became a millionaire, he became eager to advertise the grandeur of his social position by ordering up a new house, a mansion, as like as possible not to the mansions of the new rich of Europe, but to the ancient houses of the old aristocracy, especially the nobles of France and Italy. Just after Goethe had given an encouraging line to the poor or oppressed of Europe who emigrated to America, 'Du hast es besser im Amerika' (You have things better in America), an American journalist, watching the robber barons fight each other to procure the Old Master paintings and the models of the old aristocrats' houses, wrote: 'Their motto was they do things better in Europe.'

Such was the temper of the time when the most fashionable architectural firm of the day had an idea beyond the dreams of the culture-vulture robber barons. McKim, Mead & White proposed to the owners of the Pennsylvania railroad that they would like to build, not a mansion for the chairman of the board, but a railroad station for the city. To do so, they proposed to re-create a jewel of a building of ancient Rome. Stanford White was a social lion, a dandy, a ladies' man and a most remarkable architect, possibly unique in his time, as a master of pastiche. He would, at the shake of a hand or the flourish of a contract, design an early Georgian house for an Anglophile, a Venetian

340

mansion for a newspaper tycoon, a monumental arch for the George Washington centennial, a jewelled Byzantine cross for the famous actress Eleanora Duse. Why not, he suggested to the railroad company, rebuild the city's main railroad station by re-creating, if not improving on, the Baths of Caracalla, the masterpiece of Roman architecture as the Parthenon was the masterpiece of Greece. Only Charles McKim or his dashing junior partner, Stanford White, would have the audacity, and the skill, to attempt such a thing. It was done, and in 1910 it was opened to the public, who came in awestruck droves to gaze at the block-long line of stately Doric columns leading to the vast waiting room which was indeed, with its splendid vaulted ceiling, a huge image of the Baths of Caracalla. From there you passed into the great concourse, which Charles McKim had produced as a creation of steel and glass arches, domes and fan vaulting—a breathtaking development of the new glass and iron architecture of London's Crystal Palace. Americans who were not taking any train came to gaze and marvel at it. So for a time did European tourists.

But fashions in architecture, as in everything else, change. The European intelligentsia came to chuckle and to sneer. By the mid-twentieth century, America and American businessmen had been ordered to admire the revolutionary works of a German, Walter Gropius, a rebel against all classical, all romantic, all Victorian styles of architecture. He invented what he called an international style. By his time, certainly, a general reaction had set in against the gaudiness of the Victorian age, the fussiness, the elaborate writhing

341

decoration of furniture, the stuffiness which overtook everything from women's clothes to lampshades. When the Victorian style first came in, the leading Regency architects of the day had called it ugly and barbaric. Just under a hundred years later, by the 1930s, it seems even the ordinary middle classes agreed with them. And then came the führer of the revolution, the new God of modern architecture from Germany, Walter Gropius. He simply, earnestly, dogmatically reacted to everything that had gone before, from the Greeks on. He invented the monolith, the large upright plank of concrete—what an independent American pioneer, one Frank Lloyd Wright, called the new log cabin that misuses steel, faceless, characterless, god-awful rectangles of concrete and steel, leading to its peak in the United Nations buildings which he called 'an ant hill for a thousand ants'. Certainly, the towering planks of glass and steel took over America's cities.

When the Second World War was over, and the building of everything from cottages to skyscrapers could begin again, Gropius, Mies van der Rohe, the so-called Bauhaus school, became almost compulsory for any city contemplating a new airport, a city hall, a big business about to bloom. (The god himself ruled from his pulpit at Harvard.) The tycoons didn't have to like the style. It simply became essential to their social standing. And so, by the 1960s, Tom Wolfe wrote: 'There had never been a place on earth where so many people of wealth and power paid for, put up, and moved into glass-box office buildings they detested.' By then, 'every child went to school in a building that looks like a duplicating machine wholesale distribution warehouse'.

In such an atmosphere, there was only one thing more ridiculous than designing a Victorian or Georgian house, and that was retaining the huge absurdity of a re-created Roman classical building. Such is the hypocrisy of fashion that since the end of the Second World War, I don't recall a visiting friend or tourist ever saying, 'I must go down to 34th Street and look at Pennsylvania Station' as their successors would always obediently pad off to the Museum of Modern Art, the Guggenheim, the Whitney. By that time nobody had heard of the Baths of Caracalla, and nobody cared.

Except the board of directors of the Pennsylvania railroad, who decided in 1960 or thereabouts that their Roman station was an expensive burden and also something of an embarrassment. They decided to destroy it. And so at 9 a.m. on 28 October 1963 the jackhammers clawed and the wrecking ball crashed down on the Doric pillars and would soon demolish what was the last reminder in New York of the grandeur that was Rome.

There had been no pre-emptive campaign of protest that I can remember. It was only when the noisy facts of demolition assailed our eyes and ears that a collector or two, a startled author, then the intelligentsia magazines, woke up. To its credit, it was the *New York Times* that sounded the first protesting trumpet. On its editorial page, it had a leader calling the demolition 'a monumental act of vandalism'. The little spurt of public shame and horror came, of course, too late. It took three years to destroy the station and on its ashes arose what the excellent *Blue Guide* to New York calls 'the utterly graceless and unappealing Madison Square Garden . . . a 20,000-seat arena in a pre-cast concrete drum, a movie theatre, a bowling alley and an office building'.

But out of this calamity, out of that ill October wind, there came one great and good thing. In the last year of the demolition, when the long block at 34th Street began to look like a pre-vision of Ground Zero, the small clique of outraged artists, authors, art lovers and citizens, petitioned the Mayor and then the city council and formed a body called the Landmarks Preservation Commission. Since 1965, their agents have snooped around the city with the zeal of the FBI, ticketing period relics of every style to be preserved. There was a big move in the 1970s on the part of the owners of the brilliant and majestic Grand Central Station to have it demolished and replaced by a 54-storey glass-and-steel Gropism. The squabble was fierce and prolonged. Thanks, however, to the tenacity of two members of the Landmarks Commission (one, Brendan Gill, a witty, Irish-American staff writer on the *New Yorker* magazine in its heyday, the other, the Presidential widow Jacqueline Kennedy), the fight was taken all the way to the Supreme Court, which upheld the protest, and in 1978 decreed that Grand Central Station was to be immortal and never to be subjected to the jackhammer and the wrecking ball.

Charlie Addams

23 January 2004

Opening my morning mail (why do I say 'morning' mail? There is no other), I find a letter from a lady in Massachusetts who is about to write a biography of the late, incomparable cartoonist Charles Addams (maybe you remember the Addams Family on television).

As I look up and out, as usual, at the rolling park, I am almost blinded by the ice-blue sky, the blazing sun and the landscape of snow. And I chuckled at this deceptive picture, since the temperature outside was 12 below freezing and no place for yours truly to patter into. The chuckle was a taproot into a famous cartoon by Charlie Addams. First, let me tap your memory of him and his cartoon family: a butler, the spitting image of Boris Karloff as the Frankenstein monster; his boss, a long, thin, weedy young woman with mean, slit eyes, long black hair and a black soul like the two villainous, cross-eyed little kids on the floor cooking up the neighbour's cat for Thanksgiving dinner. The famous cartoon I recalled after glancing at snowbound Central Park was a simple drawing of a slightly surprised skier whizzing downhill and looking backwards after passing a tree. The marks of his track ran parallel coming towards the tree but then curved out around the tree and met again on the downside. He had evidently successfully skied through the tree, and was as surprised as we were.

Charlie Addams was of my generation. He was very tall—I'd guess about six foot three or four, a shambling, rumply faced man with a five o'clock shadow and hair as black as any of his characters. He was also, like many writers of horrid things, extraordinarily gentle. My most vivid memory of him, to which our lady biographer is very welcome, was of one time (there were many times) when my wife and I had driven over to the south shore of Long Island to a party with a magazine editor, who was a friend we had in common. While the party dawdled and chatted out on the hot terrace, Charlie and I moved into the shady indoors. He was at the time much in love with a rather stunning movie actress, not present. It had been going on for some time but, after two failed marriages, he was not about to embark on a stormy third. We sat down with our drinks and I remember saying, 'So, Charlie, how's your love life?' He sipped and paused and slowly shook his head. In his high squeaky voice, he said: 'You know, Alistair, the trouble with women is—they always want a poimanent relationship.' A short story, but a poignant one to many men who are coasting along in a very agreeable relationship but dread any mention of wedding bells.

Charlie Addams was only one of that stable of great cartoonists at the *New Yorker* magazine from the 1930s through the 1970s, each of whom was recognizable at thirty paces, both for a personal style and expert craftsmanship: Addams and Peter Arno and Helen Hokinson and Whitney Darrow and George Price (the artist of the lumpenproletariat) and on and on. Dear me! Looking at the magazine and newspaper cartoonists of today, in both Britain and the United States, I have to lament how far we have fallen into the Dark Age of comic draughtsmanship.

A day or two after the lady biographer's letter, I had an even more touching reminder of Charlie Addams and an unforgettable cartoon, of which I hope to get a laser copy. Must be thirty-odd years ago. Scene: a small bedroom. Present, two middle-aged women, one whispering behind her palm to the other. A bed, containing evidently a husband, bandaged from head to foot; both arms; only his eyes are visible. Clearly, as old American gentlemen used to say, 'not a well man'. On the other side of his bed is an extraordinary figure—a witch doctor, half-naked and tattooed to the waist, face painted like a leopard, hair curled and tied in a high knotted rope. Smoke coming out of his nostrils and ears. He has one knee bent in some sort of ritual dance. The wife across the bed is whispering to her alarmed friend: 'At least he makes house calls.'

The punchline gave a comic twist to—even thirty-odd years ago—a new, sad fact of life. The fact, simply, that not long after the Second World War doctors ceased to make house calls. I'm talking about the cities, and specifically New York. But I'm reliably told that the comfortable habit has spread to small towns. Why, I wonder. It can only be because of the rapid spread, in the past fifty years or so, of specialization. What used to be called in Britain the 'GP' is over. Here is an American dictionary definition of 'general practitioner': 'A physician whose practice covers a wide variety of medical problems in patients of all ages.' A note says '(mainly British)'. When you think of it now, what a marvellously accomplished being he must have been—able, without timidity, to face everything from cancer and diabetes to ingrowing toenails. In this country, even the word 'doctor' is going out. On all printed forms—hospital entrance, health insurance, reimbursement bills—the phrase is 'primary care physician'. And he has always called himself here not a GP but an internist—a practitioner of everything to do with the internal organs that can be treated without surgery. That leaves a lot to other doctors.

I very rarely see my 'primary-care physician' because seven years ago, within half an hour of a diagnosis, he sent me off to a heart specialist, whom I see all the time. You go to the primary man once a year for your annual check-up and call him when you feel ill. He thereupon sets a date for you to call on him. Not, I've just figured, since the 1960s has a doctor called on me. You totter off to him. If your symptoms alarm him, he puts you in the hospital, where about four or five specialists can tend to you. (Cost of ambulance and two splendid paramedics to whisk you five blocks away—$750—£500! Thank the Lord, as I regularly do, I'm over 65—when the blessed national (federal) system, Medicare, takes over and pays 90 per cent.)

I said that these medical memories, especially about the disappearance of house calls, were triggered by the request for a tale or two about Charles Addams. But the subsequent recital was due to a telephone call, only two days ago, an astounding, unique call. It was from a doctor, a specialist I had set a date with and then cancelled three times because of the Arctic weather—even a

348

sniff of which the heart man will not allow. Well, this much-pestered doctor asked me if it would be all right for her to come to me, here, at my apartment, to take care of me!! After I'd been revived from the fainting fit, I fell into a Gershwin response. I said it would be 'wonderful, marvellous that you should care for me'. And so she did.

The Democrats' Growing Confidence

20 February 2004

Propped up there against my usual three pillows and having reluctantly just finished a favourite bed book—the collected ribald musings of an old friend, Charles McCabe, I was feeling chipper enough to glance across at two bedside piles and hope for a perfect lullaby before drifting into sleep.

I found it—on one page of a pocket reference book. A very brief history of a short war—so short, so well and briskly fought, the villain so effectively punished, the peace treaty so fair but demanding enough to put an end to any remaining fears about the war-waging villain . . . It was a model of how all United Nations exploits should begin and end.

Listen! It is very short and very satisfying. 'Saddam Hussein, declaring that the Persian Gulf state of Kuwait belonged to him sent his army into that country in August 1990. The United Nations Security Council promptly demanded his withdrawal. He paid no attention. In late November, the Council urged the UN members who were willing, to use "all means" to expel

Saddam. Saddam ignored the UN. And 29 countries volunteered to go to war.' (Note that all United Nations use of arms must be voluntary— the great weakness of the UN from its birth has been that it has no forces of its own. It can only ask members if they're interested and would like to come in.) In January 1991, under an American General, American, French, British and Saudi aircraft bombed Saddam's strategic bases. He bombed in kind, firing Scud missiles into Riyadh and the country of the non-belligerent but still the real ancient enemy, Israel.

Enough, said the gallant United States President —one George Bush—we must act, and he directed half a million allied troops to mount a ground offensive and liberate Kuwait. One hundred hours later, the war was over. Saddam's famous Republican Guard was a broken army abandoning hundreds of tanks, battered trucks, wounded aircraft—staggering north on foot in such numbers that General Schwarzkopf ordered all shooting to end. 'It would have been', he said, 'a total massacre.' Within six weeks, Saddam had signed a ceasefire and agreed 'to destroy all his chemical, nuclear and biological weapons'. That is the end of the fairy tale, the lullaby.

The epilogue is sorrowful. Saddam did not give proof of obeying his ceasefire promise. The Security Council passed a resolution ordering him to do so, and threatening 'serious consequences'. Twelve years and sixteen threatening resolutions later, UN inspectors had found much of the condemned material but nobody was sure if he hadn't hidden more. The United Nations Security Council voted to go on and pass more resolutions and offer consequences that never happened.

So what, as Shakespeare asked, is the concernancy? The concernancy is that in February 1991, only a day or two after the fairy tale had come to a happy end, a Gallup poll was taken to gauge the popularity of President Bush (the first). It stood at an unprecedented 89 per cent. I did a talk, I remember, suggesting that even though the next Presidential election was twenty months away, it would save an awful lot of time, sweat and money if some constitutional way might be found to skip or abolish the Presidential election of 1992. I'm sorry to say nobody ever took me up on this. The 1992 election was held and the heroic warrior-king Bush was handsomely defeated by a nationally unknown former Governor of Arkansas, a Southern state which had never before been the cradle of a President.

So, by one of those inscrutable, perhaps cruel turns of fate, the son of the heroic President George Bush came to play over the fairy tale of his father.

All those threatening, non-performing UN resolutions had been going on all throughout the two-term Presidency of Mr Clinton; and don't think he sat back and shared the Security Council's yawn. He went on receiving lots of alarming intelligence about Iraq and Saddam's nuclear and chemical projects, was troubled by the memory of the devastating use of poison gas in Iran and Kurdistan, and must have heard the sentence, attributed to one of Saddam's top advisers but never confirmed: 'Next time, it'll be a chemical fire-storm over Israel.' In all the preliminary twelve-year concern about Saddam's intentions, this fear never failed to haunt the White House: the fear of an overnight Saddam attack and either the outbreak of a whole Middle Eastern war, or the death of the state of Israel. President Clinton fretted over this problem as much as anyone and had plans to go into Iraq (to enact, on his own if must be, 'serious consequences') when Miss Lewinsky became a figure of fate as significant as Napoleon's mistress Madame Walewska. By the time Clinton was ready to mobilize an American or allied force, he didn't possess the moral authority to invade Long Island.

When George W. Bush came in, there came with him a small group of advisers, at least three of them veterans of the Gulf War, who thought that at last the United States should foil the Iraqi intentions it feared, and invade. That is the beginning of the second Bush fairy tale. Under the guidance of Secretary of Defense Rumsfeld, who had proved himself a brilliant wager of the new special-services, precision-bombing kind of war in Afghanistan, President Bush asked him to do the same in Iraq. And it surely was astonishing to see, after only weeks, the vanishing of the fourth largest army in the world, the flight of Saddam and the ever-memorable toppling of his statue on to the streets of Baghdad.

End of second Bush family fairy tale. Shortly after this swift and picturesque victory, the Gallup Poll measured President G.W.'s popularity. It was at 69 per cent.

I do not need to detail or even sketch in bulk the subsequent turmoil and religious conflict, the accursed insurgency that is so woefully successful not only in wounding the Americans and British and Spanish and Poles and Hungarians—in a word, the allies—but seems to do even better decimating the legions of Iraqis who gamely line up to serve as a police force.

Throughout most of the tumult in Iraq, the wholly unexpected weight and range and murderous force of the Iraqis' opposition to the allied occupation, President Bush's public approval has stayed above 60 per cent. But then came the fateful testimony, before the Senate Armed Services Committee, of David Kay, the Central Intelligence Agency's retired chief weapons inspector. 'We got it all wrong,' he said, finally driving a stake in the heart of the administration's main declared reason for going into Iraq. All we found, said David Kay, and are likely to find, are the relics of an abandoned chemical warfare arsenal and of a primitive nuclear programme. Within a week of the Kay testimony, the President's approval rating—for the first time since he arrived in the White House—fell below 50 per cent. A ten-point drop after that simple sentence: 'We got it all wrong.'

If one body, one institution, in the United States was more affected by that sentence than any other it was the Democratic Party. All through the winter and the early primaries, eight Democrats fought each other on domestic issues in the hope of becoming their party's nominee by the spring. Of course, the more they fought each other, the more the White House was delighted. The eight Democrats were often apart on several issues. Only one man, a doctor, former Governor of Vermont, sensed the rising tide of popular feeling against the war, galvanized the young, and in all the public

353

polls was way ahead of the other seven. But, as a campaigner, he was fickle, shooting ideas from the hip, next day reversing his stand, or saying he was sorry he said that. Not the man to have his finger on the button. In the actual primaries, he was time and again a dim, distant third. This week, he joined the other dear departed. But what President Bush's ten-point drop did to the hopeful Democrats was to let them say now without fear that the war was fought for a false reason, and it generated a wholly new conviction, which had little to do with the issues. The three problems which the national polls say are popularly paramount: (1) To recover the two million jobs lost during this administration; (2) reform of the health care system; and, quite a way down, (3) Iraq.

The new, invigorating party conviction is a belief the Democrats had not dreamed of so far. It is the belief that George Bush can be beaten in November. This thought apparently took hold on the primary voters long before it dawned on the Democratic Party as a whole. Hence the fifteen out of seventeen primaries won by the Massachusetts Senator John Kerry, who since the campaign's beginning has sounded an odd and lonely boast: 'George Bush must be driven from the White House, and I'm the man to do it.'